The Book of Isaiah

The Book of Isaiah

Enduring Questions Answered Anew

Essays Honoring
Joseph Blenkinsopp
and His Contribution to the Study of Isaiah

Edited by

Richard J. Bautch and J. Todd Hibbard

William B. Eerdmans Publishing Company
Grand Rapids, Michigan / Cambridge, U.K.

Published 2014 by
Wm. B. Eerdmans Publishing Co.
2140 Oak Industrial Drive N.E., Grand Rapids, Michigan 49505 /
P.O. Box 163, Cambridge CB3 9PU U.K.

Printed in the United States of America

20 19 18 17 16 15 14 7 6 5 4 3 2 1

Library of Congress Cataloging-in-Publication Data

The book of Isaiah: enduring questions answered anew:
essays honoring Joseph Blenkinsopp and his contribution to the study of Isaiah /
edited by Richard J. Bautch and J. Todd Hibbard.
pages cm
Includes bibliographical references.
ISBN 978-0-8028-6773-5 (pbk.: alk. paper)
1. Bible. Isaiah — Criticism, interpretation, etc. I. Blenkinsopp, Joseph, 1927- honouree.
II. Bautch, Richard J., editor of compilation.

BS1515.52.B66 2014
224´.106 — dc23

2013046673

www.eerdmans.com

Contents

Introduction

Isaian scholarship is a story of milestones. The 1892 commentary of Bernard Duhm, for example, gave rise to the model of a tripartite Isaiah that influenced the study of the book for more than a century and has begun to be supplanted only relatively recently.[1] Another instance is Joachim Begrich's seminal article of 1934, "Das priesterliche Heilsorakel," which had an enduring impact on studies of Second Isaiah and the Psalms as well.[2] The publication between 2000 and 2003 of Joseph Blenkinsopp's 3-volume Anchor Bible commentary on Isaiah is proving to be another significant development in Isaiah studies.[3] The commentary has had a marked effect on scholarship as interpreters of Isaiah routinely consult these three volumes to gain perspective on the text through the sage eyes of Joseph Blenkinsopp. Virtually all published articles and books now cite Blenkinsopp, evidence of how his commentary is influencing the field and helping to shape the future direction of Isaiah studies.

In this volume, thirteen of today's leading scholars on the Book of Isaiah contribute essays that explore a distinct issue that arises with critical study of the text. The essays as a whole reflect the highest echelon of Isaiah studies. This volume is distinctive in that each essay acknowledges and comments upon, to the degree that it is appropriate, the exegetical contributions of Joseph Blenkinsopp. In certain essays the discussion of Blenkinsopp's work is more robust,

1. B. Duhm, *Das Buch Jesaia*, HKAT 3/1 (Göttingen: Vandenhoeck and Ruprecht, 1892).

2. J. Begrich, "Das priesterliche Heilsorakel," *ZAW* 52 (1934): 81-92.

3. J. Blenkinsopp, *Isaiah 1–39, Isaiah 40–55, and Isaiah 56–66,* AB 19, 19A, and 19B (New Haven, Conn.: Yale University Press, 2000, 2002, and 2003).

while in others it occurs largely in footnotes. Explicit or implicit, the references to this influential scholar provide coherence and distinction to the collection of essays assembled in his honor. The book as a whole provides a fresh window on Isaiah studies in the 21st century, with a focus on the contributions of Joseph Blenkinsopp.

Devoted readers of the Book of Isaiah, and especially those who work in the area of Isaiah studies, will appreciate how this volume parallels the biblical book itself. In antiquity, later biblical writers working in the Isaian tradition commented upon and at times reissued oracles of their predecessors, as in the case of the vineyard related in Isaiah 5 and later in Isaiah 27. Similarly, the contributors here have written about a portion of Isaiah with attention to the interpretive frame that Blenkinsopp has provided for a clearer understanding of the text. The volume models the rereading of Isaian traditions as exegetes engage and extend the insights of one of their own, Joseph Blenkinsopp, and comment on his commentary over the 66-chapter Book of Isaiah. In this sense, the volume as a whole invites thinking of the Isaiah collection holistically, a trend in current scholarship.

While this book features "state of the question" scholarship on the Book of Isaiah, there is an important personal dimension. Colleagues and friends of Joseph Blenkinsopp have contributed to this collection, and the editors wrote their dissertations under his direction (now some years ago). To the community of scholars, Blenkinsopp's erudition is matched by his generosity and good nature. To the readership of this book, his understanding of Isaiah is made newly available through the studies written by fellow scholars in gratitude to him.

In Praise of Joe Blenkinsopp

Philip Davies

Biblical scholars deal with some of the best-known and best-loved writings in the world, which is the great privilege of our profession. But we suffer from almost complete ignorance of their authors. The voices we hear come from a void. We do not know their identities — indeed, for the most part we do not even have their real names. One can see everywhere, in books, on church windows, carved in stone, the figures and faces of prophets or evangelists, Abraham, Moses, or David. But these images are projections of a piety or a devotion to imagined personalities. But how much even of our scholarly interpretation of the Bible has been sculpted around such figures. As a teenage schoolboy, the textbook for my Religious Education was called *Personalities of the Old Testament,* by Fleming James.[1] The last half-century has seen James' colourful parade replaced largely by the pens of anonymous scribes, while real authors have given way to implied authors or narrators. Even the laments of Jeremiah are now largely excluded from the personal experience of that prophet.

Biblical literary critics of recent fashion have doubted the validity and relevance of the historical-critical method, have championed the Bible as a modern text, to be read and understood as timeless, its meanings determined by each reader reading in her or his own culture. Even so, many of them have been reluctant to celebrate the death of the author, to relinquish the notion of a gifted individual behind the text. Ideological criticism, for example, requires an ideologically motivated author (and reader?): texts do not have ideologies,

1. New York: Charles Scribner's Sons, 1939.

but merely mediate them. We do not really like disembodied voices. We can, and do, dissolve individual authors into "communities," but wouldn't every reader of a biblical text, even the most critical scholar (especially the most critical scholar, perhaps), desire to meet the real author(s), if only to realize how poorly we have read, or imagined them, or even, out of curiosity, just to put faces to the voices?

I have a memory from my undergraduate days of seeing a photograph of the great Martin Noth, complete with cigar and looking very Germanic and somewhat inscrutable, but at least human. As an undergraduate I met in the flesh the likes of H. H. Rowley (another lover of cigars) and John Bright, previously only authors of books. In my postgraduate days, I got to know Roland de Vaux rather more. I could never read any of these again merely as authors. My opinions of their ideas did not change, but I read them with an added awareness that I was not reading a label, the bearer or author of a set of opinions, but a person of whom these opinions were a *part.* There are still numerous scholars whom I know only as authors, but there remain relatively few of whom I can say, when I read their books or articles, that I can really hear their voice in my ear and hear *what* they are saying differently. For we must surely realize sooner or later that scholarship is not merely part of what we *do.* This is another of the privileges of our profession: we do not merely improve at our craft, so that we can, for example, simply say that scholar *x* is better at the job than scholar *y.* In the end, aren't we all unique in the way we do our work — because what we do is part of what we *are?* The most enjoyable, and often instructive, aspect of a public scholarly debate lies not in the interplay of ideas but of personalities.

This preamble leads me, of course, to Joe Blenkinsopp, a favourite author, favourite scholar and favourite human being. I am fairly sure he will find being praised somewhat distasteful. He is a modest man, and only partly because he is also a very English man is his modesty not assumed. But he is, let's be honest, *old-fangled.* What other word will serve for a man who still uses WordPerfect and saves his files on floppy disks and would not be seen dead with an e-book reader? He has an old-fangled belief in truth, in scholarship and in life. He would argue (maybe I remember him doing it?) that without the value of truth there is no point in knowledge, or accuracy, or even scholarship itself, because knowledge and accuracy are the hallmarks of his scholarship. So he does not do postmodernism, or literary theory (of the new-fangled kind), and does not generally get "playful" with texts — the "generally" is important, for he has a wonderful playfulness that informs the kind of imagination he brings to his exegesis. Let me express all this in the words of someone else who knows him very well: "he is a scholar's scholar, tireless, painstakingly careful, fearless about following through wherever the texts and arguments lead him, always focused on that simplest and most elusive of scholarly aims, simply getting it right."

The major interests of Joe Blenkinsopp's scholarship might seem to be Pentateuch and Prophecy, with Genesis and Isaiah (the latter celebrated in this volume) as foremost in these two. But there is no part of the Old Testament/ Hebrew Bible or of the life of ancient Israel that he has left untouched.[2] To all of his writing, moreover, he brings a width of what we nowadays call "cultural literacy" (the old-fangled term would be "wide reading"). He is a very well-educated man, who can (and did once) identify the play *plus act and scene* of a Shakespearian couplet quoted to him. He did earn a University of London degree in English as well as History (his *Curriculum Vitae* omits the former, but I have it on good authority, yet I doubt that his favourite poet, Housman, or the ghost-stories of M. R. James were on the curriculum at London University, and I can thank him for recommending to me a number of good contemporary novels. Joe's love of ghost stories, incidentally, inspired his interest in 1 Sam. 28).[3] At this point I need to introduce the sense of humour that always threatens to break the surface. Seated beside me at a particularly geriatric society meeting, he breathed to me the lines from James's story "Count Magnus,"[4] where the hero is warned of "persons walking who should not be walking. They should be resting, not walking." I cannot repeat here his comment on the baggy pants worn by his (then much younger) son Martin, who had just acquired a skateboard, but at the refurbished basilica (no other word for it) at Notre Dame University, on a Palm Sunday with about thirty priests in full regalia, he commented, "Here you see just a few of the reasons for the Reformation." I could cite numerous other examples of a dry but lively sense of humour.

His writing draws extensively on archaeological research, and not always at second-hand. He has dug at Gibeon and Tel Dan, and was a coordinator at the Capernaum excavations in 1980-87. (His doctoral thesis at Oxford, pub-

2. See, among his other writings, J. Blenkinsopp, *Wisdom and Law in the Old Testament: The Ordering of Life in Israel and Early Judaism* (Oxford: OUP, 1983); idem, *Sage, Priest, Prophet. Intellectual Leadership in Ancient Israel* (Louisville: Westminster Press, 1995); J. Blenkinsopp et al., *Families in Ancient Israel* (Louisville: Westminster Press, 1997).

3. "Saul and the 'Mistress of the Spirits' (1 Sam. 28.3-25)," in Alistair G. Hunter and Philip R. Davies, eds., *Sense and Sensitivity: Essays on Reading the Bible in Honour of Robert Carroll* (London: Sheffield Academic Press, 2002), pp. 49-62.

4. In *Ghost Stories of an Antiquary* (London: Edward Arnold, 1904), pp. 65-79.

lished in 1972,[5] typically ignited a new controversy with its argument that the Gibeah of Saul was in fact Gibeon.)[6] Of his experiences at Tel Dan I should not say too much in order to protect the guilty, but he could not resist playing a practical joke by planting a most unlikely object for retrieval from the rubble. During 1978 he served as the Rector at the Tantur Ecumenical Institute, in those days located between Jerusalem and Bethlehem. He has always had an interest in early Judaism, and was also responsible for the Program(me) for the Study of Judaism and Christianity in Antiquity at Notre Dame. But while he has his own views about the politics of modern Palestine, he does not mix them with his religion or his scholarship. This again is old-fangledness, perhaps, but religion is in any case not something about which he talks a great deal, at least to me. The English are anyway famous for regarding it as a matter between the Englishman and God (or, if public-school educated, one's manservant and God).

I could — and maybe I really should — say more about the academic achievements of by some distance the finest Old Testament/Hebrew Bible scholar of his generation (no, I mean "generations"). But the personality behind the scholarship is the real theme of this encomium. Here is an old-fangled, learned, painstaking and sometimes reactionary friend (not politically reactionary, I hasten to add: he has a well-developed sense of social justice and the obscenity of great wealth improperly used). To these epithets I must add "indefatigable," used *ad nauseam* by our friend Robert Carroll whose insouciance I have often seen matched by Joe's own. I mentioned earlier his dry sense of humour, but not his love also of the zany and the absurd. He admires the war veteran, manic-depressive and wildly funny Spike Milligan, whose epitaph ("I told you I was ill") he loves to quote. He reads the British satirical journal *Private Eye*, which I pass on in large batches, often during conference sessions (and you thought they were offprints?). He has a party piece that demonstrates the repertoire of Italian hand gestures and their (impolite) meanings, performed with an appropriate mixture of respect and disapproval. Those acquainted with his offbeat sense of humour can also find it in his academic writing now and then (one of his articles is entitled "Deuteronomy and the Politics of Post-mortem Existence"). It actually blends well with his love

5. *Gibeon and Israel* (Cambridge: CUP, 1972).

6. The suggestion seems to have originated in fact with K.-D. Schunck, *Benjamin: Untersuchungen zur Entstehung und Geschichte eines israelitischen Stammes* (Berlin: Topelmann, 1963), pp. 131-38, and the issue is still running; see most recently I. Finkelstein, "Tel el-Ful Revisited: The Assyrian and Hellenistic Periods (with a New Identification)," *PEQ* 143 (2011): 106-18.

of pedantry and his keen observation of matters cultural, especially the contrast of American and English society. So his CV begins: *Personal:* U.S. citizen and U.K. subject. He does have an ear for the cultural inflections of language, as when, for example, he asks me for my "beverage of preference."

More than a brief biographical account would trespass on Joe's modesty and much-valued privacy. He was born in County Durham, England, into a coal-mining family and educated at a Roman Catholic junior seminary in preparation for the priesthood. I have been told that Joe's early years were not particularly happy, his father having died when Joe was very young. His wish to be conscripted into the armed forces in the Second World War was unsuccessful and according to his best schoolmate, who was conscripted and travelled widely as a result, Joe regretted a missed opportunity for adventure (rather than for warfare as such). As it was, he took degrees in English and History from the University of London and then continued his seminary studies in philosophy and theology, including a few years in Rome. After his doctoral studies at Oxford, he taught for three years at a theological college. But a firm commitment to biblical studies and a departure from the priesthood inaugurated a belated but thankfully long career in that discipline. Unable to secure a post in the U.K., he commenced a series of temporary positions in the U.S. — at Vanderbilt, Chicago, Hartford — before arriving at Notre Dame (which he insists is in South Bend, to which he refers as the "City of Shame" after a certain scandal in the Kitty Kat lounge, an "adult entertainment establishment"). But while he has remained there since 1970 he has always loved travel and even now flies many times a year across the Atlantic to England, to Rome or wherever the next conference lies, perhaps making up for the lost wartime experiences. He has also been Visiting Professor in numerous places, including Rome, his favourite city. But he retains an affection for Oxford and for the northeast of England, especially Durham. In this region lies Blenkinsopp Castle near Hadrian's Wall in Northumberland. Whether or not he is really descended from Bryan de Blenkinsopp, the castle does boast its own ghost, the White Lady.[7]

The most interesting travel story involves a trip in his younger days to Guatemala, where he was to be the Rector. He relates learning Spanish on the flight, then deciding that his Spanish was not adequate to the task, so trying Italian, then Latin. In some way he managed to displease the military author-

7. "The White Lady of Blenkinsopp" in John and Jean Lang, *Stories of the Border Marches* (Teddington: The Echo Library, 2007). The legend can also be read at http://www.blenkinsoppcastle.com/html/index.htm.

ities there and had to leave. In addition, he was invited to use the consulate swimming pool there, but his use of it apparently (and unawares to him) implied some sort of affiliation with a clique that provoked further diplomatic complications. Of this, and other stories, I look forward to hearing more from Joe in due course.

I must not finish without a comment on sociability: though he enjoys a little less after his retirement, Joe likes company. No International SBL meeting, for example, was perfect without a drink or two in his hotel room. He has always been an accomplished and knowledgeable — but not excessive — drinker, his "beverage of preference" being the very English gin and tonic, but also sambucca, grappa, ouzo, for he is an alcoholic tourist too. He is wont to express approval of a companion as a "competent drinker," a compliment acknowledged by the grateful recipient as a mark of esteem from a demanding tutor. To spend Thanksgiving at his home, with its mix of scholarly discussion, drinking and reminiscence makes the long wintry limo trip from O'Hare worthwhile. In his older years, like all of us, Joe has acquired some of the hallmarks of the "absent-minded professor," but there is a remarkable transformation once the conversation turns to matters scholarly, as it inevitably will: the mind and the memory are sharp and the attention focused. The appetite, the hunger, are still there, as witnessed by his continuing productivity.

And not just productivity, but innovation, of which I give two examples. One is Jewish sectarianism, in which he has been interested for many years.[8] Recently, however, he has developed ideas about its growth through material in Isaiah, Ezra,[9] and the *Damascus Document.*[10] The other example is a brilliant essay, "Remembering Josiah," in a recently published volume on the reception of biblical figures in the Second Temple period.[11] Typically, he contributes here to the current themes of reception theory and cultural memory simply by pursuing his own historical-critical methods of exegesis, liberally annotated

8. See "A Jewish Sect of the Persian Period," *CBQ* 52 (1990): 5-20.

9. On which he has a commentary: *Ezra-Nehemiah. A Commentary* (Philadelphia: Westminster, 1988).

10. "The Qumran Sect in the Context of Second Temple Sectarianism," in J. G. Campbell, W. J. Lyons and L. K. Pietersen, eds., *New Directions in Qumran Studies* (London: T&T Clark, 2005), pp. 10-25; updated in "Isaiah at the Beginnings of Jewish Sectarianism," in J. Blenkinsopp, *Opening the Sealed Book* (Grand Rapids: Eerdmans, 2006), pp. 56-88. See also in that same volume his "Reading Isaiah at Qumran," pp. 89-128.

11. J. Blenkinsopp, "Remembering Josiah," in D. Edelman and E. Ben Zvi, eds., *Remembering Biblical Figures in the Late Persian and Hellenistic Periods* (Oxford: Oxford University Press, 2013), pp. 236-56.

with cross-cultural examples from ancient Greece and modern Israel, and evoking from a range of texts the shape of an orally-transmitted, popular memory of a martyred royal hero that counterpoints the literary memory of the canonized texts. I'd say it is at least as good, from his ninetieth decade, as anything he has written before.

The privilege of reading Joe Blenkinsopp should be enough for any biblical scholar, and for most this will have to suffice. For myself and the contributors to this volume, there is the additional reward of knowing more than an author, of knowing the wisdom and humour of a serious seeker after truth. I have wished at times that I had been among his own students. Recently, however, I was told that he had once applied unsuccessfully for a position at the University of Sheffield. If only . . .

Exegetical Studies

"An Initial Problem": The Setting and Purpose of Isaiah 10:1-4

H. G. M. Williamson

"An initial problem," Joe Blenkinsopp has written in his valuable commentary on Isaiah, "is the connection between the series 5:8-24 and the isolated woe-saying in 10:1-4."[1] In experiencing a degree of uncertainty about the position of 10:1-4 Blenkinsopp is by no means alone, as we shall see. Solutions offered have varied. His suggestion is to treat 10:1-4a as "a displaced unit of the woe-series that has been subsequently accommodated to the poem on the divine anger by the addition of the refrain at 10:4b."

In support of this, he observes that the indictments in 5:8-24 are directed against the leadership of the people, as is 10:1-4, whereas the poem about the divine anger (which includes, at least, 9:7-20[2]) threatens rather the people as a whole. Furthermore he regards it as probable that its original position was at the beginning of the series — just before 5:8, therefore. Positively, in dependence upon the earlier work of Barth,[3] he finds that the material in 10:1-4a runs on naturally into 5:8-10; negatively, at the end of the series, 5:24b sounds like a final recapitulation (and this is now followed by an equally displaced section of the poem on the divine anger in 5:25). With characteristic wisdom Blenkinsopp comments that "it is important to resist the temptation either to

1. Joseph Blenkinsopp, *Isaiah 1–39: A New Translation with Introduction and Commentary*, AB 19 (New York: Doubleday, 2000), p. 211.

2. Verse numbers in Isaiah 9 differ between the Hebrew text and the English versions. In this article I shall use the Hebrew verse numbers throughout.

3. Hermann Barth, *Die Jesaja-Worte in der Josiazeit: Israel und Assur als Thema einer produktiven Neuinterpretation der Jesajaüberlieferung*, WMANT 48 (Neukirchen-Vluyn: Neukirchener Verlag, 1977), pp. 110-11.

impose more order on the book than was ever intended by its redactors or to privilege unduly putative original arrangements" (pp. 211-12). Nevertheless he tentatively links his proposal with possible ways that the text might have been read during the period of the reign of Josiah or in the early post-exilic period.

The displacements that Blenkinsopp proposes, though shared to a greater or lesser degree by many others, are relatively dramatic. At least his have the advantage that he sees them as a deliberate redactional move rather than a series of scribal accidents. Nevertheless it may be asked whether they are necessary or whether there is an alternative to explain the features he has so carefully observed. As part of our ongoing discussion about Isaiah as well as many other topics of mutual interest I share a possible alternative for him to consider as a mark of deep respect for his scholarship and friendship.

It may help to ground this discussion if I briefly review the range of possibilities on this subject that have been canvassed over the years. The observation that the addressees in 10:1-4 differ from those in the poem that precedes in ch. 9 goes back some way in the history of critical biblical scholarship, so that suggestions that the paragraph once stood elsewhere precede the insight that the movement might have been due to conscious redactional considerations.

The first, spasmodic discussions of this topic,[4] which noted in particular such matters as the fact that there are six woe-sayings in chapter 5, so that the addition of that in chapter 10 would make up a series of seven, and the contrasts between 9:7-20 and 10:1-3 (e.g. the orphans and widows appear to lack divine pity in 9:16 but despoiling widows is condemned in 10:2), and which therefore suggest either that the verses should be moved elsewhere or that some material had fallen out between chapters 9 and 10, do not appear to have convinced the major commentaries which followed them. Duhm, for instance, accepted that there were uncertainties, including the question whether the verses were directed towards Israel or Judah, but he nevertheless considered either hypothesis unnecessary.[5] Marti noted the same points of difficulty as

4. G. Studer, "Zur Textkritik des Jesaja," *JPT* 7 (1881): 160-86 (172-74); Friedrich Giesebrecht, *Beiträge zur Jesaiakritik nebst einer Studie über prophetische Schriftstellerei* (Göttingen: Vandenhoeck & Ruprecht, 1890), pp. 3-24 (with an astonishing degree of re-ordering of the relevant material); H. Hackmann, *Die Zukunftserwartung des Jesaia* (Göttingen: Vandenhoeck & Ruprecht, 1893), pp. 54-56.

5. Bernhard Duhm, *Das Buch Jesaia,* HKAT 3/1 (Göttingen: Vandenhoeck & Ruprecht, 1892), p. 73; not long after, but in shorter compass, John Skinner also considered proposals to

his predecessors and was prepared to go a little further than Duhm; he agreed that 10:1-3 could hardly be a direct continuation of the preceding passage and that they had probably come from elsewhere among the remaining Isaianic sayings. But he was reluctant to go any further in identifying where that might have been. Previous suggestions all disagreed with one another, and given the fact that ch. 5 was already somewhat fragmentary he concluded that any attempted reconstruction should be avoided ("sehr gewagt und von grossen Schwierigkeiten begleitet").[6] Finally Gray seems to be undecided. He sees the essence of the problem to lie in the uncertainty whether the oracle is addressed to Israel or to Judah. If it refers to Israel (Ephraim), then it will have been a strophe in the poem on divine anger — and Gray is clearly impressed by the fact that it is of the same length as his version of the other strophes. If it refers to Judah, however, then it probably did not belong in its present position originally but he remains reluctant to specify further, not least because "the question and the address in 10^3 differentiates this section no less from the 'Ah's' of 5^{8-24} than from the other strophes of the poem."[7]

It seems that a change to mainstream opinion followed in the wake of the later work of Karl Budde. Although in his textual comments he argued conventionally that his preferred order of material in this regard was 5:22; 10:1; 5:23; 10:2-4a; 5:24[8] (which may or may not seem plausible), his major contribution was an earlier broader discussion of the composition history of this whole part of Isaiah in which he insisted that Isa 6:1–9:6 was an originally separate composition dubbed the "Isaiah Memoir."[9] Noting that there is not a precise join between the end of ch. 5 and 9:7 but equally that there are close links between the series of woes in ch. 5 and the start of ch. 10 as well as the fact that there are parts of the refrain poem both before and after the memoir, Budde suggested in an uncharacteristically vague manner that in the course of the insertion of the memoir into its present position there was some serious accidental disruption to the material which now surrounds it, leading to the present untidy order.[10]

---

include these verses with ch. 5 as "unnecessary"; *The Book of the Prophet Isaiah, Chapters i-xxxix*, CBSC (Cambridge: Cambridge University Press, 1897), p. 82.

6. Karl Marti, *Das Buch Jesaja*, KHAT 10 (Tübingen: Mohr [Paul Siebeck], 1900), p. 101.

7. G. Buchanan Gray, *A Critical and Exegetical Commentary on the Book of Isaiah I–XXVII*, ICC (Edinburgh: T & T Clark, 1912), pp. 189-90.

8. Karl Budde, "Zu Jesaja 1–5," *ZAW* 50 (1932): 38-72 (67-68).

9. Karl Budde, *Jesajas Erleben: Eine gemeinverständliche Auslegung der Denkschrift des Propheten (Kap. 6,1–9,6)* (Gotha: Leopold Klotz, 1928).

10. He writes on p. 3 of "eine verwirrende Verschiebung, eine Stellentausch, der sich

Whatever doubts we may now entertain about the hypothesis as a whole,[11] its impact on the study of the first part of Isaiah was immense, and many commentaries since have more or less taken it for granted as a starting point. Consequently, this made it easier to accept as a consequence that aspects of the present ordering of the material might be accidental, so that the notion that, for instance, 10:1-4 might be shifted elsewhere seemed less controversial than it had before. Little more demonstration of this is necessary than to observe that an element of such a rearrangement has even been incorporated into an official translation of the Bible for use in public worship.[12]

It continues to be a ground for concern, however, that even as many commentators have agreed that some such displacement took place, so they equally remain as divided as ever in their suggestions for the recovery of the hypothetical original order.[13] In agreement with the position that Blenkinsopp himself favors, that is to say, slotting in 10:1-4a at the very start of the series, before 5:8, we may cite as examples Clements and Barth.[14] The major alternative proposal is that of such commentators as Fohrer, Schoors, Jacob and Wildberger, who put 10:1-3/4 after 5:24 and 5:25-29/30 after 9:20[15] (and similarly

zwischen der letzten Worte vorher und der ersten nachher vollzogen hat," and on p. 4 he adds that "wir werden nicht fehlgehn mit der Annahme, daß diese Verwirrung eben bei der Einfügung der Denkschrift an ihrer jetzigen Stelle entstand, uns auch nicht wundern, wenn dabei in den Fugen der Wortlaut im Einzelnen Schaden gelitten hat."

11. I have set out some reasons against the theory as a whole in my book *Variations on a Theme: King, Messiah and Servant in the Book of Isaiah* (Carlisle: Paternoster, 1998), pp. 73-86.

12. In the NEB 5:24-25 is moved to follow 10:1-4. This is simply noted, not explained in any way, by L. H. Brockington, *The Hebrew Text of the Old Testament: The Readings Adopted by the Translators of the New English Bible* (Oxford: Oxford University Press, and Cambridge: Cambridge University Press, 1973), p. 176.

13. It should be noted that others continue to defend the present order of the material; see, for instance, Stuart A. Irvine, who uses primarily historical arguments to uphold his case: *Isaiah, Ahaz, and the Syro-Ephraimitic Crisis,* SBLDS 123 (Atlanta: Scholars Press, 1990), pp. 121-25 and 235-50, and Marvin A. Sweeney, *Isaiah 1–39 with an Introduction to Prophetic Literature,* FOTL 16 (Grand Rapids: Eerdmans, 1996), 188-96, and William P. Brown, "The So-Called Refrain in Isaiah 5:25-30 and 9:7–10:4," *CBQ* 52 (1990): 432-43, who both advance more literary (though different) considerations.

14. Ronald E. Clements, *Isaiah 1–39,* NCB (Grand Rapids: Eerdmans, and London: Marshall, Morgan & Scott, 1980); Barth, *Die Jesaja-Worte,* pp. 110-11. Gerald T. Sheppard, "The Anti-Assyrian Redaction and the Canonical Context of Isaiah 1–39," *JBL* 104 (1985): 193-216, also follows Barth with regard to most aspects of the composition history of the relevant parts of chapters 5 and 10, though he does not in fact state explicitly where he thinks 10:1-4a stood originally.

15. Georg Fohrer, *Jesaja 1–23,* Zürcher Bibelkommentare AT 19.1, 3rd ed. (Zurich: Theologischer Verlag, 1991); Anton Schoors, *Jesaja,* De Boeken van het Oude Testament 9A (Roer-

Kaiser, who has 10:1-2 following 5:23, both being subsequently expanded[16]). Other possibilities include Mowinckel, who favoured the order 5:1-7; 9:7-20; 5:25-30; 10:1-4; 5:8-24;[17] Donner, who left 10:1-4 where it is but moved 5:25-29 to follow it;[18] Fey, who does the same except that he included 5:25 in the middle of 9:16;[19] and Vermeylen, who altered the order of several of the woe sayings in such a way as to include 5:8-10 followed by 10:1-3 at the end of the series.[20]

This brief survey, which is far from exhaustive, produces sufficiently diverse results to justify our asking once again if the starting point is correct.

The observation that there are currently six woe-sayings in Isa 5, so that the addition of 10:1-4 would bring the figure up to the significant number of

mond: Romen & Zonen, 1972); Edmond Jacob, *Esaïe 1–12,* CAT 8a (Geneva: Labor et Fides, 1987); Hans Wildberger, *Jesaja,* 1: *Jesaja 1–12,* BKAT 10/1, 2nd ed. (Neukirchen-Vluyn: Neukirchener Verlag, 1980 (ET, *Isaiah 1–12,* Continental Commentary [Minneapolis: Fortress, 1991]).

16. Otto Kaiser, *Das Buch des Propheten Jesaja, Kapitel 1–12,* ATD 17, 5th ed. (Göttingen: Vandenhoeck & Ruprecht, 1981) (ET, *Isaiah 1–12: A Commentary,* OTL [London: SCM, 1983]).

17. Sigmund Mowinckel, "Die Komposition des Jesajabuches Kap. 1-39," *Acta Orientalia* 11 (1932-33): 267-92 (275).

18. Herbert Donner, *Israel unter den Völkern: Die Stellung der klassischen Propheten des 8. Jahrhunderts v. Chr. zur Aussenpolitik der Könige von Israel und Juda,* VTSup 11 (Leiden: Brill, 1964), pp. 66-75.

19. Reinhard Fey, *Amos und Jesaja: Abhängigkeit und Eigenständigkeit des Jesaja,* WMANT 12 (Neukirchen-Vluyn: Neukirchener Verlag, 1963), pp. 83-104.

20. J. Vermeylen, *Du prophète Isaïe à l'apocalyptique: Isaïe, I–XXXV, miroir d'un demi-millénaire d'expérience religieuse en Israël,* 1, EBib (Paris: Gabalda, 1977), pp. 169-72. A detailed critique of Vermeylen's analysis of chapters 5–10 as a whole was offered by Conrad E. L'Heureux, "The Redactional History of Isaiah 5.1–10.4," in W. Boyd Barrick and John R. Spencer, eds., *In the Shelter of Elyon: Essays on Ancient Palestinian Life and Literature in Honor of G. W. Ahlström,* JSOTSup 31 (Sheffield: JSOT Press, 1984), pp. 99-119. L'Heureux describes 10:1-4 as a "supplementary strophe" to the outstretched hand poem, "put together by a redactor at a later time" (p. 112). This is comparable to the position that will eventually be favored here as well. He also traces a careful redactional purpose behind the arrangement of the materials and so is resistant to attempts to reconstruct earlier orders. In this, see too (though very differently) Andrew H. Bartelt, "Isaiah 5 and 9: In- or Interdependence?" in Astrid B. Beck et al., eds., *Fortunate the Eyes That See: Essays in Honor of David Noel Freedman in Celebration of His Seventieth Birthday* (Grand Rapids: Eerdmans, 1995), pp. 157-74, and Erhard Blum, "Jesajas prophetisches Testament: Beobachtungen zu Jes 1–11," *ZAW* 108 (1996): 547-68, and 109 (1997): 12-29. Bernhard W. Anderson also seeks an intelligible redactional shape for the material as it currently stands, though he recognizes more candidly that this was probably a second stage in the composition history; " 'God with Us' — In Judgment and in Mercy: The Editorial Structure of Isaiah 5–10(11)," in Gene M. Tucker, David L. Petersen and Robert R. Wilson, eds., *Canon, Theology, and Old Testament Interpretation: Essays in Honor of Brevard S. Childs* (Philadelphia: Fortress, 1988), pp. 230-45.

seven,[21] may be countered by an alternative solution which I have quite separately advanced elsewhere.[22] Starting from the observation that Isa 1 seems as a whole to be a relatively late assemblage of material, some parts of which, at least, look as though they have a good claim to reach back to the time of Isaiah of Jerusalem, the question arose as to whence the final redactor of the chapter derived his source material that he carefully forged into an introduction to the book of Isaiah as (more or less) a whole. Since the only obvious source of such material was the form of the book that he inherited,[23] my proposal was that in several cases one could make a plausible case for observing where the different units might have originally stood. So far as the woe-saying in Isa 1:4 is concerned (a verse which should not be joined in terms of original composition with vv. 5-9), I suggested that it originally stood at the head of the series in chapter 5. Apart from the fact that woe-sayings generally seem to have been in sequences, the single most important reason for this suggestion is the close comparability between 1:4b and 5:24c: "they have abandoned the Lord, they have spurned the Holy One of Israel" in the first case, and "they have rejected the instruction of the Lord of Hosts, and they have spurned the word of the Holy One of Israel" in the second (both my translations). As well as the general comparability of content here, we should note the use in both cases of the verb נאץ, the divine title "the Holy One of Israel," and the repeated use of the prose particle את.

Furthermore, the general sentiments expressed are suggestive of a shift from the more specific indictments of the woe-sayings themselves in the direction of the more Deuteronomic-like judgment that could well characterize redactional application of the woe-sayings in or near the exilic period.

21. This still remains the sole argument for joining 10:1-4 with 5:8-19 in, for instance, Scholastica Deck, *Die Gerichtsbotschaft Jesajas: Charakter und Begründung*, FzB 67 (Würzburg: Echter Verlag, 1991), p. 209, and Frank Crüsemann, *The Torah: Theology and Social History of Old Testament Law* (Edinburgh: T & T Clark, 1996), p. 20. Otto Procksch, *Jesaia I*, KAT 9/1 (Leipzig: Deichert, 1930), p. 91, also considered the argument from the number seven to be significant, but he solved the problem by the imaginative step of postulating that a woe-saying had been lost between verses 13 and 14.

22. H. G. M. Williamson, "Relocating Isaiah 1:2-9," in Craig C. Broyles and Craig A. Evans, eds., *Writing and Reading the Scroll of Isaiah: Studies of an Interpretive Tradition*, VTSup 70/1-2, 2 vols. (Leiden: Brill, 1997), 1: 263-77, and *A Critical and Exegetical Commentary on Isaiah 1–27, 1: Isaiah 1–5*, ICC (London: T & T Clark, 2006), pp. 37-40.

23. The almost inevitable nature of this conclusion is strongly underlined by the wholly implausible nature of the only alternative that, to my knowledge, has been advanced, namely that some form of the chapter circulated previously (i.e. for several centuries!) "as an independent collection"; so Wildberger, *Isaiah 1–12*, p. 9 (*Jesaja*, 1, p. 8).

It is therefore plausible to suppose that these two lines were introductory and concluding redactional comments on the whole woe-series, and also that if 1:4 had originally stood at the head of the series it would have naturally been in the sort of prominent position that might have attracted the attention of the later compiler of chapter 1. It follows from this suggestion that no other woe-saying is likely to have been included in any earlier form of the series in chapter 5.

A second reason for questioning whether 10:1-4 ever stood in a position other than its present one relates to the integrating role which it plays in its present position. On the assumption that it once stood elsewhere, it has long been recognized that the last line of v. 4 must have been added later in order to join it with the refrain poem which precedes it; this might have been either by the person who consciously brought vv. 1-4a here or by somebody else if the displacement was accidental. Either way, the point is acknowledged that this line was added deliberately to bind the passage to its present context.

In addition to that one line, however, it should be further noted that the verses share exactly the same length and structure as the preceding stanzas in the refrain poem (allowance made, of course, for some later additional elements in the present text).[24] It would certainly be a striking coincidence if this were the result of a chance move of some material to which the refrain element had subsequently been added.

We should observe next, however, that the passage is also followed by a woe-saying, beginning in v. 5. Admittedly, 10:5 seems to set out on a major new section in the book, as its focus is clearly anti-Assyrian. Nevertheless, given the evident fondness for woe-sayings to be grouped, the use of such a saying at 10:1 works well as an integrating feature looking forwards,[25] just as 10:4b does backwards. Furthermore, as several of the more recent studies noted above have shown, the use of a woe-saying at this point leads to a neatly chiastic structure around the so-called memoir (woes — outstretched-hand poem — memoir — outstretched-hand poem — woe).

In short, factors of differing kinds and from several different directions combine to suggest that this unprecedented combination of a woe-saying and

24. See especially the analysis by Gray, *Isaiah I–XXVII*, p. 177; note also L'Heureux, "Redactional History," pp. 112-13.

25. This point is emphasized strongly by Olof Bäckersten, *Isaiah's Political Message: An Appraisal of His Alleged Social Critique*, FAT 2. Reihe 29 (Tübingen: Mohr Siebeck, 2008), pp. 135-60. Indeed, it forms part of his argument that the passage is, in fact, anti-Assyrian. Regardless of whether that suggestion be accepted, his conclusion that our passage serves as an "editorial bridge" is close to that advocated here.

the outstretched-hand refrain serves its present position extremely well, both as a satisfactory conclusion to all that precedes by its combination of these two distinctive elements from the preceding chapters and as a help with the transition to the next section immediately following.

If this is correct, it is worth then moving on to ask next whether the content of the passage is generally suitable for a redactional conclusion to a considerable block of preceding material. The matters described in the following paragraphs are not of such a kind as would by themselves lead to the conclusion that this passage must be later. On the other hand I believe that they show how suitable the passage would be for this purpose, so that to that extent they support the case already made on other, independent grounds.

In the first case some elements in the composition seem to reflect knowledge of the surrounding context but to reverse or otherwise develop them in a heightened manner, so suggesting that it is our passage which is the dependent one. This applies in particular to the indictment in vv. 1-2. The language of the first line of v. 2, for instance, seems to be clearly indebted to 3:13-15 ("judgment" [דין], "steal" [גזל], "legal rights" [משפט], "poor" [עניי], and "my people" [עמי]), but it is made more shocking by referring not to God's exercise of judgment on behalf of his oppressed people but to the perversion of due legal process. Again, the use of "spoil and plunder" (שלל and בזז) in vv. 2 and 6 indicates that what might be expected of the Assyrian invader in v. 6 is now made more horrifying by being referred to the oppression of the local needy by their compatriots, while the application of the injustice to widows and orphans, which is admittedly a stereotyped element, may have been prompted in particular by the reference to them in 9:16. By allusions such as these, the indictment develops the force of earlier uses of similar sounding material.

Second, the expression of judgment is suitable to a writer who is living with some clearer expectation or knowledge of the eventual fate of Judah. In the eighth century Isaiah himself seems to have anticipated judgment exclusively in the form of defeat and destruction in the land,[26] and this is certainly the case with the various expressions relating to judgment that we find in chapters 5 and 9. Verses 3-4a of our passage point further than just that, however. Some of the vocabulary used does not appear elsewhere in the early parts of Isaiah 1–39 but is found, by contrast, in the second half of the book where it includes the ex-

26. I realize that this is rather a bold claim to make and that it needs more justification than can be briefly offered here. For indications of the line that the argument might take I refer to my essay "In Search of the Pre-exilic Isaiah," in John Day, ed., *In Search of Pre-exilic Israel: Proceedings of the Oxford Old Testament Seminar,* JSOTSup 406 (London: T & T Clark, 2004), pp. 181-206, as well as comments on relevant passages in my commentary *Isaiah 1–5*.

perience of exile. אסיר, "prisoner," for instance, occurs elsewhere in the Hebrew Bible only at 42:7 (a central passage in the reference to the deliverance from exile; one might also compare the use of the related form אסורים in 49:9 and 61:1) and 24:22, a later passage where in any case it is applied to foreign kings, not the people of Judah. The verb that describes part of their fate, כרע, is otherwise completely absent from the first half of the book, but it recurs, albeit with different referents and semantic nuances, in 45:23; 46:1, 2; 65:12.[27] Equally,

27. I am well aware that the first line of v. 4 is difficult. For a full discussion, see my forthcoming ICC commentary. There is no evidence from the main textual witnesses to suggest any corruption, so that if a solution is sought by emendation it can only be conjectural. While there is room for doubt at the margins, the present form of the text can be construed satisfactorily ("so as to avoid crouching among the prisoners and among the slain who have fallen"). It is difficult to suppose that בלתי could not be used in poetry as an equivalent of לבלתי without requiring emendation (cf. GK §163*c;* JM §160*l-m;* RSV, 'so as not to crouch . . .'; NEB). This must, however, be followed by an infinitive construct, so that the vocalization כְּרֹעַ should be preferred; I assume that the Masoretes thought of בלתי as a conjunction that could be followed by a finite verb; בלתי אם occurs twice with a finite verb following at Amos 3:3, 4, and they may have (wrongly) supposed, on the basis of the nominal clause at Gen 43:3, that the אם was optional (cf. Budde, 'Jesaja 1–5', 69); but in any case the problem of the switch in subject remains. For יפלו, however, no emendation is required; we may follow the proposal of Theodor H. Gaster, "Notes on Isaiah," in Abraham I. Katsh and Leon Nemoy, eds., *Essays on the Occasion of the Seventieth Anniversary of the Dropsie University* (Philadelphia, 1979), pp. 91-107 (92), in construing it rather as a relative clause without אשר, so that both תחת phrases in the line are dependent on כרע, a perfectly regular poetic form (see v. 3a, to go no further). Sense suggests that תחת does not literally mean "under," but rather "in place of" (BDB, p. 1065B), hence "among" (NRSV). There is no need for more radical emendations, such as Edward J. Kissane, *The Book of Isaiah, Translated from a Critically Revised Hebrew Text with Commentary,* 1: *i-xxxix* (Dublin: Browne and Nolan, 1941), p. 117, כי תכרעו, "when ye bow down . . . ," or the once very popular proposal of Paul de Lagarde, *Semitica* 1 (Göttingen: Dieterich, 1878), p. 105 (involving only one redivision of words so far as the consonantal text is concerned): בלתי כרעת חת אסיר, "Beltis is crouching, Osiris is shattered"; the thought may be compared with 46:1 and Jer 50:2. However, neither deity is attested elsewhere in the OT and there is no reason why Egyptian gods should be introduced at this point; appeal to the obscure chapter 28 is not sufficient justification. August Dillmann, *Der Prophet Jesaia,* KeHAT, 5th ed. (Leipzig: Hirzel, 1890), p. 102, dismissed the proposal as an "Einfall"! Similarly there is no need to follow C. J. Labuschagne, "Ugaritic *blt* and *biltî* in Is. x 4," *VT* 14 (1964): 97-99, who suggested that בלת was an equivalent of Ugaritic *blt,* a negative exclamation, and so moved the *yod* to the following word to read יכרע: "No, he will crouch among the prisoners" (somewhat similarly John H. Hayes and Stuart A. Irvine, *Isaiah, the Eighth-Century Prophet: His Times and His Preaching* [Nashville, 1987], p. 193). Apart from being somewhat speculative, the problem of the verbal subjects remains, despite what Labuschagne states, for it would be singular here but plural in the parallel. As an improvement on Labuschagne, Wildberger, *Jesaja,* 1, p. 180 (*Isaiah 1–12,* p. 194), followed by Renatus Porath, *Die Sozialkritik im Jesajabuch: Redaktionsgeschichtliche*

שואה does not feature elsewhere in the first part of Isaiah, but is attested later in 47:11 as the climax of a string of words referring to the end of Babylon. Finally, it is worth mentioning that the judgment is addressed to the readers in the second person plural.[28] This is not true of any of the judgment elements in the preceding divine anger poem, so that it becomes even less likely that this was once an original stanza of that poem. Rather it gives the impression of making the judgment more immediate to the readers, something which we might well expect in the aftermath of the later catastrophe.

Given that some of the other vocabulary items in these verses, such as פקדה and הרוגים, are not diagnostic, this may seem like small pickings on which to base a case. I should emphasize again, therefore, that my argument is not to say that this passage must be exilic on this basis but rather that on the other grounds described above this passage has all the appearance of being a later redactional conclusion to a previous section in the book and that, in the light of that more firmly based conclusion, the phraseology used to describe the nature of the judgment is fully compatible with a date later than the surrounding material.[29]

I conclude, therefore, that the "initial problem" perhaps turns out to be an important clue not so much to the early stages of the composition of Isaiah but rather to the processes by which original sayings from Isaiah were gradually drawn together with other material in the long process which led to the eventual book which we have inherited. In my opinion, an important step in that process was the realization that Isaiah's prophecies had come to a measure of fulfilment in the destruction of Jerusalem and the exile of some of the elite population to Babylon, from which the second half of the book goes on to announce their liberation. Isaiah 10:1-4 may be seen to take its natural place within this unfolding scenario.

Analyse, Europäische Hochschulschriften 23/503 (Frankfurt: Peter Lang, 1994), p. 161, takes בלתי as an independent negative (cf. Num. 11:6), "No! All in vain!," and then vocalizes כרע as an infinitive absolute. This is possible, but it is not clear that Num. 11:6 is really a parallel for the proposed usage; it seems rather to introduce an exceptive clause.

28. This is correctly observed by Uwe Becker, *Jesaja — von der Botschaft zum Buch,* FRLANT 178 (Göttingen: Vandenhoeck & Ruprecht, 1997), p. 156. He also considers that this makes unlikely an original setting among the woe-sayings; however, 5:8 (admittedly the only example) means that this argument is not watertight.

29. Among others who have also concluded that 10:1-4 may be a redactional composition I have noted Rudolf Kilian, *Jesaja 1–12,* Die Neue Echter Bibel 17 (Würzburg: Echter Verlag, 1986), p. 79; Wolfgang Werner, *Studien zur alttestamentlichen Vorstellung vom Plan Jahwes,* BZAW 173 (Berlin: de Gruyter, 1988), pp. 13-14; L'Heureux, "The Redactional History of Isaiah 5.1–10.4"; Becker, *Jesaja,* pp. 155-59; Bäckersten, *Isaiah's Political Message.*

On the Structure and Formation of the Book of Deutero-Isaiah

Rainer Albertz

At the end of the last century, when I wrote my book on the history and literature of the Babylonian exile, which included — among other issues — a study on Deutero-Isaiah,[1] I was not aware that Joseph Blenkinsopp had prepared a commentary on Isaiah 40–55 nearly at the same time (published 2002),[2] which was part of the enormous project of interpreting the entire book of Isaiah in three volumes.[3] I am happy to be given the opportunity to appreciate this sophisticated and thoughtful commentary, which I think is one of the best written since the commentary of Bernhard Duhm.[4] For me, as one who tries to resist the pressure of specializing in our field, Joseph Blenkinsopp is an outstanding example of a learned Old Testament scholar. He has a competent overview of all research fields in scholarship, not only of all the books of the Hebrew Bible, including their ancient Near Eastern background and their

1. See Rainer Albertz, *Israel in Exile: The History and Literature of the Sixth Century* B.C.E., Studies in Biblical Literature 3 (Atlanta: Society of Biblical Literature, 2003), pp. 376-438. The German original is titled: Rainer Albertz, *Die Exilszeit: 6. Jahrhundert v. Chr.*, Biblische Enzyklopädie 7 (Stuttgart: Kohlhammer, 2001).

2. See Joseph Blenkinsopp, *Isaiah 40–55: A New Translation with Introduction and Commentary*, The Anchor Yale Bible 19A (New Haven and London: Yale University Press, 2002).

3. See Joseph Blenkinsopp, *Isaiah 1–39: A New Translation with Introduction and Commentary*, The Anchor Yale Bible 19 (New Haven and London: Yale University Press, 2000) and Joseph Blenkinsopp, *Isaiah 56–66: A New Translation with Introduction and Commentary*, The Anchor Yale Bible 19B (New York, London, Toronto, Sidney, and Auckland: Doubleday, 2003).

4. See Bernhard Duhm, *Das Buch Jesaia*, 5th ed., Göttinger Handkommentar zum Alten Testament III/1 (Göttingen: Vandenhoeck & Ruprecht, 1968). The first edition was published in 1892.

Wirkungsgeschichte,[5] but also of the historiography of all periods including archaeology.[6] Therefore, it is a great privilege for me to contribute some ideas about the structure and formation of the book of Deutero-Isaiah to this volume in his honor.

1. Basic Insights in the Structure of Isaiah 40–55

Blenkinsopp discussed the structure of Deutero-Isaiah in some length.[7] He was aware of many different proposals, but wisely did not follow one fixed scheme. He rightly maintained, against Kiesow,[8] that the two parts of the book, the Jacob/Israel section (Isa 40–48) and the Zion/Jerusalem section (Isa 49–55), conceptually belong together.[9] Therefore the call to flee from Babylon (48:20-21) constitutes just the end of the first section, but not an end of an earlier book. Interestingly, he observed that the second section is structured by an alternation between Servant and Zion passages, but suggested that the last sequence, the fourth servant song (52:13-53:12) and promises for Zion (54:1-17a), "might . . . appear to have been added subsequently."[10]

Perhaps one could emphasize a little bit more explicitly than Blenkinsopp that the joyous report of YHWH's arrival at Zion in 52:7-12, which runs parallel to 48:20-21 at its end, constitutes a first epilogue, where several visions of the prologue in 40:1-11, the announcement of good news and YHWH's return to Zion, become true. Because of this obvious *inclusio* already Elliger concluded that 52:7-12 may have constituted the end of the book at an earlier stage.[11] This view, which is now shared by several recent scholars,[12] is supported by the

5. Cf., with regard to the book of Isaiah, the interesting study of Joseph Blenkinsopp, *Opening the Sealed Book: Interpretations of the Book of Isaiah in Late Antiquity* (Grand Rapids and Cambridge, U.K.: Eerdmans, 2006).

6. Cf. for example, Joseph Blenkinsopp, "The Age of the Exile" in *The Biblical World*, vol. 1, ed. John Barton (London and New York: Routledge, 2002), pp. 416-39.

7. *Isaiah 40–55*, pp. 59-61.

8. Cf. Klaus Kiesow, *Exodustexte im Jesajabuch: Literarkritische und motivgeschichtliche Analysen*, Orbis et Biblicus Orientalis 24 (Fribourg and Göttingen: Universitätsverlag and Vandenhoeck & Ruprecht, 1979), p. 165.

9. Following Hans-Jürgen Hermisson, *Studien zur Prophetie und Weisheit*, Forschungen zum Alten Testament 23 (Tübingen: Mohr-Siebeck, 1998), pp. 117-23, 148-49.

10. *Isaiah 40–55*, p. 61.

11. See Karl Elliger, *Deuterojesaja in seinem Verhältnis zu Tritojesaja*, Beiträge zur Wissenschaft vom Alten und Neuen Testament 63 (Stuttgart: Kohlhammer, 1933), pp. 265-67.

12. Thus, Odil Hannes Steck, *Gottesknecht und Zion: Gesammelte Aufsätze zu Deuteroje-*

observation that only Isa 40:1–52:7 are structured by so-called "eschatological hymns" (42:10-13; 44:23; 45:8; 48:20-21; 49:13; 52:9-10) into meaningful segments.[13]

It is generally acknowledged that the present book of Deutero-Isaiah comes to its end in Isa 55:13. Among others, Kiesow has convincingly shown that 55:6-13 constitutes a second epilogue, whose praise of YHWH's creative word in 55:10-11 refers back to 40:6-8* of the prologue, where the eternity of the divine word is reflected.[14] These verses constitute an outer *inclusio.* From these observations Elliger concluded that an earlier Deutero-Isaiah collection (40:1–52:7*) was expanded by the fourth servant song (52:13–53:12) first, and by chapters 54–55 later. He regarded Trito-Isaiah as responsible for these later editions of the book.[15] This last suggestion became less convincing, since it turned out that Isa 56–66 do not originate from a single person, but constitute a multi-layered composite in itself. His basic insight, however, that the doubled structure of the book points to two major editions of the book of Deutero-Isaiah, remains true; likewise that the second edition generally shows a closer relationship with Isa 56–66 than the first.

---

saja, Forschungen zum Alten Testament 4 (Tübingen: Mohr-Siebeck, 1992), p. 125; Reinhard Gregor Kratz, *Kyros im Deuterojesaja-Buch: Redaktionsgeschichtliche Untersuchungen zu Entstehung und Theologie von Jesaja 40–55,* Forschungen zum Alten Testament 1 (Tübingen: Mohr-Siebeck, 1991), p. 217; Jürgen van Oorschot, *Von Babel zum Zion: Eine literarkritische und redaktionsgeschichtliche Untersuchung,* Beihefte zur Zeitschrift für die alttestamentliche Wissenschaft 206 (Berlin and New York: de Gruyter, 1993), p. 345; Ulrich Berges, *Das Buch Jesaja: Komposition und Endgestalt,* Herders Biblische Studien 16 (Freiburg, Basel, Vienna, Barcelona, Rome, and New York: Herder, 1998), p. 549; Jürgen Werlitz, *Redaktion und Komposition: Zur Rückfrage hinter die Endgestalt von Jesaja 40–55,* Bonner Biblische Beiträge 122 (Berlin and Bodenheim: Philo, 1999), pp. 319-23. This view is also indicated by Blenkinsopp, *Isaiah 40–55,* p. 372.

13. Cf. Roy F. Melugin, *The Formation of Isaiah 40–55,* Beihefte zur Zeitschrift für die alttestamentliche Wissenschaft 141 (Berlin and New York: de Gruyter, 1976), pp. 90-175. Isa 51:3 is just a fragment of such a hymn at best; it will prove to be a late insertion; see below. Isa 54:1-2 is no religious hymn at all, but a call to joy, *pace* Claus Westermann, *Das Buch Jesaja: Kapitel 40–66,* 5th ed., Das Alte Testament Deutsch 19 (Göttingen and Zürich: Vandenhoeck & Ruprecht, 1986), pp. 19-20.

14. Kiesow, *Exodustexte,* pp. 65-66, 165.

15. Cf. Elliger, *Verhältnis,* pp. 265-71.

2. Consequences for Reconstructing the Formation of Isaiah 40–55

In his commentary, Joseph Blenkinsopp deals with the formation of Isa 40–55 in some detail.[16] After having referred to the theories of some scholars, Blenkinsopp identified a "current confused situation" and maintained that "our text exhibits a relatively high level of coherence,"[17] especially in chapters 40–48, where he noted only a few possible additions.[18] With regard to chapters 49-55 he accepted the evidence of a Trito-Isaianic editor, who has added the last three servant songs (49:1-6; 50:4-9; 52:13–52:12) including the comments to the first two (49:7, 9-12; 50:10-11). He also added some smaller passages in their immediate surroundings (50:1-3; 51:1-6) and some sporadic insertions in chapters 54–55.[19] Thus, Blenkinsopp sensitively noticed different styles and concepts in such passages,[20] but he hesitated to go further in order to differentiate and classify these insertions. That may be wise for writing a commentary, which will still be read when most of the recent redactional theories will have been forgotten.

The current situation, however, is not as confused as Blenkinsopp has stated.[21] Nearly all proposals for reconstructing the formation of the book which have been recently published converge — in spite of all differences in detail — on the result that there is ample evidence to distinguish two major editions of the book of Deutero-Isaiah, an earlier one, which was restricted to Isa 40:1–52:12* and a later one, which comprised Isa 40:1–55:13*. What was identified as "Jerusalem redaction" by van Oorschot (Dtjes Z) in the earlier edition, substantially corresponds to Berges's "Golah redaction" and "first Jerusalem redaction" and Werlitz's "book edition."[22] Even the "supplementary Cyrus stratum" reconstructed by Kratz is similar.[23] The four scholars even agree on dating; they all propose the origin of the earlier edition around the year 520 B.C.E., although they concede the incorporation of older material. With regard to the later book edition, three of these scholars argue for a later

16. See Blenkinsopp, *Isaiah 40–55*, pp. 69-81.

17. For both citations see Blenkinsopp, *Isaiah 40–55*, p. 73.

18. So Isa 46:12-13; 48:16b, 17-19, 22; see Blenkinsopp, *Isaiah 40–55*, pp. 73-74, 80.

19. For example Isa 54:17b; 55:13b; see Blenkinsopp, *Isaiah 40–55*, pp. 74, 80, 366.

20. Especially in Isa 48; cf. Blenkinsopp, *Isaiah 40–55*, pp. 288-90, going beyond the introductory remarks.

21. For a more detailed study of the research history see Albertz, *Israel*, pp. 378-93.

22. See the schemes or summaries mentioned above in note 12.

23. Kratz, *Kyros*, p. 217, mainly differs as far as he included also the fourth servant song into this stratum and suggested Isa 55:3-5 as a possible end. But there is no need to go beyond 52:12.

redaction during the fifth century, be it the "Servant Israel stratum" of Kratz, the "secondary Zion stratum" of van Oorschot, or the "second Jerusalem redaction" of Berges.

Among these recent attempts to reconstruct the earlier edition of the book of Deutero-Isaiah, the methodological reflections of Jürgen Werlitz are of major importance.[24] Werlitz connects the diachronic literary critical and redaction historical approach, on the one hand, with a synchronic composition critical approach, on the other hand. In his view, the composition criticism must provide a constant frame of reference and corrective for redaction criticism, and vice versa. A satisfactory literary and redactional study must yield a book with a distinct beginning and end, a clear structure, and a meaningful sequence of texts. By this methodological innovation, the redaction critical results can be controlled much better and provided with a higher degree of probability. Following these methodological lines, Werlitz was able to reconstruct a first book edition, which runs from a reduced prologue (40:1-2, 3-5*) through the Jacob/Israel and the Zion/Jerusalem portions to an epilogue (52:7-12).[25] Both portions are linked by the second servant song (49:1-6), including its commentary (49:8-12). The entire book is structured by the eschatological hymns in two introductions (40:12-31; 49:14–50:2*) and five segments (41:1–42:13; 42:14–44:23; 44:24–48:21; 49:1-13*; 50–52*). Interestingly, Werlitz has recognized that the structuring elements — the prologue, epilogue, eschatological hymns, and the commentaries on the first two servant songs — are all editorial. By these, the prophetic editor not only brought the older material into a meaningful sequence, but also actualized it for a new purpose. According to Werlitz, this older material also includes the first three servant songs and parts of the polemics against the idols, because they are firmly anchored in the composition. Thus, the composition critical approach detected the original compositional setting of some of those texts, which, since Bernhard Duhm, were often regarded as secondary.[26]

3. A Possible Reconstruction of the Formation of Isaiah 40–55

Along the methodological lines elaborated by Jürgen Werlitz, I presented a reconstruction of the book of Deutero-Isaiah, which comprised the first three

24. See Werlitz, *Redaktion,* pp. 237-82.
25. See his summary, Werlitz, *Redaktion,* pp. 319-23.
26. See for example Duhm, *Jesaia,* pp. 14-15; Westermann, *Jesaja,* pp. 27-28.

editorial stages, the first book edition (40:1–52:12*: DtIE^1), the appendix of the fourth servant song (52:13–53:12), and the second edition of the book (40:1–55:13*: DtIE^2).[27] These strata include about 87 percent of the present text. The book of this stage, however, was later expanded by a number of insertions, which I did not deal with before in detail, because my earlier publication was restricted to the exilic period. Thus, I would like to take the opportunity to complete my view of the formation of Isa 40–55 here.

3.1 The First Edition of the Book of Deutero-Isaiah (DtIE^1)

The first book edition, which was already reconstructed and described elsewhere in detail,[28] consists of the following passages:

DtIE^1
Isa 40:1-2, 3aβ-5bα, 9-11, 12-31*; 41:1–42:16, 18-19a, 20, 22-24aα$_1$, 25; 43:1–44:8, 10-17, 20, 21-24, 26b-28; 45:1-8, 11a, 12-13bα, 14-15,[29] 18-20a, 21-25; 46:1-7, 9-13; 47:2, 5-8a, 10-15; 48:1abα, 3, 6-7a, 8a, 11aα, 11b-16a, 20-21; 49:1-6, 8-21*; 50:1-2, 4-9; 51:4-5, 9-10, 17-19; 52:1-2, 7-12

According to my view, it was written during the years 521-520 B.C.E., after the group of the anonymous prophet, who had preached before among the Babylonian exiles from about 547 B.C.E. onwards, came to Judah in order to bring the good news to Zion that YHWH had decided to show pity to his people, to release his capital and bring the exiles home (40:1-2, 9-11; 52:9-10). The political events in the background are probably the usurpation of Gaumata by Darius I, the following revolts against Darius throughout the empire, especially those in Babylon during the years 522 and 521, and the suppression of these revolts by Darius. Under these conditions, Darius was probably ready to repatriate a loyal group of

27. See Albertz, *Israel*, pp. 393-438.

28. See Albertz, *Israel*, pp. 393-425.

29. In contrast to the table in Albertz, *Exilszeit*, p. 297, I include also the difficult verses Isa 45:14-15 in the first edition. They seem to reflect — like 43:3b-4 — the conquest of Egypt by Cambyses (525 B.C.E.); for additional reasons, see Rainer Albertz, "Loskauf umsonst? Die Befreiungsvorstellungen bei Deuterojesaja," in *Freiheit und Recht*, ed. Christof Hardmeier, Rainer Kessler and Andreas Ruwe (Gütersloh: Chr. Kaiser and Gütersloher Verlag, 2003), pp. 360-79, esp. pp. 366-75. In the English edition (Albertz, *Israel*, p. 398), these verses are already included (see also p. 415). But in the table on p. 398 the misprint of the first line (40:12-1) should be corrected to 40:12-15.

Judean exiles around Zerubbabel and Joshua in order to stabilize the western wing of his empire. Against these dramatical historical events, the book describes how the message of comfort — from the first victories of Cyrus to the conquest of Babylon by Darius — extended from Babylonia to Jerusalem through all resistances and disappointments. The book proclaims divine salvation without any conditions, but its probable public recitation was intended to encourage the lethargic and reserved population of Judah to grab the opportunity of salvation and welcome the returnees from Babylonia. As shown elsewhere in detail,[30] this reconstructed edition can be understood as a well-structured, coherent, and meaningful rhetorical unit in a concrete historical situation.

3.2 *The Appendix of the Fourth Servant Song*

That the fourth servant song (52:13–53:12) has to be regarded as an appendix was already seen by Elliger.[31] As shown by the framing divine speeches in 52:13-15 and 53:11aβ-12 it is a rhetorical unit of its own. The fact that this song follows a call to leave Babylon as does the second one (48:20-21; 49:1-6), which was rightly observed by Blenkinsopp,[32] may be one reason for adding it at this place. There is a link to the given context: the term "arm of YHWH" in 53:1 refers back to 52:10. Thus, the song was composed with knowledge of the final passage of DtIE[1]. Since 49:7, which constitutes a second divine answer to the complaint of the Servant (49:4) and is completed by 49:8-12, directly refers to the beginning of the fourth servant song (cf. 52:15), it serves to link this song with DtIE[1]. Its position indicates that the fourth servant song should be read as a commentary to the second one, especially to the universal salvific task of the Servant mentioned in 49:6. Here, it is not the place to discuss the highly disputed meaning of the fourth servant song. Considering the given links to 49:1-7 and 52:10, however, one should rather think of a collective understanding: By all his suffering during the exile the Servant Israel has taken on an atoning and salvific function for all the nations. These deep reflections about a possible positive meaning of the distress of exile may come from the years after 515 B.C.E., when Israel's "renewal" had begun but was not yet complete. The author was still a member of the Deutero-Isaiah group, but — as some differences in language and concept show — not the redactor of the DtIE[1].

30. Cf. Albertz, *Israel,* pp. 404-25.

31. See Elliger, *Verhältnis,* pp. 266-67.

32. Blenkinsopp, *Isaiah 40–55,* p. 74.

3.3 *The Second Edition of the Book of Deutero-Isaiah (DtIE²)*

The author of the second edition of the book (DtIE²) added the new chapters Isa 54–55* and tied them to the DtIE¹ through a framework of appeals to hear around the appendix of the fourth servant song (51:1-2, 7-8; 55:1-5). In addition, by inserting 40:6, 8 into the prologue and composing a new epilogue (55:6-13), the editor created a new framework for his entire book (55:10-11), which intended to emphasize the persistence and effectiveness of the divine word in the face of all earthly obstacles. Thus, he sporadically intervened also in the first edition. As explained elsewhere in more detail,[33] DtIE² consists of DtIE¹ including its appendix plus probably the following passages:

DtIE²
Isa 40:3aα, 6, 8; 44:25-26a; 45:9-10, 11b, 13bβ; 47:3-4, 8b-9; 51:1-2, 7-8, 12-15, 20-23; 52:3; 54:1-17a; 55:1-6, 8-13[34]

The message of the DtIE² cannot be unfolded here in detail.[35] But it should be mentioned that the second edition of the book is characterized by a defense of the prophetical message against substantial obstacles and doubts. In the beginning of the fifth century, the reality lagged far behind the enthusiastic message of the Deutero-Isaiah group. It is true that a sizable group of exiles had returned and the temple had been rebuilt, but Jerusalem lay still in ruins until the middle of the fifth century, and several foreign leaders whom the Persians settled in Samaria interfered in Judah (Ezra 4:9-10). With several exhortations, the author of DtIE² intended to encourage those faithful adherents, who still waited for the complete fulfillment of the announced salvation, to maintain their hopes against all obstacles, threats and mockeries (51:1-2, 7-8, 12-15; 55:1-5). He never tired of assuring the ruined capital of YHWH's irremovable love (54:4-6, 7-9), of its wonderful reconstruction (54:11-13) and a peaceful existence (54:10, 14-17a). Since the new book edition reveals fear about

33. See Albertz, *Israel,* pp. 428-33.

34. In the table of Albertz, *Israel,* p. 429, the verses Isa 45:11a, 13bα have to be corrected to 45:11b, 13bβ. Isaiah 51:12-15 has to be added to the list, because in this divine answer to the lament of 51:9-10, which is secondary with regard to the primary answer in 51:17-19, the warning about fear of human beings, who are transient like grass, reminds one of 40:8, a verse which certainly belongs to DtIE². The gloss in 40:7b, which relates the grass to people, is wrong; the enemies of Israel are meant. Also Oorschot, *Babel,* pp. 253-55, includes the passage in his "secondary Zion stratum."

35. See for more details Albertz, *Israel,* pp. 430-33.

new military threats (51:12-13, 20-23; 54:15-17a), it was perhaps prompted by Xerxes' campaigns against Greece (484-479 B.C.E.), which were accompanied by new uprisings of Babylon (cf. 47:3-4, 8b-9). In DtIE² the prologue was converted by small intrusions (40:3aα, 6) into a kind of call narrative corresponding to Isa 6:4, 8. Now, the commission of comforting the people and Zion (40:1-2) was interpreted as an explicit annulment of the heavenly judgment of doom, which the prophet Isaiah had experienced (6:9-11). Thus, it may have happened at this stage of redactional history that the enlarged book of Deutero-Isaiah was physically connected with the existing book of Isaiah (roughly Isa 1–32*).

3.4 Alignments with the Book of Trito-Isaiah (DtIT)

After the second book edition, Deutero-Isaiah seems to have been subject only to sporadic insertions or smaller redactions. One group of insertions is characterized by the intention of aligning the book of Deutero-Isaiah with topics that can be found in the book of Trito-Isaiah. The following passages can be ascribed to it:

DtIT
Isa 48:16b; 49:22-23, 24-26; 54:13

The secondary character of 48:16b is generally acknowledged.[36] After a divine oracle, which commissioned an anonymous king — after the fall of Babylon (Isa 47) probably Darius I[37] — to carry through the salvific will of God (48:12-16a), the short self-report of a prophetical figure about his call seems to be out of place. It may even be an anacoluthon: "And now Adonay-YHWH has sent me, and his spirit . . . ," as Blenkinsopp considered.[38] The phrase takes up the

36. Duhm, *Jesaia,* p. 365; Elliger, *Verhältnis,* pp. 213-15; Oorschot, *Babel,* 277-78; Werlitz, *Redaktion,* p. 275; Blenkinsopp, *Isaiah 40–55,* p. 294; Blenkinsopp, *Isaiah 56–66,* p. 64, among many others.

37. For the thesis that the commission of Cyrus (Isa 41:1-4; 44:24-28; 45:1-7) is tacitly substituted for that of Darius in the DtIE¹ (42:5-9; 45:11a, 12-13abα; 48:12-16a), see Albertz, *Israel,* pp. 399-404, 408-9, 418, and Albertz, "Darius in Place of Cyrus: The First Edition of Deutero-Isaiah (Isaiah 40.1–52.12) in 521 BCE," *Journal for the Study of the Old Testament* 27 no. 3 (2003): 371-83.

38. See Blenkinsopp, *Isaiah 40–55,* p. 294. Nowhere else is the divine spirit an object of God's sending.

presentation of the Servant Israel in 42:1 and clearly refers to the self-presentation of the prophetical Servant in 61:1. The anacoluthon may even have the rhetorical function that the reader should complete it from there in the sense: "and his spirit is laid on me." In my view, the insertion has two intentions: on the one hand, it aims at relating the royal oracle to the prophetical figure, whom we call Trito-Isaiah. It was no longer the Persian king Darius, but the Israelite prophet in the succession of Deutero-Isaiah and his group who would conduct the salvific will of YHWH in the future. On the other hand, the insertion indicates where Trito-Isaiah's promises for Zion (Isa 60–62), which run partly parallel to those of Deutero-Isaiah (49:14–54:17), should be placed in the process of Israel's salvation: just before the return of the prophetical group to Jerusalem (48:20-21).

In the contentious comfort of Zion (49:14-26), the last two passages, 49:22-23 and 49:24-26, probably constitute later additions.[39] In contrast to the announcement of 49:14-21, which belongs to DtIE[1], both small units use the messenger formula in their introduction. They both end with recognition formulas, whose stylistic features (with *waw*-perfect) remind one more of Ezekiel (Ezek 16:62; 22:16; 25:11, 17 passim) than of Deutero-Isaiah (with *lĕmaʿan* and imperfect in 45:3); a similar construction occurs in Trito-Isaiah (60:16). Moreover, 49:22 gives an answer to Zion's question (49:21), although it was only rhetorical, and 49:24-25 imitate the rhetorical question-answer play of 49:14-15 in an artificial and slightly unclear manner. As Elliger already pointed out,[40] the language and motives of the two passages remind one of Trito-Isaiah. The first passage intends to support the hopes in the repopulation of Jerusalem with the notion that YHWH would stimulate the nations by his banner (similar to 62:10) announcing his intentions to bring home the sons and daughters of Zion (49:22). This notion is not totally absent from the DtIE[1] (43:6), but is displayed in detail by Trito-Isaiah (cf. 60:4, 9; 66:20). The idea that kings and queens will serve Zion and its people like vassals (49:23) has its closest parallels in the descriptions of salvation of Trito-Isaiah (60:16; 61:5-6; cf. already 49:7). Against the fear that mighty earthly powers might cost YHWH his victory, the

39. Westermann, *Jesaja*, pp. 175-80, regarded Isa 49:14-26 as a compositional unity following the three addressees of complaint, but this was already questioned by Melugin, *Formation*, pp. 148-52. Oorschot, *Babel*, pp. 151-52, 247-48, and Hans-Jürgen Hermission, *Deuterojesaja, 3. Teilband: Jesaja 49,14–55,13*, Biblischer Kommentar Altes Testament XI/3 (Neukirchen-Vluyn: Neukirchener Verlag, 2007), pp. 17-18, 25, attribute the first passage (49:22-23) to an early book edition, but regarded the second (49:24-26) as clearly secondary. The secondary character of both passages is stressed by Werlitz, *Redaktion*, pp. 308-13.

40. See Elliger, *Verhältnis*, pp. 124-29.

second passage (49:24-26) encourages the audience to believe that YHWH himself will litigate with the nations and save Zion's children. The somewhat cruel notion that YHWH will feed Zion's enemies with their own flesh and make them drunk from their own blood has no parallel at all, but the final recognition formula is a citation of Isa 60:16. It is possible that especially the second passage responds to a similar military threat during the first part of the fifth century B.C.E., like $DtIE^2$.

Finally, 54:13 interrupts the report of the wonderful reconstruction of Jerusalem (from $DtIE^2$) by interpreting the precious stones of Zion's gates as its sons, who would all become "pupils of YHWH" and enjoy peace.[41] This idea reminds one of the pupils of the prophet Isaiah (8:16) and the Deutero-Isaiah group (50:4), but is also paralleled by the notion of 61:6 that all inhabitants of restored Judah will become priests and servants of YHWH. Isaiah 54:13 intended to emphasize that not only the city but also its inhabitants would have to be transformed in the direction of a close relationship with the divine, as shown by the prophetic group itself.

It is not quite clear whether all these additions come from the same hand and from the same time, but they all intend to replenish the salvific notions of Deutero-Isaiah with ideas developed by the prophetic circle behind Trito-Isaiah. Since these ideas all are taken from the kernel of this book (Isa 60–62), these alignments must not be much later than $DtIE^2$ and probably still belong to the first part of the fifth century B.C.E.

3.5 *The Scholastic Redaction (DtIS)*

A more coherent reworking of the book happened by the so-called scholastic redaction, which is characterized by a closer relationship to styles and concepts of Deuteronomistic literature and other prophetic books, such as Jeremiah and Ezekiel. This redaction was first discovered by Hans-Christoph Schmitt long ago,[42] but meanwhile can probably be expanded by some other secondary verses. In my view, it comprises the following passages:

41. The verse was regarded as secondary to its context by Oorschot, *Babel*, p. 268. The variant reading of 1QIs[a] ("your builder" instead of "your sons") can be regarded as an attempt to align the verse a little bit more with its context. Its intrusion also disturbs the *stichoi* of the passage.

42. See Hans-Christoph Schmitt, "Prophetie und Schultheologie im Deuterojesajabuch: Beobachtungen zur Redaktionsgeschichte von Jes 40–55*," *Zeitschrift für die alttestamentliche Wissenschaft* 91, no. 1 (1979): 43-61. Schmitt calls this redaction "schultheologische Bearbeitung."

DtIS

Isa 42:19b, 21, 24aα$_2$b; 46:8; 48:1bβ, 2, 4-5, 7b, 8b-10, 11aβ, 17-19; 50:10-11; 55:7

The best evidence for this redaction comes from Isa 48, a chapter which is thoroughly reworked in the course of this redaction.[43] Originally, 48:1-11 was an editorial unit, by which the redactor of DtIE^1 intended to prepare his Judean audience for the surprising message (48:6) that YHWH had decided to commission anew a king with the salvation of his people (48:12-16a), who — after the fall of Babylon (47:1-15*, referred to in 48:1) — could only be Darius I. He would carry through God's salvific will, what Cyrus had only started, but not completed.[44] This preparation for a salvific message was secondarily converted into a penitential sermon:[45] In 48:1bβ, 2, which constitutes a doublet to 48:1abα, the people are accused of referring to Zion and YHWH in a dishonest and immoral way. The delay of fulfilling the given prophetic announcements (48:3) is now secondarily founded on the stiff-necked character of the people (48:4; cf. Ezek 2:4; 3:7), who would rather ascribe the fulfillment to their idols (48:5). The surprising character of the good news (48:6-7a) is interpreted as a divine strategy against the arrogant attitude of the people that they already knew all that the prophets would say (48:7b). Finally, the divine statement that YHWH would save Israel for his own sake (48:11aα, b) is interpreted by a long accusation (48:8b-10, 11aβ), in which Israel is characterized as a treacherous and notorious rebel from its origins (cf. Jer 3:8, 11; 5:11; 9:1; Isa 1:2). Only because YHWH wanted to care for his name did he remain patient and not destroy Israel (cf. Ezek 20:9, 14, 22), but tested it in the smelting furnace of exile (cf. Jer 6:27-30; Ezek 22:18-22). Thus, the scholastic redaction (DtIS) used an earlier text, which reflected the delay of salvation in some way, for the purpose

43. See already Duhm, *Jesaia*, pp. 360-66, Westermann, *Jesaja*, pp. 159-62, and Werlitz, *Redaktion*, pp. 348-53. Also Blenkinsopp, *Isaiah 40–55*, pp. 288-90, 295, noticed in Isa 48 passages of a different language and concept, which are "difficult if not impossible to reconcile with the outlook, the tone, and even the religious vocabulary of the 'prophet of consolation'" (p. 290).

44. As is known, Cyrus did not conquer Babylon in 539 B.C.E., but cooperated with its aristocracy and its Marduk priests, not with the exiled Judean groups. He only sent some temple vessels back to Jerusalem at best (Ezra 1:7); see Albertz, *Israel*, 113-32.

45. Some recent scholars argue that the passage gains its specific profile only by the accusations (cf. Kratz, *Kyros*, pp. 114-17; Hans-Jürgen Hermission, *Deuterojesaja, 2. Teilband: Jesaja 45,8–49,13*, Biblischer Kommentar Altes Testament, XI/2 [Neukirchen-Vluyn: Neukirchener Verlag, 2003], pp. 210-13), but they seem to overlook its important function to introduce the commission of a new Persian king after the fall of Babylon.

of introducing accusations of the pre-exilic prophets of doom — not only of Isaiah, but also of Jeremiah and Ezekiel — into the book of Deutero-Isaiah. It intended to demonstrate that Israel, not God, is to be blamed for the delay of salvation. From his post-exilic experience the redactor wanted to make Deutero-Isaiah's unconditional message of salvation conditional.

The intention of providing the salvific message of Deutero-Isaiah with a strong ethical commitment becomes obvious in 48:17-19, which the redactor put in the mouth of the prophet introduced by DtIT in 48:16b. Here YHWH is presented as a helpful guide of Israel who wishes to keep Israel on the right way (48:17). But God has to complain that the people missed the chance to obey his commandments and reflects about how Israel could have been multiplied and lived in peace, if it had done his will (48:18). According to the scholastic redactor, the misery of the people from the exilic past up to the present was a consequence of its disobedience (48:19 with a reference back to 48:9). The concept expressed in these verses is clearly Deuteronomistic; the language partly reminds one of Trito-Isaiah (60:17; 66:12), but also of patriarchal promises (Gen 22:17; Exod 32:13) and of Ps 81:14-17 (13-16).

The scholastic redactor seems to have reworked also Isa 42:18-25, the first one of the two judgment speeches on Israel (cf. 43:22-28*) in DtIE^1.[46] Here Deutero-Isaiah had criticized his companions in Babylon for being blind and deaf to his message of salvation, because they did not understand that their exilic situation was caused by YHWH and nobody else (42:18-19a, 20, 22-24aα_1, 25).[47] Thus, for the prophet and his group, the acceptance of the divine punishment was crucial for salvation, but that did not explicitly include new rules of conduct. The scholastic redactor wanted to make this explicit. He probably inserted the repeating questions of 42:19b in order to emphasize the scandal that even "Meshullam," the post-exilic substitute for the dead exilic generation, persisted in the blindness of YHWH's servant.[48] He interpreted

46. Cf. the identical expression *hālak b^{e}derek* "to go on the way" in Isa 42:24bβ and 48:17; 55:7, and the similar phrases *šāmaʿ b^{e}tôrâ* in 42:24bβ and *qāšab* hif. *l^{e}miṣwôt* "to listen to the torah/commandments" in 48:18. All these phrases have their parallels in Deuteronomic and Deuteronomistic texts (Deut 8:6; 1 Kgs 3:14; Jer 32:23; Neh 9:34).

47. Hans-Christoph Schmitt, "Erlösung und Gericht: Jes 43,1-7 und sein literarischer und theologischer Kontext," *Alttestamentlicher Glaube und Biblische Theologie: Festschrift für Horst Dietrich Preuß*, ed. Jutta Hausmann and Hans-Jürgen Zobel (Stuttgart: Kohlhammer, 1992), pp. 120-31, ascribed the ground level to the DtIS and the additions to a late Torah piety (pp. 122-25), but such a solution would distort the clear structure of DtIE^1.

48. Meshullam is a very common personal name given to a child who is regarded as a substitute for his elder brother who has died. Thus there is no reason for believing that it should have a completely different meaning as a symbolic name for Israel.

Israel's disorientation as divine strategy of magnifying the Torah as a new rule of conduct (42:21).[49] And he inserted an explicit confession of sins through 42:24aα_2b in order to clarify that only an honest repentance of the people would pave the way of salvation. According to the scholastic redactor, Israel's sin was characterized by its unwillingness to listen to the Torah and to follow God's way, similar to 48:17-18. Thus, Israel's lesson to learn from the exile should be to keep God's Torah in the future.

After the third servant song (50:4-9), there is a short admonition that takes the faithful prophet as an example for the pious, but as a warning to his enemies (50:10-11). The text clearly depends on the song, but interprets it in a generalized way. Since 50:10 partly speaks in Deuteronomistic language,[50] the admonition probably also belongs to the DtIS. Anyone who is still living in darkness but "leans on his God" should be encouraged by the faithful confession of the prophet (50:10). But all those who no longer wait for the light of salvation, but kindle their own fire, are warned that they will be killed by their own hostile actions (50:11). This argument reveals that the scholastic redactor seems to belong to a prophetic group in succession of Deutero-Isaiah, which enjoyed some agreement but suffered much rejection. According to him, Israel, or at least the pious, did not only have to listen to the Torah but also to the voice of YHWH's prophet.

There are two other small admonitions, secondary to their context, which can probably be ascribed to the scholastic redaction. The first, 46:8, addresses the "rebels" (cf. 48:8) and warns them about the idols in which they may trust: they are not able to save human beings (48:7). The verse depends on its context, but draws a conclusion that moves clearly beyond.[51] The accusation of idolatry corresponds with 48:5b. The second admonition, 55:7, addresses the "wicked" *(rāšāʿ)* and calls him to leave "his way" *(darkô)* (cf. 42:24; 48:17) and return to YHWH. For this case, it promises him the pity and the forgiveness of "our God" (55:7; cf. 50:10; 42:24). The verse shows its secondary character by doubling the final admonition ("seek YHWH!") of DtIE^2 in 55:6 and focusing it on the specific group of the wicked *(r^{e}šāʿîm)*. It takes up terms from its context but uses them in a different sense: in 55:7 *derek* denotes, for example, no longer

49. The personal pronoun *w^{e}hûʾ* "but he" in Isa 42:22 refers back to the subject of 42:20b and proves that 42:21 is an insertion.

50. For the phase *šāmaʿ b^{e}qôl* "to listen to one's voice" cf. Deut 4:30; 8:20; 1 Sam 8:19; 15:22 and others. These affinities in language are the main reason why I no longer assign this passage to DtIT as done before in Albertz, *Israel,* p. 397, note 778.

51. The addressees in the second person plural of Isa 46:5, 9 are not the evildoers, but all the Israelites.

the plan for salvation as in 55:8, but the way of life. The call for repentance is typical for the Deuteronomistic theology (cf. 1 Kgs 8:33-34; Jer 36:3 among others). Thus the language and the concept of Isa 55:7 fit the characteristics of the scholastic redactor. From Isa 46:8; 50:10-11; and 55:7 it becomes clear that the scholastic redactor already knows a split of the Judean society into "the pious" and "the wicked" factions. This points to the social reality of the middle of the fifth century (cf. Neh 5). For the redactor, however, this split is not completely settled. He still tried hard to lead the wicked to repentance, so that they would listen to the Torah and the prophetic word and would improve their conduct. Verbal and conceptual parallels to later layers of the book of Trito-Isaiah (especially, Isa 59) suggest that the scholastic redactor — or a companion of his — was also involved in the formation of that book; but this suggestion needs further study.

3.6 Late Idol Additions

While earlier scholars regarded all idol polemics as later additions,[52] Jürgen Werlitz has shown that a major portion of them are well integrated into the composition (Isa 40:19-20; 41:6-7; 44:10-17, 20; 46:6-7).[53] They already belong to DtIE[1] and function to convince the audience of the monotheistic belief in a more amusing manner.[54] From these early passages, which reflect the Babylonian polytheistic background in a sarcastic way, those later polemics have to be distinguished. The late idol additions are secondarily placed into their contexts, and they criticize the producers and venerators of idols in a more schematic way:[55]

Late idol additions
Isa 42:17; 44:9, 18-19; 45:16-17, 20b

These passages accuse all those who create idols for their own needs, trust in them (42:17), pray to them (45:20b), and call them "our gods" (42:17). The idolators all have no understanding and will be ashamed, because these idols

52. For example, Elliger, *Verhältnis,* pp. 305-7, Westermann, *Jesaja,* p. 27.

53. See Werlitz, *Redaktion,* pp. 221-37.

54. These passages have an impressive rhetorical function: When a student group in my seminar in 2002 performed a recitation of DtIE[1] on stage, the audience laughed every time during the polemical idol passages.

55. See Werlitz, *Redaktion,* pp. 231-32.

would not save them (45:20b), in contrast to YHWH (45:16-17). Since the DtIS is also concerned with adherents of idols (46:[6-7], 8; 48:5), these late idol additions may come from a similar background. That some kind of idolatry became popular in post-exilic Judah can be seen from Isa 57:5-8; 66:17.

3.7 A Great Isaianic Redaction (DtIG)

Odil Hannes Steck elaborated several indications that the entire book of Isaiah including Proto-, Deutero- and Trito-Isaiah may have undergone *"großjesajanische Fortschreibungen."*[56] Steck observed several redactional links running through the book of Isaiah. According to him Isa 34–35 played a major role in connecting the books of Proto- and Deutero-Isaiah. He dated this redaction in the early Hellenistic period.[57] Meanwhile, several scholars postulate such a redaction,[58] but neither its scale nor its date is settled. In my view, within Isa 40–55, the following passages could most likely belong to such a redaction:

DtIG
Isa 40:5bβ; 48:22; 51:3, 11, 16; 52:4-6(?); 54:17b

The concluding formula in Isa 40:5bβ "For the YHWH's mouth has spoken" turns out to be secondary, because the order to build a "highway of YHWH" through the desert was originally spoken by the prophetic group ($DtIE^1$), and later — in the sight of $DtIE^2$ — by a heavenly figure (cf. 40:3aα), but not by God himself. All the more, the formula is not integrated in the poetic structure of the text. Since it also appears in Isa 1:20, its major function seems to be in aligning the beginning of Deutero- with that of Proto-Isaiah. What is said in both parts of the book comes from the very voice of YHWH. In Trito-Isaiah, the formula occurs a third time (58:14), but not in such a prominent position. At any rate, the promises of the book's third part are also provided with the same divine sanction as the first two.

At the end of Isa 48 an isolated statement is made in v. 22: "There is no peace — says YHWH — for the wicked," which has no connection to the

56. Thus, in Odil Hannes Steck, *Bereitete Heimkehr: Jesaja 35 als redaktionelle Brücke zwischen dem Ersten und dem Zweiten Jesaja,* Stuttgarter Bibelstudien 121 (Stuttgart: Katholisches Bibelwerk, 1985), p. 76.

57. Cf. Steck, *Heimkehr,* pp. 65-80.

58. See the discussion in Werlitz, *Redaktion,* pp. 332-41, and the considerations of Berges, *Buch,* pp. 533-46, 551.

following second servant song (49:1-6) and only a weak linguistic link with the preceding context in 48:18 ("peace"). While the admonition speech calls all Israel to repentance (48:17-19), v. 22 presupposes a manifest split into a "pious" and a "wicked" faction. Thus, the verse is clearly an addition to its context. Nearly the same statement about the wicked is made in Isa 57:21, where it is much better integrated into its context (57:20-21; cf. the contrasting frame with 57:1-2). There, it functions to restrict the cited promise of Trito-Isaiah (57:14-19) to the pious. Thus, the Great Isaianic editor clearly borrowed the statement from 57:21. When he inserted it in 48:22, just before the prophetic group had returned from Babylon to Jerusalem (48:20-21) and passed the good news to Zion (49:14-26), he intended to exclude the wicked *(rešāʿîm)* from all the salvific promises to Jerusalem and the Judean population given in Deutero-Isaiah (49–55). They would not be included into the eternal "covenant of peace" (54:10) that YHWH would establish with Jerusalem in the future. In contrast to the scholastic redactor, the Great Isaianic book editor presupposed a manifest split of the Judean society, which can likewise be noticed in the latest layers of Trito-Isaiah (Isa 57; 65–66). Thus, he erected a barrier in the "book of consolation," which should hinder the arrogant, anti-social, and godless people from getting an easy access to its promises.

In 54:17b there is a concluding statement which defines all the promises for Zion given in that chapter as the heritage of the "servants of YHWH." Since such "servants" are never mentioned before, the statement is clearly secondary to its context. With the same terminology ("my servants") the pious faction is named at the end of Trito-Isaiah (65:8-9, 13-15; 66:14).[59] Thus, the restriction comes from a similar milieu as 48:22 and probably also belongs to the DtIG. Both statements, 48:22 and 54:17b, constitute brackets around the promises for Zion and its people, which intended to protect the treasure of the "book of consolation" in between from any misuse by the wicked faction.

Among the promises for Zion, there are some extensions, which can probably be ascribed to DtIG. The complaint of the people in 51:9-10 that YHWH has forgotten his mighty deeds of the days of chaos and the time of the exodus is amplified by a description of the joyful wanderings of the released to Zion in 51:11. The complaint does not only burst the shape of the *Gattung*, but also has a parallel in Isa 35:10. Since the verse is firmly anchored in the salvific description of 35:1-10, where it constitutes its final climax, it is highly probable that the verse was taken from there and inserted in 51:11. According to Steck, Isa 35, which reminds one of Isa 40 in many aspects (cf. 35:2b-4 with 40:5, 9-10), was

59. Cf. the similar assessment of Blenkinsopp, *Isaiah 40–55*, pp. 74, 366.

created for the purpose of connecting the books of Proto- and Deutero-Isaiah.[60] Thus, the primary function of 51:11 would be to fasten this redactional bridge by stretching a rope back to chapter 35. In that case, we would have to do with a basic editorial work of the DtIG. There are, however, some doubts about such an appraisal. According to my observations the literary connection between Proto- and Deutero-Isaiah was rather established already by $DtIE^2$.[61] Moreover, Joseph Blenkinsopp has rightly pointed out that Isa 35 presupposes not only Deutero- but also Trito-Isaiah (cf. 35:1-2a with 60:13, 61:10; 65:18-19; 66:10).[62] According to him, chapters 34–35 — the final judgment of the nations, exemplified by the destruction of Edom, and the final salvation of Zion including a miraculous transformation of nature (35:2, 7-9) — should rather be regarded as an eschatological interpretation of Deutero- and Trito-Isaiah's prophecies, which were intended to conclude the first part of the Isaiah book (cf. the references of 34:8, 17 back to 13:9, 17). Thus, the effort of the Great Isaianic redactor was of a smaller scale: he already presupposed the literary connections between the three parts of the book including the eschatological finale of the first part (34–35), but he wanted to align the prophecies of Deutero-Isaiah with the eschatological message already addressed in Isa 35. Since 51:10 speaks of the "released" *(gᵉʾûlîm),* who have passed through the chaos waters, and 35:9 also mentions the "released" *(gᵉʾûlîm)* on their wonderful way back to Zion, the redactor saw an appropriate place here to include a reminder of the eschatological events described by Isa 35 in the Deutero-Isaianic context of Isa 51. By this, he intended to synchronize the process of salvation between the first and second part of the book of Isaiah. Zion's preparations for the arrival of salvation dealt with in chapters 51–52 should be understood by the reader as that period when the eschatological events of chapter 35 would take place.

It is probable also that 51:3, sometimes regarded as a displaced fragment of an "eschatological hymn,"[63] belongs to the same reworking of the chapter, because it includes the identical expression "joy and gladness" *(śāśôn wᵉśimḥâ),* found in both 35:10 and 51:11.[64] Through this insertion the Great Isaianic redactor intended to focus the scope of the entire chapter on Zion; in addition, he described the wonderful transformation of the city into the garden of Eden in accord with the visions of Isa 35.

Finally, the surprising address to a prophetic figure in 51:16 may be also

60. See Steck, *Heimkehr,* pp. 13-64.

61. See above p. 29.

62. See Blenkinsopp, *Isaiah 40–55,* pp. 44-46.

63. See for example Westermann, *Jesaja,* p. 192.

64. Apart from these passages the expression only occurs in Isa 22:13 and Ps 51:10(8).

ascribed to the DtIG. The verse is clearly an insertion, after the divine answer to the lament (51:12-15a) has ended with a concluding hymnic formula in 51:15b (DtIE^2).[65] If one takes the verse as it is transmitted in the Masoretic text the prophet is commissioned to "plant" *(nāṭaʿ)* heaven and to ground earth through the divine word, before he should assure Zion of God's solidarity with its people. The motives are partly taken up from the context (cf. 51:13; 49:2); the commission also reminds one of Jer 1:9-10.[66] While the prophet Jeremiah was ordered to pull out and plant the nations through his divine message, the Isaianic prophet would be able to plant a new heaven through his divine word. Steck has proposed to interpret Isa 51:16 in such an eschatological horizon.[67] Then, it would refer to the creation of a new heaven and a new earth announced in 65:16b-23, which also aims at a wonderful transformation of Jerusalem and the circumstances of its inhabitants. If such an interpretation is accepted, the verse will fit perfectly the concept of the Great Isaianic redactor. In the same Deutero-Isaianic chapter, where he referred back to Proto-Isaiah, he also pointed forward to Trito-Isaiah. By doing so, he united the three parts of the book under the same eschatological perspective. According to him, at that moment (Isa 51), when the wonderful salvation of Zion described in Isa 35 is prepared, the Isaianic prophet of the book is commissioned to start the creation of the new world according to Isa 65.[68] Since DtIG lacks historical allusions, it is difficult to date. Its fully developed eschatological concept, however, points to the end of the fifth or to the fourth century B.C.E.

3.8 Apocalyptic Additions

Within Isa 40–55 there are two additions, which can be labeled as "apocalyptic," since they describe a cosmological dissolution of heaven and earth (Isa

65. The insertion probably caused the textual problem that resulted in the addressee of the divine speech varying between the female (Zion) and male (prophet) gender.

66. In the phrase "I put my words in your mouth" only the verb differs (*śîm* instead of *nātan*). The verb *śîm* is used also in Exod 4:15; Num 23:5; and Isa 59:21. Whether the last verse, which indicates a succession of the prophetic office, also belongs to DtIG, is not clear, because it is formulated in prose.

67. See Steck, *Zion,* pp. 70-72.

68. Steck, *Heimkehr,* p. 80; Steck, *Zion,* pp. 124-25, also ascribed the prose extension, Isa 52:4-6, to the DtIG. The passage, however, has more interest in historical connections than in an eschatological unification of the book. Thus, the affiliation is rather improbable. Whether one has to distinguish different Great Isaianic redactions needs further research.

50:3; 51:6). They may have to do with the insertion of Isa 24–27 in the book of Isaiah. Especially 51:6 could perhaps be assigned to the DtIG described above. But since a similar apocalyptic perspective seems to be an expansion even in 34:4, the apocalyptic additions may be later.[69]

4. Conclusion

The redaction historical hypothesis elaborated above covers about 98 percent of the text of Isa 40–55 with an explanation of its formation. This is not a bad portion. Many redaction-critical proposals in our research field suffer from the fact that they are not tidied up for the entire text unit. It is not necessary to emphasize that my results are hypothetical to one degree or another. They can only be regarded as preliminary, as long as they are not controlled, revised and expanded by similar redactional and compositional critical studies of Proto- and Trito-Isaiah. Joseph Blenkinsopp would be one of the few scholars in the world who would be able to carry out such a tremendous task, since he has thoroughly studied all three parts of Isaiah. But I am afraid he would not like to do so, even in his younger years. I wish him more healthy years of study and hope that he may acknowledge that my attempts at reconstructing the formation of the book of Deutero-Isaiah are not totally superfluous, but can lead to a better understanding of some difficult passages.

69. A few additions to the book can be characterized as glosses: Isa 40:7a, 7b, 14bα; 43:28a; 49:21bα_1.

The Legal Capacity of Women in the Biblical Tradition of the Persian Period

Klaus Baltzer and Peter Marinkovic

I. Introduction

In the following article texts taken from the book of Isaiah are linked with others from Ezra-Nehemiah. This is unusual, but it is the result of extensive research which we are here presenting for discussion to a wider circle. Approaches for it were already developed in the Hermeneia commentary on Deutero-Isaiah and in the later article "The Book of Isaiah."[1] The basic contention is that Deutero-Isaiah and Nehemiah are contemporaries, and that they are also linked with each other in a literary respect. We believe that the Servant of God texts (Isa 42:1-4; 49:1-6; 50:4-11; and 52:13–53:12) have their origin in the Moses tradition, but that it was impossible in the Persian era to acknowledge publicly that Israel's liberator had an Egyptian name and came from Egypt. That is one of the reasons for the anonymity of the Servant of God. Deutero-Isaiah is a document which has its place in the new constitution after the Exile. Other corresponding themes in the two literary works, Isaiah and Ezra-Nehemiah, include the traditions which have been taken up there (the early traditions, such as the theology of divine kingship, Zion-Jerusalem, etc.), down to the building of the wall of Jerusalem. This already raises the problem of the book of Isaiah, as a whole and as a historical work. Questions touching on the Pentateuch also belong here — its literary form, its traditions, and the dating of the whole work as be-

1. Klaus Baltzer, *Deutero-Isaiah: A Commentary on Isaiah 40–55*, Hermeneia (Minneapolis: Augsburg Fortress, 2001); Klaus Baltzer, "The Book of Isaiah," *HTR* 103 (2010): 261-70.

longing to the Persian era. These texts and themes in the Pentateuch, in the book of Isaiah, and in Ezra-Nehemiah are also focal texts in the scholarly work of Joseph Blenkinsopp.

Our purpose here is to discuss questions of this kind in the context of a particular example. The starting point for the following investigation is the observation that in Neh 10 women are explicitly mentioned. The context in Neh 9–10 is an agreement for a new constitution for Judah/Jerusalem after the exile. In a solemn act of penitential worship, past history is remembered. It ends with the "conclusion of a covenant." Nehemiah 9:38 states: "Because of all this we make a firm agreement in writing, and on that sealed document are inscribed the names of our officials, our Levites and our priests."[2] The list of the names of the nobility of the "people of Israel" follows (Neh 10:1-27), headed by Nehemiah: "Upon the sealed document are the names of Nehemiah the governor, son of Hacaliah, and Zedekiah" (Neh 10:1). The summary in Neh 10:28-30 reads as follows:

> ". . . all who have separated themselves from the peoples of the lands to adhere to the law of God, their wives, their sons, their daughters, all who have knowledge and understanding, [29]join with their kin, their nobles, and enter into a curse and an oath to walk in God's law, which was given by Moses the servant of God, and to observe and do all the commandments of the LORD our Lord and his ordinances and statutes. [30]We will not give our daughters to the people of the land or take their daughters for our sons."

According to this text the women participate in this official legal enactment. They have legal and cultic capacity. The consequences will be described in what follows. Sectors in which this legal capacity can be established are: 1) marriage laws; 2) the treatment of dowries and the right to dispose over them; 3) the possession of land; 4) occupational descriptions/characteristics; and 5) laws of inheritance. These points can be illustrated by examples. Our thesis is that the background for the struggle against mixed marriages (Ezra 9; Neh 13:23-30) is also the conflict about the right to inherit and to possess land, especially when the land in question lies in the border area, such as Moab and Edom.[3]

2. Unless otherwise noted, all translations are from the NRSV.

3. See Richard J. Bautch, *Glory and Power, Ritual and Relationship: The Sinai Covenant in the Postexilic Period,* Library of Hebrew Bible / Old Testament Studies, vol. 471 (New York and London: T. & T. Clark, 2009), esp. pp. 99-103; also Gary N. Knoppers, "'Married into Moab': The Exogamy Practiced by Judah and His Descendants in the Judahite Lineages" in *Mixed*

Text groups which are of relevance are the historical works of the Pentateuch, the Deuteronomistic and the Chronicler's histories, as well as the book of Isaiah as a whole, seen as a historical work in the prophetic tradition.[4] It is impossible, however, to arrive at completeness. The present study rests on a series of basic decisions, which methodologically touch above all on form criticism and tradition history, with the resulting historical approaches.

II. A Consideration of the Text Groups

II.1. Women in the Book of Isaiah (Also as an Indication of Their Social and Economic Position)

The following aspects especially should be taken into account in the "relecture" of the book of Isaiah, for which Professor Blenkinsopp provides a model: 1) feminine characteristics; 2) feminine behaviour; and 3) the Zion-Jerusalem symbolism.

1. Feminine Characteristics

The Book of Isaiah describes feminine characteristics in several places, often in uncomplimentary ways. For example, Isa 1–39 includes the critical comment that the "daughters of Zion" have become arrogant (3:16). Isaiah 3:16-24 describes their appearance, ranging from make-up and perfume to clothing and jewelry. This clearly applies to women belonging to the upper class. Women are elsewhere reproached for their "complacency" (Isa 32:8-20). Isaiah 40–55 is in accord with this judgment (Isa 47:8).

2. Feminine Behaviour / The Woman's Position

Isaiah includes several texts that touch on women's social locations and their associated responsibilities. It is of interest legally when we are told that a young woman becomes pregnant and calls her child "Immanuel" — for otherwise the naming of a child is generally the father's privilege (Isa 7:14). Elsewhere in Isaiah, women's financial independence is evident. This is ap-

---

Marriages: Intermarriage and Group Identity in the Second Temple Period, ed. Christian Frevel, LHBOTS 547 (London: Continuum, 2011), pp. 170-91.

4. Klaus Baltzer, "The Book of Isaiah," *HTR* 103 (2010): 261-70.

parent when women appeal to a man in 4:1, saying, "We will eat our own bread and wear our own clothes; just let us be called by your name." Widowhood (Isa 10:2), divorce (Isa 50:1), and childlessness (Isa 54:1-3) also present problems.

It is also surprising that in Deutero-Isaiah Abraham *and* Sarah are called Israel's "parents" (Isa 51:2: "Look to Abraham your father and to Sarah who bore you"). This recalls Gen 2 and the appearance of Adam *and* Eve at the beginning of the human race. In Isaiah, Abraham and Sarah are named in place of the triad Abraham-Isaac-Jacob, which is otherwise customary (see, e.g., Deut 29:13).

It is striking that in Deutero-Isaiah and Trito-Isaiah "the desolate heritages" (e.g. Isa 49:8) and "desolate places" (e.g. Isa 49:19) are mentioned several times. According to Isa 54 it is Jerusalem as a woman whose descendants will occupy "the desolate towns" (Isa 54:3) and will rebuild them (Isa 54:11ff.). Trito-Isaiah (58:12 and 61:4) also talks about "ancient ruins" and their rebuilding. The ruins are building land and that represents capital. According to ancient law, building was permissible on a *tell,* but not on agricultural land. There development was prevented. If land forms part of a woman's inheritance, its value increases, especially in peaceful times.

According to these texts, a woman's importance and position is different from that in the pyramid-like thinking of Roman law, with its *pater familias* outlook. It was this later standpoint which became more influential in European history than the view taken by the biblical texts — a point to which Dieter Georgi has vehemently drawn attention.[5]

3. *The Zion-Jerusalem Symbolism*

The name of Zion is a link binding together all three parts of the book of Isaiah (I: Isa. 16:1-7; II: 49:14 and 52:1; III: 62:11-12). As a woman, Zion is the city of Jerusalem and at the same time a model. In this sense the theme belongs to the same context as the question about the position of women in biblical tradition. Thus Zion/Jerusalem also takes the place of a city goddess.[6] Isaiah 52:1

5. See D. Georgi, *The City in the Valley: Biblical Interpretation and Urban Theology* (Atlanta: SBL, 2005).

6. See Klaus Baltzer, "Die Stadt als Frau: Personifikation versus Stadtgöttin — am Beispiel der Figur 'Zion/Jerusalem' bei Deutero-Jesaja (Jes 40–55)" in I. Fischer, K. Schmid, H. G. M. Williamson, eds., *Prophetie in Israel: Beiträge des Symposiums "Das Alte Testament und die Kultur der Moderne" anlässlich des 100. Geburtstags Gerhard von Rads (1901-1971), Heidelberg 18.-21. Oktober 2001,* Altes Testament und Moderne, vol. 12 (Münster: Lit-Verlag, 2003), pp. 137-48.

reads: "Put on your strength, O Zion, put on the garments of glory, O Jerusalem, you holy city." Deutero-Isaiah probably presupposes this translation, though "city of the sanctuary" would also be a possible translation. The translations reflect different views about the function of the temple and Jerusalem. Common to them both is the association with pilgrimage. In Deutero-Isaiah the pilgrimage takes the place of the occupation of the land (Isa 55:1-5, esp. vv. 1 and 5; cf. also Isa 2:1-5). God is present as king in Jerusalem, which is his royal city[7] (see also Zech 14:16-21).[8]

According to its function, Jerusalem is the capital or residence of God, the place of the central sanctuary for "all Israel" (place of pilgrimage, holy city/city of the sanctuary) and seat of the prophet in the Mosaic tradition. The pilgrimage also has an economic and social significance. Thus the goldsmiths play a part in the rebuilding of Jerusalem's walls (Neh 3:8, 31-32). Their trade is at the service of the public and the private cult (cf. Exod 35:30-35, esp. v. 35, as well as 31:1-6; Isa 40:19; 41:7; esp. 46:6; Jer 10:9, 14; 51:17; see also Acts 19:24). This does not mean that there were not other important towns in Israel which have to be described in various ways according to their function, above all in the Persian period — for example Ramat Rahel was a possible administrative center in the province of Yehud[9] — and it does not do away with the importance of Jerusalem as the place of the sanctuary. The relationship between Bethel and Samaria is comparable.[10] In the Persian empire, several cities acted as "chief" cities, with specific functions in each given case. Thus, for example, Pasargadae served as ceremonial city (for the royal ritual and royal ancestor cult, with the tomb of the founder king Cyrus), Persepolis as financial capital (with the "imperial treasury"; cf. the presentation of the tribute-bearers on the relief on the staircase leading to the *apadana*), as well as Susa (with the winter palace of the great king) and Ecbatana (with the king's summer palace) as

7. See Peter Marinkovic, *Stadt ohne Mauern: Die Neukonstitution Jerusalems nach Sacharja 1-8*, Diss., University of Munich, 1996.

8. See Melody D. Knowles, *Centrality Practiced: Jerusalem in the Religious Practice of Yehud and the Diaspora in the Persian Period*, SBL — Archaelogy and Biblical Studies (Leiden: Brill, 2007).

9. Cf. Oded Lipschits, "Achaemenid Imperial Policy, Settlement Processes in Palestine and the Status of Jerusalem in the Middle of the Fifth Century B.C.E." in Oded Lipschits and Manfred Oeming, eds., *Judah and the Judeans in the Persian Period* (Winona Lake IN: Eisenbrauns, 2006), pp. 19-52; see also Oded Lipschits, Manfred Oeming, Yuval Gadot and Benjamin Arubas, "The 2006 and 2007 Excavation Seasons at Ramat Rahel: Preliminary Report," *IEJ* 59 (2009): 1-20.

10. Cf. Gary Knoppers, "Revisiting the Samarian Question in the Persian Period" in Lipschits and Oeming, eds., *Judah and the Judeans in the Persian Period*, pp. 265-89.

further administrative centers (with a wealth of administrative tablets in the various indigenous languages).[11]

II.2. Women in the Pentateuch

1. Numbers 27:1-11 and 36:1-13: The Right of Daughters to Inherit

If we take the Pentateuch as starting point, two texts from the book of Numbers speak to important issues facing women in ancient Israel. First, Num 27:1-11 is a text of essential importance since it shows that women/daughters had the right to inherit. The law is associated with the Moses tradition and must therefore be viewed as foundational.

> Then the daughters of Zelophehad came forward. Zelophehad was son of Hepher son of Gilead son of Machir son of Manasseh son of Joseph, a member of the Manassite clans. The names of his daughters were: Mahlah, Noah, Hoglah, Milcah, and Tirzah. [2]They stood before Moses, Eleazar the priest, the leaders, and all the congregation, at the entrance of the tent of meeting, and they said, [3]"Our father died in the wilderness; he was not among the company of those who gathered themselves together against the LORD in the company of Korah, but died for his own sin; and he had no sons. [4]Why should the name of our father be taken away from his clan because he had no son? Give us a possession among our father's brothers."
>
> [5]Moses brought their case before the LORD. [6]And the LORD spoke to Moses, saying: [7]The daughters of Zelophehad are right in what they are saying; you shall indeed let them possess an inheritance among their father's brothers and pass the inheritance of their father on to them. [8]You shall also say to the Israelites, "If a man dies, and has no son, then you shall give his inheritance to his daughter. [9]If he has no daughter, you shall give his inheritance to his brothers. [10]If he has no brothers, then you shall give his inheritance to his father's brothers. [11]And if his father has no brothers,

11. See David Stronach, *Pasargadae: A Report on the Excavations Conducted by the British Institute of Persian Studies from 1961-63* (Oxford: Oxford University Press, 1978); Erich Friedrich Schmidt, *Persepolis,* vols. 1-3 (Chicago: University of Chicago Press, 1953-1970); Heidemarie Koch, *Verwaltung und Wirtschaft im persischen Kernland zur Zeit der Achämeniden,* Beiheft zum Tübinger Atlas des Vorderen Orient, Series B, Geisteswissenschaften No. 89 (Wiesbaden: Reichert, 1990); Muchammed A. Dandamaev, *A Political History of the Achaemenid Empire* (Leiden: Brill, 1989); Josef Wiesehöfer, *Das Antike Persien, Von 550 v. Chr. bis 650 n. Chr.,* 3rd ed. (Düsseldorf: Albatros, 2005).

> then you shall give his inheritance to the nearest kinsman of his clan, and he shall possess it. It shall be for the Israelites a statute and an ordinance, as the LORD commanded Moses." (Num 27:1-11)

The issue is addressed further by the addendum of Num 36:1-13. This text seeks to ensure that the daughter's right to inherit, a right stipulated in Num 27, does not become a condition for the loss of tribal land. Hence, to ensure that this does not occur, women are required to marry within their ancestral tribes so that a clan's inheritance does not pass from one tribe to another. As the conclusion to the book of Numbers, the text stands in a prominent place within the Pentateuch.

2. *Deuteronomy 29:10-15: Women in the Covenant*

This text closes the legal enactments in Deuteronomy with a renewal of the covenant. Here again the women are explicitly mentioned, as they are at the conclusion of the covenant in the book of Nehemiah.

> [10]You stand assembled today, all of you, before the LORD your God — the leaders of your tribes, your elders, and your officials, all the men of Israel, [11]your children, your women, and the aliens who are in your camp, both those who cut your wood and those who draw your water — [12]to enter into the covenant of the LORD your God, sworn by an oath, which the LORD your God is making with you today; [13]in order that he may establish you today as his people, and that he may be your God, as he promised you and as he swore to your ancestors, to Abraham, to Isaac, and to Jacob. [14]I am making this covenant, sworn by an oath, not only with you who stand here with us today before the LORD our God, [15]but also with those who are not here with us today.

The picture which we can deduce from the Pentateuch about the position of women coincides which that which can be detected from the Wisdom texts. In this respect the approaches of the legal and the Wisdom texts (*torah* and *chokma*) do not diverge from one another.

II.3. Wisdom Texts

1. Job 42:13-15: Job's Learning Process

> [13]He also had seven sons and three daughters. [14]He named the first Jemimah, the second Keziah, and the third Keren-happuch. [15]In all the land there were no women so beautiful as Job's daughters; and their father gave them an inheritance along with their brothers.

At the beginning Job sacrifices for his sons' party (see Job 1:5). In Job 42:13-15 his daughters are also given their share.

2. Proverbs 31:10-31: Women as Entrepreneurs

The text is distinguished by its artistic structure; it is an *acrostic* which follows the Hebrew alphabet:

> [10]A capable wife who shall find?
> She is far more precious than jewels.
> [11]The heart of her husband trusts in her,
> and he will have no lack of gain.
> [12]She does him good, and not harm,
> all the days of her life.
> [13]She seeks wool and flax,
> and works with willing hands.
> [14]She is like the ships of the merchant,
> she brings her food from far away.
> [15]She rises while it is still night
> and provides food for her household
> and tasks for her servant-girls.
> [16]She considers a field and buys it;
> with the fruit of her hands she plants a vineyard.
> [17]She girds herself with strength,
> and makes her arms strong.
> [18]She perceives that her merchandise is profitable.
> Her lamp does not go out at night.
> [19]She puts her hands to the distaff,
> and her hands hold the spindle.
> [20]She opens her hand to the poor,
> and reaches out her hands to the needy.

> [21]She is not afraid for her household when it snows,
> for all her household are clothed in crimson.
> [22]She makes herself coverings;
> her clothing is fine linen and purple.
> [23]Her husband is known in the city gates,
> taking his seat among the elders of the land.
> [24]She makes linen garments and sells them;
> she supplies the merchant with sashes.
> [25]Strength and dignity are her clothing,
> and she laughs at the time to come.
> [26]She opens her mouth with wisdom,
> and the teaching of kindness is on her tongue.
> [27]She looks well to the ways of her household,
> and does not eat the bread of idleness.
> [28]Her children rise up and call her happy;
> her husband too, and he praises her:
> [29]"Many women have done excellently,
> but you surpass them all."
> [30]Charm is deceitful, and beauty is vain,
> but a woman who fears the Lord is to be praised.
> [31]Give her a share in the fruit of her hands,
> and let her works praise her in the city gates.

It is worth noting the headings given to this text in the respective translations of the text, with their interpretations of a woman's tasks, e.g.:

- Ode to a Capable Wife (NRSV)
- Epilogue: The Wife of Noble Character (NIV)
- Lob der tüchtigen Hausfrau [Praise of the capable housewife] (Luther)
- Das Lob der tüchtigen Frau [Praise of the capable woman] (Einheitsübersetzung)

The position and function of women hardly find expression in these headings. But Prov 31:10-31 brings out the woman's role in her varied tasks and functions as being that of an independent, legally responsible business woman or entrepreneur.

III. Summary of Results, Further Questions, and Perspectives

The full legal capacity and independence of women which emerges from the book of Isaiah and from the Pentateuch, as well as from the Wisdom texts and passages in Ezra-Nehemiah, also led to conflicts. From texts belonging to the Persian period we can deduce that there was a demand for separation from foreign women. From our contemporary viewpoint this demand is a measure that is hard to accept. Various justifications for such demands have been put forward in the past, and today as well. They can be summed up as follows:

1. cultic impurity (to the point of an actual cult of foreign gods)
2. failure to speak the language (see Neh 13:23-25)
3. cultural differences (extending from, e.g., hostility towards strangers to racist objections; cf. the commentaries).

It is important to be clear about the social position of women as exemplified in the book of Isaiah, the more so since the book of Nehemiah in its final version stems from the Persian period and provides evidence of significant activity (the building of the wall, the expansion of the city of Jerusalem).

Our investigation has shown the legal capacity and independence of women. We believe that in the case of conflict a special feature of the order laid down by Persian constitutional law played a part. This was pointed out in Peter Calmeyer's pioneer study "Die 'Statistische Landcharte' des Perserreiches."[12] His thesis is that recognition as an independent political unit within the Persian empire always presupposed:

1. a capital city (with walls)[13]
2. an area surrounded by a boundary
3. a common language and custom.

These criteria clearly apply to Yehud as province, and to Jerusalem as capital city. The investigation has shown that foreign women were by no means always members of the lower classes, but in fact belonged rather to the upper class. It

12. P. Calmeyer, "Die 'Statistische Landcharte' des Perserreiches I und II" in *Archäologische Mitteilungen aus Iran* (Berlin, 1982), pp. 109-87, and AMI 16 (Berlin, 1983), pp. 141-222.

13. On the building of the walls cf. Neh 2–7, especially the account of the inspection of the walls in Jerusalem after Nehemiah's appointment, Neh 2:11-16.

was probably the case that women possessed considerable amounts of land, either inherited or expanded by way of purchase. If, especially in the border area of Edom and Moab, women took their landed property with them in the event of a separation, this was not merely a problem in civil law; it also gave rise to an inter-state conflict about the boundary line. In this context, the list of those returning, their families, and the places to which they belonged would again require examination (Neh 7; 1 Chron 9; Ezra 2). In view of the opportunities for communication which the Persian empire opened up, a comparison with the legal traditions of Egypt and Mesopotamia in their bearing on the legal capacity of women or its limitation would require special development. The family archives found on the Nile island of Elephantine, a Jewish military colony, as well as the newly discovered texts from *ir jehud*[14] in southern Babylon would be of particular interest.

A particularly cogent example of the position and function of women is offered by Neh 5. According to this text, women played an active part during the economic crisis that followed the first globalization, after the beginning of Persian rule (coin currency, gold/silver/bronze, with their respective standards; the hoarding of gold in the Persian "treasure houses"). The women bring their accusation directly before Nehemiah, the governor — and are successful (Neh 5:1-4, 6-7a). They are "fearless women":

> Now there was a great outcry of the people and their wives against their Jewish kin. For there were those who said, "With our sons and our daughters, we are many; we must get grain, so that we may eat and stay alive." There were also those who said, "We are having to pledge our fields, our vineyards, and our houses in order to get grain during the famine." And there were those who said, "We are having to borrow money on our fields and vineyards to pay the king's tax." . . . I was very angry when I heard their outcry and these complaints. After thinking it over, I brought charges against the nobles and the officials.[15]

The text has retained its topical force down to the present day.[16]

14. The texts are being worked on by Cornelia Wunsch in co-operation with others.

15. Text according to NRSV. On the expression "we are many," see Heribert Prantl, "Wir sind viele. Anklage gegen den Finanzkapitalismus," Verlag Süddeutsche Zeitung, Munich, 2011.

16. We would like to thank Margaret Kohl for her kind help in preparing the English translation.

The Lament in Isaiah 63:7–64:11 and Its Literary and Theological Place in Isaiah 40–66

Lena-Sofia Tiemeyer

Introduction

This article[1] has two interconnected aims. First, I wish to shed new light upon the rhetorical function and *Sitz-in-der-Literatur* of the lament[2] in Isa 63:7–64:11 within Isa 40–66. Second, I aim to show that the lament expresses the same kind of theology as the voice of Daughter Zion in Isa 49. This shared theological outlook is best explained in terms of a shared origin, both in time and in place. The persona of Daughter Zion in Isa 40–55 embodies the community

1. It is an honour to dedicate this article to my friend Joseph Blenkinsopp. Without our conversations, my understanding of the book of Isaiah would have been found wanting.

2. There is much debate as to whether Isa 63:7–64:11 is a lament, a penitential prayer, or something in between. Many scholars see it as a penitential prayer. For example, Rodney A. Werline, *Penitential Prayer in Second Temple Judaism: The Development of a Religious Institution* (Early Judaism and Its Literature 13; Atlanta: Scholars Press, 1998), pp. 41-45, regards Isa 63:4-7 as a confession of sins. See also Richard J. Bautch, *Developments in Genre Between Post-Exilic Penitential Prayers and the Psalms of Communal Lament* (SBLAB 7; Atlanta: Society of Biblical Literature 7, 2003), pp. 61-63, who interprets Isa 63:7–64:11 as a proto-penitential composition/communal lament, and stresses its combination of complaints of God's perceived absence with confession of sins. See also Mark J. Boda, *A Severe Mercy: Sin and Its Remedy in the Old Testament* (Siphrut 1; Winona Lake, IN: Eisenbrauns, 2009), pp. 216-18 (esp. p. 218). However, the content of Isa 63:7–64:11 fits the genre of "lament" better. See further my discussion in "The Doubtful Gain of Penitential Prayer: The Fine Line between Lament and Penitential Prayer," in *Spiritual Complaint: Theology and Practice of Lament* (ed. Tim Bulkeley and Miriam Bier; Eugene, Ore.: Paternoster, 2013), pp. 102-21.

in early post-monarchic Judah (i.e. 586-520 B.C.E.)[3] and her statements/thoughts in Isa 49:14, 21, 24 reflect the concerns of this community. Likewise, the lament in Isa 63:7–64:11 reflects the opinions of many people in Judah at the same time. The theological affinity between Isa 49:14-26 and Isa 63:7–64:11 can shed light upon the formation of Isa 40–66. In particular, I shall argue that Isa 63:7–64:11 fits well within the wider Isaianic tradition which allows for lament and protest against God.

1. Dating and Geographical Origin of Isaiah 49:14-26

The dating of the various strands of material in Isa 40–55 is debated. Most critical scholars today fall into one of two schools of thought. Those scholars who regard Isa 40–55 as the work of one author tend to date that work to shortly before 539 B.C.E. The majority argue that that author lived in Babylon,[4] while a small number place him in Judah.[5] In contrast, those scholars who regard Isa 40–55 as a composite work mostly detect an early core in Isa 40–48/52*, written in Babylon around 539 B.C.E. This core underwent several redactions and new material was added (Isa 49–55*) in Judah sometime after 520/515 B.C.E.[6] My own view forms a middle position: Isa 40–55 is likely to be

3. I use the term "early post-monarchic Judah" to denote the sixth century B.C.E. following the fall of Judah in 586 B.C.E. It is preferable to terms such as "exilic" and "post-exilic" as it does not presuppose a drastic change in the conditions of the people in Judah in 539 B.C.E. and as it does not define the situation in Judah by the experience of the people in exile.

4. E.g. Shalom M. Paul, *Isaiah 40–66: Introduction and Commentary* (2 vols.; Jerusalem: Magnes, 2008) (Hebrew), p. 1:3.

5. E.g. Christopher R. Seitz, *Zion's Final Destiny: The Development of the Book of Isaiah: A Reassessment of Isaiah 36–39* (Minneapolis: Fortress, 1991), pp. 130-48, 206; Michael Goulder, "Deutero-Isaiah of Jerusalem," *Journal for the Study of the Old Testament* 28 (2004): 350-62. Hans M. Barstad has also written on the topic but focused more on the geographical origin of the *text*. See, for example, Hans M. Barstad, *The Babylonian Captivity of the Book of Isaiah: "Exilic" Judah and the Provenance of Isaiah 40–55* (Oslo: Instituttet for Sammenlignende Kulturforskning, 1997).

6. See, e.g., Klaus Kiesow, *Exodustexte im Jesajabuch: Literarkritische und motivgeschichtliche Analysen* (OBO 24; Fribourg: Editions Universitaires, 1979), pp. 197-201; Rosario P. Merendino, *Der Erste und der Letzte: Eine Untersuchung von Jes 40–48* (VTSup 31; Leiden: Brill, 1981), p. 544; Ulrich Berges, *Das Buch Jesaja: Komposition und Endgestalt* (HerBS 16; Freiburg: Herder, 1998), pp. 368-87; Jürgen Werlitz, *Redaktion und Komposition: Zur Rückfrage hinter die Endgestalt von Jesaja 40–55* (BBB 122; Berlin and Bodenheim bei Mainz: Philo, 1999), pp. 313-14; Rainer Albertz, *Israel in Exile: The History and Literature of the Sixth Century B.C.E* (trans. D. Green; Studies in Biblical Literature 3; Atlanta: Society of Biblical Literature, 2003), pp. 397-99 (chart); 402-3.

the work of several authors and its development probably stretches over several decades. Yet, given its description of Jerusalem in ruins, its lack of references to the temple, and the eagerly awaited return of the exiles, most of the texts, although possibly not in their present form, were composed prior to 520/515 B.C.E. Furthermore, as I do not detect a move from Babylon to Judah within Isa 40–55, and as I do not see the material in Isa 40–55 as written from an exilic perspective by a group of (returned) exiles, I regard all of Isa 40–55 as the product of Judah. The earliest layers were written by those remaining in Judah. As to any subsequent layers composed after 520/515 B.C.E., it is unwarranted to distinguish between indigenous Judahites and returned exiles as other texts from that time period (Haggai, Zech 1–8) do attest to a sharp conflict between the two groups of people.[7] As to the particular case of Isa 49:14-26, relevant in the present article, the criteria for dating depend on whether the text reflects the concerns of the community in Judah or in Babylon. In my view, its focus on Jerusalem and its ruined condition favours a Judahite origin in the latter quarter of the sixth century B.C.E.

2. Dating and Geographical Origin of Isaiah 63:7–64:11

As Isa 49:14-26, the lament in Isa 63:7–64:11 probably stems from early post-monarchic Judah.[8] Its date can be inferred from the references in 63:18 to the temple being trampled by enemies and by the references in 64:9-10 (Eng. 64:10-11) to the ruins of Jerusalem and to a temple that has been destroyed by fire. Its geographical origin is supported by its resemblance to other early post-monarchic Judahite texts (Lamentations, Neh 9).[9] In addition, it is likely that Isa 63:7–64:11 preserves a lament that had a liturgical function in the community in early post-monarchic Judah.[10]

7. See further Lena-Sofia Tiemeyer, *For the Comfort of Zion: The Geographical and Theological Location of Isaiah 40–55* (VTS 139; Leiden: Brill, 2011), pp. 32-51.

8. I view Isa 63:7–64:11 as an authorial unity. See further my discussion and bibliographic references in Lena-Sofia Tiemeyer, "Two Prophets, Two Laments, and Two Ways of Dealing with Earlier Texts," in *Die Textualisierung der Religion* (ed. J. Schaper; FAT 62; Tübingen: Mohr Siebeck, 2009), p. 188, n. 13.

9. See my discussion and cited bibliography in Lena-Sofia Tiemeyer, *Priestly Rites and Prophetic Rage: Post-Exilic Prophetic Critique of the Priesthood* (FAT II/18; Tübingen: Mohr Siebeck, 2006), pp. 57-60, and "Two Prophets, Two Laments," pp. 187-89.

10. H. G. M. Williamson, "Isaiah 63,7–64,11: Exilic Lament or Post-Exilic Protest?," *Zeitschrift für die alttestamentliche Wissenschaft* 102 (1990): 48-58 (here 55-58).

Scholars who agree on an early post-monarchic Judahite origin of Isa 63:7–64:11 tend to treat it as an independent lament which originated outside of the Isaiah tradition. A redactor incorporated it into Isa 56–66 only at a relatively advanced stage in the formation of Isa 56–66, when he also furnished it with a response.[11] Thus, although the lament may be the earliest text in Isa 56–66 in terms of its date of composition, it is among the latest texts in terms of being incorporated into the book of Isaiah. Scholars maintain this position for one or both of the following reasons:

1. Positively, scholars have detected many similarities between Isa 63:7–64:11 and the psalms of lament and argue that, although it cannot be proven, the lament was composed for liturgical recital, either at the site of the ruined temple or at some other religious centre in Judah.[12]
2. Negatively, noting few links between Isa 63:7–64:11 and the surrounding material in Isa 40–66, scholars have concluded that the lament is of non-Isaianic origin.[13] Koenen, for example, suggests that, as the lament lacks the (for the rest of the material in Isa 56–66) typical links to Isa 40–55, it stems from neither the basic layer of Isa 56–66 nor a later redactor. Instead, the lament was included into Isa 56–66 by the redactor responsible for Isa 65:1-7.[14]

In contrast, a smaller, predominantly German-speaking group of scholars reject an early date of Isa 63:7–64:11 and instead place its composition in the Hellenistic period. This late date is often combined with the view that Isa 63:7–64:11 was composed especially for its current place in Isa 56–66, and therefore should be interpreted only in view of its Isaianic context (see further below). There are two distinct interpretative models:

11. See further Tiemeyer, "Two Prophets, Two Laments," p. 189.

12. See, e.g., Joseph Blenkinsopp, *Isaiah 56–66* (AB 19B; New York: Doubleday, 2003), p. 259. See also R. Norman Whybray, *Isaiah 40–66* (NCBC; London: Marshall, Morgan & Scott, 1975), p. 42, who regards the lament in Isa 63:7–64:11 as incorporated in the Isaiah material.

13. E.g. Brooks Schramm, *The Opponents of Third Isaiah: Reconstructing the Cultic History of the Restoration* (JSOTSupp 193; Sheffield: Sheffield Academic Press, 1995), p. 150; Wolfgang Lau, *Schriftgelehrte Prophetie in Jes 56–66: Eine Untersuchung zu den literarischen Bezügen in den letzten elf Kapiteln des Jesajabuches* (BZAW 225; Berlin: de Gruyter, 1994), pp. 286-87; 315.

14. Klaus Koenen, *Ethik und Eschatologie im Tritojesajabuch. Eine literarkritische und redaktionsgeschichtliche Studie* (WMANT 62; Neukirchen-Vluyn: Neukirchener, 1990), pp. 158-59, 168.

1. A few scholars regard the composition of the lament as part of the redactional *Fortschreibung* of the book of Isaiah as a whole. Steck, for example, maintains that Isa 63:7–64:11 was composed shortly before the final redaction of Isaiah, at the turn of the fourth century B.C.E. The lament thus never existed independently from its current place in Isaiah and it never had any original liturgical or other societal function.[15]
2. Other scholars see the writing of Isa 63:7–64:11 as an individual instance of *Fortschreibung* that is not directly connected with the formation of the book of Isaiah. Goldenstein in particular argues that the lament was composed to follow the material in Isa 62:8-9; 62:10-12; and 63:1-6 (see further below).[16] The lament was thus written for its present place in Isaiah and thus belongs to the Isaiah tradition. In fact, Goldenstein suggests that the lament was at one point the intended end of the book of Isaiah.[17]

   Zapff likewise maintains that, rather than being written to fit the surrounding material in the growing book of Isaiah, the lament forms a single occasion of *Fortschreibung*. Moreover, as the lament and the subsequent material in Isa 65–66 have divergent views of the cult (the latter being much more critical), they must have been written by different hands. As to its dating, Zapff argues that the lament was written at a time when people sought an explanation for the delay of salvation promised in Isa 40–55 and 60–62.[18]

According to both models, the lament in Isa 63:7–64:11 never had a *Sitz-im-Leben*, only a *Sitz-in-der-Literatur*. Even though the lament shares many of the structural and thematic aspects of a communal lament, it is a literary work from beginning to end and any liturgical use is secondary.

Evaluating these proposals, a Hellenistic date of Isa 63:7–64:11 must be deemed unlikely. As pointed out by Blenkinsopp, the occupation of Jerusalem by Ptolemy I in 302 and 301 B.C.E., which, according to Steck, is referred to in Isa 63:18 and 64:9-10(10-11), does not qualify since the temple was not burnt down. Likewise, the similarity between the last verse in 64:11(12) and Lamentations, "practically eliminates the later dates proposed."[19]

15. Odil H. Steck, *Studien zu Tritojesaja* (BZAW 203; Berlin: de Gruyter, 1991), pp. 233-42.

16. Johannes Goldenstein, *Das Gebet der Gottesknechte: Jesaja 63,7–64,11 im Jesajabuch* (WMANT 92; Neukirchen-Vluyn: Neukirchener, 2001), pp. 170-90, esp. pp. 188-90.

17. Goldenstein, *Das Gebet der Gottesknechte*, pp. 193, 197-98.

18. Burkard M. Zapff, *Jesaja 56–66* (DNEB; Würzburg: Echter, 2006), pp. 405-6.

19. Blenkinsopp, *Isaiah 56–66*, pp. 259, 265.

It should also be mentioned that those predominantly early scholars who uphold the authorial unity of all of Isa 56–66 accordingly view the lament as an integral part of Isa 56–66. Odeberg, for instance, states that the language of Isa 63:7–64:11 is clearly "Trito-Isaianic" and thus belongs to the tradition of Isa 56–66.[20] From a widely different perspective, Hanson maintains that the lament was written by the same Levites responsible for all the texts in Isa 56–66. For Hanson, the lament is thus in line with, and an integral part of, the surrounding material.[21] However, for different reasons, neither of these theories has won any broader appeal. On the one hand, in view of the diversity in terms of theological outlook and literary genre, it is unlikely that one person wrote all of Isa 56–66. On the other hand, Levitical authorship of Isa 56-66 must remain a conjecture, given the absence of any concrete reference to Levites in these chapters.[22]

To conclude: although it is impossible to determine with any kind of surety when exactly Isa 63:7–64:11 was written, it probably stems from before 539 B.C.E., given the lack of awareness of Cyrus and of any return of the exiles from Babylon.[23] This dating opens the possibility that the authors of Isa 40–55, and in particular the author of Isa 49, were familiar with the lament. As to the question whether the lament is of independent origin or written for its current place in the book of Isaiah, the lament probably originated outside of the Isaiah tradition.

3. The Relationship of Isaiah 63:7–64:11 with the Rest of Isaiah 56–66

Although I ultimately disagree with Steck's and Goldenstein's dating of the lament, their theories are important insofar as they challenge us to ask pertinent questions related to the *Sitz-in-der-Literatur* of Isa 63:7–64:11. If we maintain that the lament is of non-Isaianic origin, given the difference in genre between the lament and the rest of Isa 56–66, we need to explore the reasons

20. Hugo Odeberg, *Trito-Isaiah (Isaiah 56–66): A Literary and Linguistic Analysis* (UUÅ; Uppsala: Lindequistska Bokhandeln, 1931), pp. 19, 277-79.

21. Paul D. Hanson, *The Dawn of Apocalyptic: The Historical and Sociological Roots of Jewish Apocalyptic Eschatology* (Philadelphia: Fortress, 1975), pp. 91-99. See also idem, *Isaiah 40–66* (Interpretation; Louisville: John Knox Press, 1995), p. 235, where Hanson states that the author of Isa 56–66 speaks in the lament.

22. See further Tiemeyer, *Priestly Rites*, pp. 10-13.

23. E.g. Whybray, *Isaiah 40–66*, p. 256. Cf. also the discussion in Jan L. Koole, *Isaiah*, III/3 (HCOT; Peeters: Leuven, 2001), pp. 347, 372-73.

as to why it was preserved together with the Isaianic texts and what its function is in its current place in Isaiah.

Scholars looking at the redaction of Isa 56–66 have so far not delved too deeply into this issue. For example, Stromberg's recent monograph on the role of the final redactor of Isa 56–66 does not discuss the function of the lament in Isa 63:7–64:11 to any great length. He argues convincingly that the author of Isa 56:9–59:21 and 65:1–66:17 is the redactor of all of Isa 56–66, and maintains that Isa 63:7–64:11, together with Isa 60–62 and 63:1-6 are early texts that were incorporated into Isa 56–66 by that redactor. Stromberg further notes that the later redactional texts interact with and interpret the earlier material.[24] In the ensuing section, we shall look in detail at the relationship between Isa 63:7-64:11 and (1) Isa 65–66; (2) Isa 59:1-15; 60:1–63:6; and (3) the rest of Isa 56–66.

3.1. *The Relationship Between Isaiah 63:7–64:11 and Isaiah 65–66*

In many respects, the material in Isa 65–66 responds to the lament in Isa 63:7–64:11.[25] Steck lists thirteen lexical, stylistic, and structural links between the two texts, based upon which he suggests that Isa 65:1–66:17 provides the lament with a (negative) response.[26] Goldenstein maintains that Steck's interpretation does not fully take into consideration the dual aspects of the answer, and therefore proposes a step-by-step development. Isa 65:1-7, 16b-25 forms the original positive response, directed to the whole people. It is later enlarged in order to differentiate between the sinners and the chosen ones (Isa 65:8-16a; 66:1-6). In an even later addition, the chosen ones are identified with the children of Zion (Isa 66:7-15, 17). Finally, the concluding material in Isa 66:16, 18-24 is added.[27] However, Goldenstein's interpretation fails to convince because solid arguments support the authorial unity of Isa 65–66.[28] From a different perspective, Zapff sees Isa 65–66 as a *schriftgelehrte Fortschreibung* which seeks the reason for the people's con-

24. Jacob Stromberg, *Isaiah After Exile: The Author of Third Isaiah as Reader and Redactor of the Book* (OTM; Oxford: Oxford University Press, 2010), pp. 11-39.

25. E.g. Zapff, *Isaiah 56–66*, p. 345; Stromberg, *Isaiah After Exile*, p. 16.

26. Steck, *Studien*, pp. 221-24.

27. Goldenstein, *Das Gebet der Gottesknechte*, pp. 201-28.

28. See, e.g., Paul A. Smith, *Rhetoric and Redaction in Trito-Isaiah: The Structure, Growth and Authorship of Isaiah 56–66* (VTSup 62; Leiden: Brill, 1995), pp. 129-31.

stant desire to sin and discovers that the answer is their continuous *Verstockung*.[29]

Other scholars agree with Steck insofar as they regard Isa 65–66 as the (mixed/critical) response to the lament, but reject a Hellenistic dating as well as the idea that the lament was purposely written for its current place in the book of Isaiah.[30] Koenen, for example, regards Isa 63:7–64:11 as an older text which was inserted into the present context by a redactor who also created the response, mixing his own material (Isa 65:1-7, 8-16a) with an older text (Isa 65:16b-24).[31] Likewise, Sekine argues that Isa 63:7–64:11 must have been written by someone other than the redactor of Isa 56–66 (responsible for Isa 65–66) because of the marked stylistic difference between the two sets of writings, and because of the different views on salvation: while the lament is interested in the salvation of Israel alone, the response looks beyond Israel to the nations.[32] Independently from Sekine, Fischer also argues that Isa 65–66 was composed as a response to the lament, yet reflecting the theological issues of a different, much later time.[33]

The *critical nature* of the response in Isa 65–66 to the preceding lament constitutes a potential problem. As Aejmelaeus asks pertinently, is it at all possible to assume that the lament in Isa 63:7–64:11 was incorporated in the text merely in order to argue against it?[34] Is it really plausible that a redactor includes a lament, the theological standpoints of which he disagrees with, and then furnishes it with an unfavourable response? In my view, this can indeed be a conceivable scenario, if (1) the lament was well-known among the intended audience, and (2) a substantial part of that audience shared its sentiments. The joint text of Isa 63:7–66:24 then dialogues with the audience, acknowledging their thoughts and feelings yet, at the same time, aiming to convince them to change their mindset by stating that their understanding of reality and of God's action is incorrect (65:1-2). They — rather than God — are

29. Zapff, *Isaiah 56–66*, p. 347.

30. See, e.g., Blenkinsopp, *Isaiah 56–66*, pp. 63, 257; Berges, *Das Buch Jesaja*, pp. 496-500, 532. See also Smith, *Rhetoric*, pp. 128, 132, 134, 136, 140, 142, 172, who emphasizes that Isa 65–66 is critical of the people's lament in Isa 63:7–64:11.

31. Koenen, *Ethik und Eschatologie*, pp. 159, 168, 183 (summaries), 252-56 (translation).

32. Seizo Sekine, *Die Tritojesajanische Sammlung (Jes 56–66) redaktionsgeschichtlich untersucht* (BZAW 175; Berlin: de Gruyter, 1989), p. 162.

33. Irmtraud Fischer, *Wo ist Jahwe? Das Volksklagelied Jes 63,7–64,11 als Ausdruck des Ringens um eine gebrochene Beziehung* (SBB 19; Stuttgart: Katholisches Bibelwerk, 1989), pp. 257-80 (esp. pp. 276-79).

34. Anneli Aejmelaeus, "Der Prophet als Klageliedsänger: Zur Function des Psalms Jes 63,7–64,11 in Tritojesaja," *Zeitschrift für die alttestamentliche Wissenschaft* 107 (1995): 46-47.

responsible for their situation. This dialogic character of the text explains the seeming inconsistencies in God's answer (highlighted by Goldenstein, above) as he alternates between promises of blessings and threats of punishment.[35]

3.2. *The Relationship Between Isaiah 59:1-15; 60:1–63:6; and 63:7–64:11*

Turning to the relationship between Isa 59:1-15; 60:1–63:6; and 63:7–64:11, two interrelated issues concern us here:

1. The relationship between Isa 63:7–64:11 and Isa 60:1–63:6
2. The relationship between Isa 63:7–64:11 and Isa 59:1-15

The material in Isa 63:7–64:11 and 60:1–63:6 shares key vocabulary, thus suggesting that the author of one text was familiar with the other text. What remains unclear is the *direction* of the allusions. Did the author(s) of Isa 60:1–63:6 pick up key words from the lament or did the author of the lament reuse key words from Isa 60:1–63:6?

Many scholars argue that the lament is the earlier text to which the author(s) of Isa 60:1–63:6 allude. Westermann, for example, suggests that the laments in Isa 59:1-15a and 63:7–64:11 form a framework around Isa 60–62 (identified as the work of TI). These laments originated within the tradition of Israel's worship (and outside of the Isaiah tradition) and already existed when TI wrote Isa 60–62. By presenting his own material together with the laments, the prophet showed his solidarity with the people's concerns and, at the same time, responded positively to them.[36]

Along the same lines, Smith highlights seven points of connection between Isa 63:7–64:11 and 60–62, and argues that the style of Isa 60–62 shows closer affinity with the language and interests of the lament than with Isa 40–55. Thus, even though Isa 60–62 may have been composed as a literary continuation of Isa 40–55, these chapters also had an important function in relation to the community's penitential rites.[37] In addition, Smith lists three verbal connections between Isa 63:7–64:11 and the immediately preceding ma-

35. On Isa 64:11–65:1 as a "question-answer" literary device, see Aage Bentzen, *Introduction to the Old Testament* (Copenhagen: G. E. C. Gads, 1948-49), 2:108.

36. Claus Westermann, *Das Buch Jesaja: Kapitel 40–66* (ATD 19; Göttingen: Vandenhoeck & Ruprecht, 1966), pp. 240-41.

37. Smith, *Rhetoric*, pp. 44-46.

terial in Isa 63:1-6.[38] On the basis of his findings, Smith tentatively suggests that the lament in Isa 63:7–64:11 was the background for the proclamation of salvation in Isa 60:1–63:6 and that the prophetic author of that material exercised his ministry in the context of early post-exilic services of fasting and lamentation.[39]

Fischer also emphasizes the textual relationship of the lament with Isa 60–62, evident in the relatively close verbal ties with Isa 62:1-7. She follows Westermann's relative dating and argues that Isa 60–62 at one point served as the response to the earlier lament, but she differs with regard to its authorship and function. In contrast to Westermann who maintains that the author of Isa 60–62 added the framework, Fischer argues that it stems from a later redactor. The framework of laments was created at the time of the compilation of Isa 56–66, when people had realized that the expectations of salvation in Isa 60–62 had not yet come to pass.[40]

Other scholars, in particular those who date Isa 63:7–64:11 to the Hellenistic period, detect a reverse direction in the allusions. Zapff, for instance, maintains that Isa 63:7–64:11 constitutes Israel's *response* to the preceding magnificent promises in Isa 60–62.[41] For Zapff, the material in Isa 64:1b-2 presupposes the judgement of the nations as portrayed in Isa 63:1-4.[42]

Along different lines, Ruszkowski argues that the different texts in Isa 60–66 are arranged in chronological order of their composition. Read in that way, the lament constitutes a reaction to Isa 60–62 which, from the perspective of the people lamenting, had become a failed prophecy. This reading explains the dissonance between the hopeful tone of Isa 60–62 and the lament. The lament, linked to the preceding material by verbal affinity, especially with Isa 63:1-6, thus forms a later, redactional continuation of and reaction to Isa 60–62.[43]

From a different perspective yet stressing the same point, Seitz challenges the idea that Isa 60–62/63:6 responds to Isa 63:7–64:11. He notes that neither Westermann nor Smith gives a satisfactory answer as to why, in the final text, the lament *follows* the response. Isa 65–66 constitutes the (only) intended response to the lament. Although the links backwards to Isa 60–62 are impor-

38. Smith, *Rhetoric,* pp. 46-47.

39. Smith, *Rhetoric,* p. 47.

40. Fischer, *Wo ist Jahwe,* pp. 265, 279.

41. Zapff, *Jesaja 56–66,* p. 344.

42. Zapff, *Jesaja 56–66,* pp. 405-6.

43. Leszek Ruszkowski, *Volk und Gemeinde im Wandel: Eine Untersuchung zu Jesaja 56–66* (FRLANT 191; Göttingen: Vandenhoeck & Ruprecht, 2000), pp. 52-59.

tant, they are insufficient to warrant a reading against the present order of the text. In parallel, Seitz argues that the current place of Isa 63:7–64:11 invites reading it in conjunction with God's victory over Edom in Isa 63:1-6. Together, Isa 63–64 (esp. 63:7-14) emphasize that God is Israel's redeemer now, as he was in the past.[44]

These readings do not convince for two reasons. From a technical perspective alone, the relatively small amount of shared key words does not shed any light upon the direction of the allusions. From a more general perspective, it is, in my view, likelier that promises are written in response to a lament than vice versa (cf. also below). Taken together with the conclusion above, that the lament probably dates to the very earliest time of post-monarchic Judah, I would suggest that, contrary to Goldenstein's and Zapff's claim, the material in Isa 60:1–63:6 alludes to the lament.

However, Zapff's and Ruszkowski's, as well as Seitz's observations, are important insofar as they stress the extent to which the final redactor of Isa 56–66 prioritized God's voice. According to the (non-chronological) order of the final text, God promises a wondrous future for Jerusalem in Isa 60–62, yet its inhabitants are too bogged down by their (own) issues to believe in it (Isa 63:7–64:11). The final redactors allowed for the audience's voice to be heard, yet they arranged the final text in a way that gives precedence to God's promises of salvation for Israel (Isa 60:1–63:6) and to his threats of judgment (Isa 65–66). Israel is allowed to lament, yet God's perspective has the greater weight.

Turning to the relationship between Isa 63:7–64:11 and Isa 59:1-15, most scholars note that the texts in Isa 59:1-15 and Isa 63:7–64:11 give voice to the audience and that they, in their current place in Isa 56–66, comprise a ring-structure around Isa 60:1–63:6 (cf. above).[45] Taking this reasoning even further, Childs argues that a synchronic reading of Isa 59:1–64:11 creates a coherent and progressing narrative: First, Israel confesses its unrighteousness (59:1-15). Then God promises salvation and that he will come as a redeemer (59:15-21; 63:1-6). Lastly, Israel expresses its faithfulness (63:7–64:11).[46]

While Childs's interpretation of Isa 63:7–64:11 as an expression of Israel's faithfulness is only loosely anchored in the text, his reading emphasizes cor-

44. Christopher R. Seitz, "The Book of Isaiah 40–66," in *New Interpreter's Bible Commentary* 6 (Nashville: Abingdon, 1994), p. 525.

45. E.g. Brevard S. Childs, *Isaiah* (OTL; London: Westminster John Knox, 2001), p. 448; Zapff, *Isaiah 56–66*, p. 347 (58:9-15a [*sic*]).

46. Childs, *Isaiah*, p. 522.

rectly the dialogic[47] character of Isa 56–66. The material in Isa 40–55, as well as that in Isa 56–66, is characterized by different voices and by multiple and often contradictory attitudes towards suffering.[48] Isa 56–66 contains competing voices, primarily that of the audience and that of God. The audience is given a voice, possibly alongside a prophetic speaker, in the confession in Isa 59:9-15a and in the lament in Isa 63:7–64:11. The rest of the material, an intriguing mixture of divine oracles of blessing and judgment, gives a voice to God.

3.3. *The Relationship Between Isaiah 63:7–64:11 and the Rest of Isaiah 56–66*

A small number of scholars have detected connections between Isa 63:7–64:11 and other parts of Isa 56–66. Sekine, for example, points out that the expression "to do righteousness" (עשה צדק) in 64:4(5) is attested also in 56:1 and 58:2.[49] In greater detail, Aejmelaeus argues that the emphasis on holiness in the lament (63:10, 11, 15, 18; 64:9, 10[10, 11]) is characteristic of the language of the book of Isaiah as a whole (e.g., 57:15). In addition, the view of God (Isa 63:15; cf. 57:15; 66:1-2) and of sin and righteousness (Isa 64:4-5[5-6]; cf. 57:12; 58:2; 59:1-2, 12-13) in the lament is in line with the rest of Isa 56–66, as exemplified by the use of the shared term "righteousness" (צדק) in Isa 57:12 and 64:4b-6. In view of these links, Aejmelaeus concludes that the lament was uttered by a prophet standing in the Isaianic tradition (Trito-Isaiah).[50] While I hesitate to accept Aejmelaeus's conclusion, both Sekine's and Aejmelaeus's research suggests that *all* the authors of Isa 56–66 were familiar with the lament and interacted with it to some extent.

47. Several scholars have emphasized the dialogic character of Lamentations. See, e.g., the studies by Elizabeth Boase, *The Fulfilment of Doom? The Dialogic Interaction between the Book of Lamentations and the Pre-Exilic/Early Exilic Prophetic Literature* (LHBOTS 437; London: T&T Clark, 2006); and Kurt H. Heim, "The Personification of Jerusalem and the Drama of Her Bereavement in Lamentations," in *Zion, City of Our God* (ed. R. R. Hess and G. J. Wenham; Grand Rapids: Eerdmans, 1999), p. 169.

48. See Tiemeyer, *Comfort of Zion*, pp. 212-320, and also "The Doubtful Gain of Penitential Prayer" (forthcoming).

49. Sekine, *Sammlung*, p. 160.

50. Aejmelaeus, "Der Prophet als Klageliedsänger," pp. 38-49.

3.4. Conclusion

Despite the many differences between the lament and the rest of Isa 56–66, and despite its non-Isaianic origin, the lament is integral to Isa 56–66 in more than one way. First, the shared themes and vocabulary show that the lament expresses thoughts and theological viewpoints which were common to both the authors of Isa 56–66 and their audiences. Second, the textual links to both preceding and following material demonstrate that the chronologically later Isaianic material in Isa 56–66 interacted with and responded to the lament. The strong links forward to Isa 65–66 indicate that Isa 65–66 was composed as a conscious response to the lament. The less prominent, yet still significant links backwards to Isa 60:1–63:6 suggest seeing Isa 60:1–63:6 as an alternative response to the lament. Chronologically, that response precedes the one in Isa 65–66. We can thus surmise that the lament was first given a positive response (Isa 60:1–63:6) which, at a later point, was supplemented with a negative one (Isa 65–66). The reader of the final form of Isa 56–66 is, however, guided towards a different understanding of the situation. The final redactor, who is probably also the author of Isa 65–66 (cf. Stromberg, above), presented the material in a way which emphasizes that God's glorious promises came first (Isa 60:1–63:6), then the people's complaint (Isa 63:7–64:11), and finally God's critical response (Isa 65–66).

4. The Relationship of Isaiah 63:7–64:11 with Isaiah 40–55

Turning to the relationship between the lament in Isa 63:7–64:11 and the material in Isa 40–55, my recent proposition that Isa 40–55 was composed in and also reflects the situation in Judah in the second half of the sixth century B.C.E.[51] compels me to explore the *Sitz-in-der-Literatur* of Isa 63:7–64:11 within the wider literary corpus of Isa 40–66. Phrased differently, if the lament stems from the latter half of sixth-century Judah, and if Isa 40–55 was written in the same place and more or less at the same time, given also that both texts appear in the book of Isaiah, is it not likely that they are connected in some way?

Many scholars regard the lament as having originated independently from the preceding Isa 40–55 and thus to be unconnected with its message and theology.[52] Other scholars recognize a few inter-connections. Lau, for instance,

51. Tiemeyer, *Comfort of Zion.*

52. See, e.g. J. Muilenburg, "The Book of Isaiah Chapters 40–66," in *Interpreter's Bible* 5

has detected a thematic link between the reference to the Exodus in Isa 63:12 and the motif of a "New Exodus" in Isa 42:16.[53] A close look at these two passages does not confirm Lau's point, however. While 63:12 refers to Moses and the Exodus out of Egypt, Isa 42:16 speaks of God's strength and ability to lead his people safely through periods of hardship.[54] From a different perspective, Hanson has argued that, as in Isa 40:25-26 and 41:21-29, the people in Isa 63:9 and 64:3-4 await God's return in glory to save his people.[55] However, as Williamson points out, Isa 40:25-26 and 41:21-29 speak about God's incomparability over against the idols and not about God appearing in glory as his people's saviour.[56]

Yet, there is definitely affinity between the lament and Isa 40–55, as demonstrated by Sekine, Aejmelaeus, Berges, Goldenstein, and Gärtner:

Sekine points out two points of contact between the vocabulary of Isa 63:7–64:11 and Isa 40–55:

- The phrase הסתרת פניך in 64:6b is reminiscent of 45:15 (אל מסתתר) and 54:8 (הסתרתי פני רגע ממך ובתסך).
- The expression יצרנו in 64:7b is similar to 45:9 (הוי רב את יצרו) and it brings to mind 43:1, 7, 21; 45:11; 49:5.[57]

Aejmelaeus detects five additional examples of verbal or thematic similarity between Isa 63:7–64:11 and Isa 40–55:

- Both texts emphasize God as saviour (63:8; cf. 41:14; 43:14; 47:4; 48:17; 49:7, 26; 54:5).
- Both texts refer to Abraham. However, while the references to Abraham in 41:8; 51:2 are positive, the reference in 63:16 is negative.
- Both 63:16 and 45:9-11 depict God as a father.
- Both 63:19b and 48:18 use the particle לוא.

(Nashville: Abingdon, 1956), p. 729; and Williamson, "Isaiah 63,7–64,11," p. 53. In support of his claims, Williamson cites Walther Zimmerli, "Zur Sprache Tritojesajas," in *Gottes Offenbarung: Gesammelte Aufsätze zum Alten Testament* (ThB 19; Munich: Chr. Kaiser, 1963), pp. 217-33, whose study seeks to demonstrate that there are virtually no textual links between Isa 63:7–64:11 and Isa 40–55.

53. Lau, *Schriftgelehrte Prophetie*, pp. 312-14.

54. See further Tiemeyer, *Comfort of Zion*, pp. 178-81.

55. Hanson, *Dawn of Apocalyptic*, p. 92.

56. Williamson, "Isaiah 63,7–64,11," p. 52.

57. Sekine, *Sammlung*, pp. 159-60.

- 64:8(9) contains the notion of God's anger, as do 48:9; 54:7-9; 57:16.[58]

Berges notes even more cases of affinity between the lament and Isa 40–55:

- The question "where is your zeal and your strength?" (איה קנאתך וגבורתך) in 63:15b is reminiscent of 42:13, which, using the roots קנא and גבר, describes God as a mighty man who stirs up zeal.[59]
- 63:18 draws conceptually on the idea in 52:3 that God let go of Zion for some time only then to redeem her. Furthermore, the imperative שוב in 63:17bα, directed to God, is reminiscent of the statement in 52:8bβ that God is returning to Zion (בשוב ה׳ ציון). In addition, 63:19a, where the people declare that they feel as if God has never ruled over them (היינו מעולם לא משלת בם) and that they are not called by God's name (לא נקרא שמך עליהם), is reminiscent of 52:5-6 which states that, in the past, other people took God's people for free (כי לקח עמי חנם) and ruled over them (משליו/משלו) but that now God's people will know God's name (לכן ידע עמי שמי). In view of these verbal and conceptual similarities, Berges suggests that 63:18-19a alludes to 52:3-6 as a way of reminding God to fulfill his promises to his people.[60]
- The idea that God was angry with his people and polluted his inheritance in Isa 47:6 forms the basis for the statement about God's anger in 64:4b, 8a(5b, 9a) (cf. Aejmelaeus above).[61]
- The emphasis on God as Father in 64:7 draws on the imagery in 45:9-11 (cf. Sekine above).[62]
- The lament in 64:11(12) that God has been silent (תחשה ותעננו עד מאד) is similar to the divine statement in 42:14 that God has been silent for a long time (החשיתי מעולם) but now, he will cry out like a woman in childbirth.[63]

Goldenstein also demonstrates that the lament in 63:7–64:11 shares vocabulary and themes with the material in chapters 40–55:

58. Aejmelaeus, "Der Prophet als Klageliedsänger," pp. 42-46.
59. Berges, *Das Buch Jesaja,* p. 488.
60. Berges, *Das Buch Jesaja,* p. 490.
61. Berges, *Das Buch Jesaja,* pp. 491-92.
62. Berges, *Das Buch Jesaja,* p. 493.
63. Berges, *Das Buch Jesaja,* pp. 488-89.

- The reference to "God's servants" in 63:17 (עבדיך) is connected with the notion of "God's servant" in 40–55 (e.g. 43:10).
- The command in 46:9 (זכרו ראשנות מעולם) to remember the (days of) old is reminiscent of the statement in 63:11 that the people remembered the days of old (ויזכר ימי עולם).
- There are thematic links between the lament in 63:7–64:11 and select verses in 42:10–44:5:
  a. Use of similar metaphors: for example, both 43:2 and 63:11-12 recall the Exodus out of Egypt, and both 43:6 and 63:16; 64:7 (8) refer to the relationship between God and Israel in terms of father-child.
  b. Use of contrasting imagery: for example, 42:14 speaks of God crying out while 64:11(12) complains that God is silent (cf. Berges above).
- There are contrasting thematic and literary links between 63:7–64:11 and 44:26, 28; 45:8-11: for example, the promises in 44:26, 28 to rebuild the cities of old are contrasted with the statement in 64:9-10(10-11) that the cities are ruined.[64]

Recently, Gärtner has emphasized the links between 63:17 and 43:10; 54:17 in their shared use of the Servant motif.[65]

I will offer a three-fold response to these findings. First, I would like to add to the list of parallels by highlighting the affinity, in tone and in attitude towards suffering, between Isa 63:7–64:11 and Isa 49:

- In 49:14-15a,[66] Daughter Zion exclaims that the Lord has forsaken her and forgotten her (עזבני ה' ואדני שכחני). She also accuses God of unnatural behaviour, akin to that of a woman who forgets her baby and who has no compassion for her child (התשכח אשה עולה מרחם בן בטנה). In 63:15bβ, the lamenters cry out that God's love and compassion are being withheld from them (מעיך ורחמיך אלי התאפקו). Although there is no verbal agreement between the two statements beyond the shared use of the root רחם, their content is similar.

64. Goldenstein, *Das Gebet der Gottesknechte,* pp. 156-57.

65. Judith Gärtner, "'. . . Why Do You Let Us Stray from Your Paths . . .' (Isa 63:17): The Concept of Guilt in the Communal Lament Isa 63:7–64:11," in *Seeking the Favor of God: The Origins of Penitential Prayer in Second Temple Judaism* (ed. M. J. Boda, D. K. Falk, R. A. Werline; SBLEJL 21; Atlanta: Society of Biblical Literature, 2006), pp. 145-163 (esp. pp 160-62).

66. It is likely that all of Isa 49:14-15a contains Zion's speech. See further Rosario P. Merendino, "Jes 49:14-26: Jahwes Bekenntnis zu Sion und die neue Heilszeit," *Revue Biblique* 89 (1982): 321-69 (esp. 329-30).

- Furthermore, Daughter Zion's thoughts in 49:21, expressing that she feels left alone, bereaved and barren, exiled and rejected, as well as God's statement that Zion is lying in ruins (49:19, ושממתיך) agree with the sentiments expressed in 64:9(10) that God's holy cities have become a wilderness, Zion has become a desert, and Jerusalem has become desolate (ירשלים שממה).
- Finally, Daughter Zion's doubts as to God's ability or willingness to save, expressed in Isa 49:24 ("can booty be taken from the mighty one or can a captive be delivered from an awe-inspiring one") (היקח מגבור מלקוח ואם שבי צדיק ימלט),[67] is reminiscent thematically of the questions expressed in Isa 63:18 and 64:11 about God's inactivity on behalf of his temple and his people.

Second, I wish to question the postulated *direction of influence* between Isa 40–55 and Isa 63:7–64:11. In contrast to the aforementioned scholars, two factors suggest, independently of each other, that the lament is the earlier text to which Isa 40–55 alludes. First, as both Berges and Goldenstein note, in some cases a statement in Isa 40–55 *reverses* a statement in Isa 63:7–64:11. For instance, 64:11(12) complains that God is remaining silent while 42:14 claims that God will cry out after having kept silent for a long time. In a similar manner, Isa 64:9-10(10-11) laments that the cities are ruined while Isa 44:26, 28 promises that the cities of old will be rebuilt. This kind of reversal is counter-intuitive. Although one can envision a situation wherein Isa 63:7–64:11 laments the fact that the promises in Isa 40-55 have not yet been fulfilled, the positive answers to a lament tend to post-date the lament. For instance, all scholars (as far as I am aware) agree that the promises in Isa 40–55 allude to and respond to the laments in Lamentations (cf. also the relationship between Isa 60:1–63:6 and Isa 63:7–64:11, above).[68] By analogy, it is likely that the material in Isa 40–55

67. The *Niphal* of ימלט can have both an active and a passive sense. Here, assuming that v. 24b is parallel to v. 24a, the passive sense fits best. A passive sense is also presupposed by the LXX (σωθήσεται = "be rescued"), although the whole of v. 24b in the LXX ("and if one should take [a man] captive unjustly, shall he be delivered?") appears to be paraphrasing the MT. A passive reading is adopted by, among others, Joseph Blenkinsopp, *Isaiah 40–55* (AB 19A; New York: Doubleday, 2000), pp. 313-14, including note a, and Childs, *Isaiah*, p. 388. As to the word צדיק, much favours accepting the reading of 1QIsa[a] (עריץ). In particular, both V *(a robusto)* and the Peshitta (עשינא) seem to support a Hebrew consonantal text עריץ ("awe-inspiring"). In addition, v. 25 parallels the two concepts of גבור and עריץ. Cf. Tiemeyer, *Comfort of Zion*, p. 190.

68. See especially Patricia Tull Willey, *Remember the Former Things: The Recollection of Previous Texts in Second Isaiah* (SBLDS 161; Atlanta: Scholars Press, 1997).

responds with encouragement to the lament in Isa 63:7–64:11. Second, as discussed in the beginning of this article, Isa 63:7–64:11 was probably composed before 539 B.C.E. while Isa 40–55, in particular Isa 49–55, was written around 539 B.C.E. or later.[69] The fact that the lament appears later in the book of Isaiah does not necessarily mean that its date of composition is later, only that the final editor(s) of the book wanted the readers of the book to approach the texts in this particular order. A case in point is Isa 24–27, a section which most historical-critical scholars assign to one of the later strata in the book of Isaiah.[70]

Third, I wish to shed new light upon the relationship between Isa 40–55 and Isa 63:7–64:11. In view of the similarities between Isa 49 and 63:7–64:11, I suggest that the incorporation of the lament in Isa 63:7–64:11 was carried out in continuity with the same tradition that is reflected in the short laments of Daughter Zion in the preceding Isa 49–55. Phrased differently, the authors/redactors responsible for incorporating the originally independent lament that is now found in Isa 63:7–64:11 did so in part because the theology of this lament agreed with the theology expressed by Daughter Zion in Isa 49–55. Thus, while it is unlikely that the lament in Isa 63:7–64:11 was purposely written for its present place in the book of Isaiah, it nevertheless stands in continuity with a theological view that is found elsewhere in the book of Isaiah. Moreover, in the same way as the speech of Daughter Zion in Isa 49–55 represents views found in Judah in the latter half of the sixth century B.C.E., so the lament in Isa 63:7–64:11 reflects the concerns of the people of Judah in the same time period.

At the same time, these thematic similarities, as well as those pointed out by Sekine, Aejmelaeus, Berges, Goldenstein, and Gärtner, are too vague to suggest that the relevant passages in Isa 40–55 were written for the specific purpose of responding to Isa 63:7–64:11. Rather, it is probable that the authors of Isa 40–55 were familiar with the lament, given its likely liturgical function, and sought to respond to the *type of complaints* voiced by the lament and to the *key theological issues* that it raises. The various texts in Isa 40–55 thus seek to provide answers to the important questions in the lament: Why is God silent? Why has he left his city in ruins? Why does God, although being their father, appear to be unwilling to save his people? Why has he rejected them?

69. A few scholars have argued that Isa 63:7–64:11 is the oldest text in Isa 40–66. See especially Georg Fohrer, *Das Buch Jesaja*, Vol. 3 (Zürcher Bibelkommentare; Zürich/Stuttgart: Zwingli Verlag, 1964), pp. 24-47.

70. See, e.g., J. Todd Hibbard, *Intertextuality in Isaiah 24–27* (FAT II/16; Tübingen: Mohr Siebeck, 2006), pp. 32-36.

Conclusion

In this article, I have endeavoured to show that the lament in Isa 63:7–64:11 is an integral part of Isa 40–66. Although it did not originate within the Isaiah tradition, and although it was not composed with its present place in the book of Isaiah in mind, the sentiments voiced in the lament have affinity with key aspects of the surrounding Isaianic texts. In particular, they have the same theological concerns and share the same outlook upon suffering as the voice of Daughter Zion in Isa 49. The authors/editors of Isa 40–66 did not fully agree with these sentiments, yet they recognized that the intended audience of their texts did. These authors therefore allowed for dissenting voices to be heard in order to reach their audience. At the same time, they sought to convince them that their pessimistic outlook had not taken all the relevant data concerning their situation into account, and that God would indeed be willing to save them if they decided to live their lives in accordance with his will.

Joseph Blenkinsopp as an Interpreter of "Third Isaiah"

Hans M. Barstad

Joseph Blenkinsopp has, at remarkable speed and with impressive quality, published commentaries on all the three different parts of the Isaiah scroll.[1] In the present (very modest) contribution, I want to make some comments on his third volume, the commentary on Isaiah 56–66. As one would expect from a commentary, the exegetical part makes up the bulk of the book.[2] However, I will not so much deal with the commentary itself in the present quite short essay.[3]

1. Joseph Blenkinsopp, *Isaiah 1–39: A New Translation with Introduction and Commentary,* Anchor Bible 19 (New York: Doubleday, 2000); *Isaiah 40–55: A New Translation with Introduction and Commentary,* Anchor Bible 19A (New York: Doubleday, 2000); *Isaiah 56–66: A New Translation with Introduction and Commentary,* Anchor Bible 19B (New York: Doubleday, 2003).

2. *Isaiah 56–66,* pp. 129-317.

3. The design follows the Anchor Bible style: translation, texts, critical notes, and commentary. The bibliography that precedes the detailed exegesis is very comprehensive (pp. 95-126). After the substantial commentary there follows a high quality index of subjects (pp. 319-30), and a comprehensive listing of biblical and ancient texts (pp. 331-48). Unfortunately,

I am very pleased that I was invited by the editors to take part in the celebration of Joe's contribution to Isaiah studies with this modest essay. I have known Joe for many years. He is not only a greatly esteemed colleague, but also a highly valued friend. Over the years, we have met at innumerable scholarly meetings and shared countless meals. These encounters have in themselves been like small "mini-conferences," and I always left our meetings with the feeling of having become much wiser. Even if Joe has now reduced his transatlantic travels to three yearly flights, I still hope to learn a lot also in the future.

For this reason, it may be worthwhile to reproduce here at the very start of my paper the headlines and divisions that are used throughout the commentary. These are conveniently found also at the beginning of the commentary, together with Blenkinsopp's very useful translation of the whole Trito-Isaianic text.[4] They are: "Reassurance of the Marginal" (56:1-8); "Corrupt Leaders Invite Disaster" (56:9-12); "Lament for the Dead Prophet and His Disciples" (57:1-2); "Denunciation of the Sorcerer and Her Children" (57:3-13); "A Call for a New Beginning" (57:14-21); "True Fasting, True Piety" (58:1-14); "Why God Remains Inactive and Silent" (59:1-8); "A Community Complaint" (59:9-15a); "Finally, a Reply" (59:15b-20); "The Gift of Prophecy" (59:21); "An Apostrophe to Zion" (60:1-22); "The Prophetic Disciple's Mission" (61:1-7); "Covenant of Blessing and a Hymn of Thanksgiving" (61:8-11); "The New Jerusalem" (62:1-5); "Prophets, Guardians of the City" (62:6-9); "The Processional Way" (62:10-12); "A Bloodbath in Edom" (63:1-6); "A Community Lament" (63:7–64:11[12]); "Judgement on the Syncretists" (65:1-7); "Who Are Not God's People" (65:8-12); "Eschatological Reversal" (65:13-16); "New Heaven, New Earth, New City" (65:17-25); "Vindication of the True Worshippers of God" (66:1-6); "Mother Zion and Her Children" (66:7-16); "A Sense of an Ending" (66:17-24).[5]

Duhm's Thesis

In his impressive introduction, Blenkinsopp takes up a variety of important issues that have been dealt with in Trito-Isaianic research.[6] He first discusses briefly Bernhard Duhm's hypothesis.[7] After having presented some of the main components of his ideas, he follows this up by referring to some of Duhm's main critics. The scholars mentioned by Blenkinsopp are: C. C. Torrey, L. Glahn, J. Muilenburg, M. Haran, J. D. Smart, B. D. Banwell, F. Maass, C. R. Seitz, and B. S. Childs. However, since there are weaknesses attached to the work of many of these researchers, too, Blenkinsopp wisely concludes that

there is no modern author index. It is, consequently, not possible to follow the several references to secondary literature in the many discussions throughout the book.

4. *Isaiah 56–66*, pp. 3-24.

5. In addition to these headlines, the volume has also an excursus on "Double Meanings in Isaiah 57:3-13" (pp. 162-63), on "The Sorceress of Isaiah 57:3-13" (pp. 163-66), and on "Fasting in Isaiah 58:1-14" (pp. 182-83).

6. *Isaiah 56–66*, pp. 27-91.

7. *Isaiah 56–66*, pp. 27-29.

Duhm's tripartite hypothesis cannot be discarded. Clearly, the idea suffers from obvious shortcomings. Nevertheless, it has to be retained as a valuable heuristic tool for serious exegetical work on the Isaiah scroll.

Subsequently, Blenkinsopp also discusses some of the commentators that have attempted to argue against Duhm's Trito-Isaianic textual delimitations.[8] These scholars claim that one major reason why Duhm is wrong is that what we find in Isa 56:1 does not represent the beginning of a new unit 56–66. Rather than a "gap marker," 56:1 is a verse that secures continuation. In reality, according to these researchers, Isa 56:1 binds 56–66 to the preceding parts of the Isaiah scroll.

On this point, Blenkinsopp mentions names like C. C. Torrey, O. H. Steck, W. A. M. Beuken, and R. Rendtorff as adherents of this particular view. All of them have argued that there are strong authorial and/or editorial links between 56–66 and 40–55. They do this on the basis of common vocabulary and shared themes in the two corpuses. To these scholars, Isa 56:1 represents the very key text that proves the connection. Blenkinsopp argues fairly vehemently against this particular view. The only scholar that he finds useful is Rendtorff.

As will be known, the literature dealing with the relationship between 40–55 and 56–66 is quite overwhelming, and also rather nuanced. Due to the briefness of Blenkinsopp's survey, it goes without saying that it can only touch upon a very small part of the various issues involved in the debates that have taken place. For this reason, his overview cannot be said to be "representative." Nevertheless, it may be useful to quote a small "programmatic" text from his commentary in order to attempt to understand better Blenkinsopp's own view on these intricate problems.

> Some of the ways in which chs. 56–66 mark a further stage of development and differentiation vis-à-vis chs. 40–55 will be apparent at first reading. While both sections are directed at Jewish communities, chs. 40–55 are concerned primarily with Judah's place on the international scene. YHVH's purposes are here seen to be implemented by human agents, Cyrus in the first place, and polemic is directed against cults practiced by foreign peoples. Literary forms and metaphoric language appropriate to these themes predominate, the most characteristic (especially in 40–48) being the trial scene together with much forensic terminology.
>
> In 56–66, on the other hand, interest is focused on internal affairs. The prospect held out is that of direct divine action, whether in judgement or

8. *Isaiah 56–66*, pp. 29-30.

> salvation, and no more is heard of the Persian conquests or other kinds of political agency. Alien (i.e., syncretic) cults practiced within the community are targeted rather than cults of foreign peoples.[9]

As one may see from this quotation, one of Blenkinsopp's major points is that the international outlook of Isa 40–55 is replaced by the more domestic or internal one in chapters 56–66. When viewing the two corpuses in relation to each other, we find, according to Blenkinsopp, continuities as well as breaks. Roughly, chapters 56–66 represent an exegetical extension, or *Fortschreibung* ("continuous writing"), of chapters 40–55.

The Relationship Between Isaiah 56–66 and 40–55

The quotation from Blenkinsopp's commentary above shows how important it is to him that 56–66 represents a further development in relation to 40–55. For this reason, he goes through the current debate that supports the independence of "Trito-Isaiah" from "Deutero-Isaiah" in some detail.[10]

According to Blenkinsopp, where the ideas, language, and historical context in 56–66 differ from 40–55, the theme of consolation is often present. In Isa 40–55, divine comfort takes its starting point in the state of Judah after the Neo-Babylonian invasion. Divine comfort in 56–66, on the other hand, is seen against the background of late post-exilic times. Nevertheless, comfort issues still echo in the former Deutero-Isaianic corpus.[11] A second area where there is a marked difference between 40–55 and 56–66 concerns the way divine action is described in the two parts. The role of God in 40–55 is political (against the Babylonians). In 56–66, however, ". . . the power of God is essentially and radically the power to overcome evil."[12]

Similarly, the use of terms for "way"/"path"/"road" also differs in the two parts of the Isaiah scroll. In 40–55, these lexemes have a more concrete meaning, a way from the exile to the homeland, possibly echoing a processional itinerary. In 56–66, however, the "way" idiom "is now a metaphor for a way

9. *Isaiah 56–66,* p. 30.

10. *Isaiah 56–66,* pp. 30-34. Here, he builds for convenience on Sekine's redaction historical study, and refers to this study for a more complete list: Seizo Sekine, *Die Tritojesajanische Sammlung: (Jes 56–66) redaktionsgeschichtlich untersucht,* Beihefte zur Zeitschrift für die alttestamentliche Wissenschaft 175 (Berlin: de Gruyter, 1989).

11. *Isaiah 56–66,* p. 31.

12. *Isaiah 56–66,* p. 31.

out of the mess in which the community finds itself, a way in the direction of redemption."[13] For support, Blenkinsopp refers to Zimmerli's classic (but very old) study.[14] Additionally, views on the glory of God *(kbwd yhwh)* also differ in the two corpuses. The coming of God in glory to Jerusalem, also echoing divine kingship, is shared in 40–66. However, in 56–66, it is clearer that this divine advent will take place in Jerusalem.[15] Finally, views on creation vary between the two texts. In 40–55, creation is more "universal," reflecting the world as it is. In 56–66, creation deals not with the extant world, but rather with a new "world order."

Blenkinsopp comments also on important terminology in describing the differences between 40–55 and 56–66. He discusses words like "justice" *(mšpt),* "righteousness" *(ṣdqh),* and salvation *(yšwʿh).* All of these theologically pregnant words are used differently in the two corpuses. In 56–66, the usage of all of these central terms is broadened and expanded (in particular *ṣdqh*).[16] Finally, the use of "servants" rather than "servant" in 56–66 is dealt with at some length. Here, Blenkinsopp refers to works by Beuken and himself for further discussions. This is one of the areas where Blenkinsopp himself has contributed considerably to changing our research situation.[17]

In the summing up, Blenkinsopp concludes more generally how the experience of reading 56–66 in the light of 40–55 has revealed an underlying textual and exegetical process that binds the two texts together. The best indications of continuity are instances where 56–66 reproduces, sometimes word for word, verses or phrases from 40–55. However, he also comments wisely that

13. *Isaiah 56–66,* p. 31.

14. Walther Zimmerli, "Zur Sprache Tritojesajas," *Schweizerische theologische Umschau* 20 (1950): 110-22.

15. *Isaiah 56–66,* p. 32.

16. *Isaiah 56–66,* pp. 32-33.

17. See, for instance, his important "The Servant and the Servants in Isaiah and the Formation of the Book," in *Writing and Reading the Scroll of Isaiah. Studies of an Interpretive Tradition,* edited by Craig C. Broyles and Craig A. Evans, Supplements to Vetus Testamentum 70,1 (Leiden: Brill, 1997), pp. 155-75. In the commentary at hand, Blenkinsopp refers to his own 1997 essay, as well as to one article by Beuken in support of his view: W. A. M. Beuken, "The Main Theme of Trito-Isaiah: 'The Servants of YHWH,'" *Journal for the Study of the Old Testament* 47 (1990): 67-87. However, his own engagement in this particular question goes back at least as far as Blenkinsopp's seminal essay, "The 'Servants of the Lord' in Third Isaiah: Profile of a Pietistic Group in the Persian Epoch," *Proceedings of the Irish Biblical Association* 7 (1983): 1-23.

> Interpretation of this kind is hardly ever simply reproduction, however. In almost all instances it involves a reactualization and therefore very often a problemization of the text, now considered to some degree authoritative, when introduced into a different situation. In 40-55 proselytes are acknowledged and accepted (44:5), but by the later stage represented by 56:1-8 the presence within the community of those who 'join themselves to YHVH' has become a matter of dispute.[18]

This statement is vital and brings Blenkinsopp's important work in line with a whole series of contributions that provide guidelines for sound and adequate ways of reading scripture. That reading, writing, and the very handing down of the tradition itself in fact also represents a re-interpretation is something that has been known a long time. As we know, this is an issue that has not always been fully appreciated by scholars.[19] That this particular wisdom has now been applied as a fully integrated part of a commentary on the whole Isaiah scroll will remain only one of several long-lasting effects of Blenkinsopp's magnificent *opus magnum.*

The Relationship Between Isaiah 56–66 and 1–39

For many years, as a result of the success of the Deutero-Isaianic thesis, the only debates that were regarded as relevant to this area of biblical scholarship concerned the relationship between 40–55 and 56–66. Since 1–39 was considered to stem from completely different times, it was believed to be unrelated to 1–39. However, this situation has changed drastically during the last thirty years or so. For the most part, this is due to a renewed interest also among academics in the "unity" of the book of Isaiah. Among several names, I can only mention a few in the present context: P. R. Ackroyd, W. Brueggemann, R. Clements, J. H. Eaton, R. Rendtorff, J. D. W. Watts, J. Vermeylen, C. R. Seitz, and H. G. M. Williamson.[20]

18. *Isaiah 56–66,* p. 34.

19. Among important contributions in this area, one classic on "inner-biblical exegesis" is Michael Fishbane, *Biblical Interpretation in Ancient Israel* (Oxford: Oxford University Press, 1985). The most recent volume that I have come across is the fine study by Sidnie White Crawford, *Rewriting Scripture in Second Temple Times,* Studies in the Dead Sea Scrolls and Related Literature (Grand Rapids, MI: Eerdmans, 2008).

20. Particular mention should here be made of Hugh Williamson's pivotal contribution. See H. G. M. Williamson, *The Book Called Isaiah: Deutero-Isaiah's Role in Composition and*

Blenkinsopp is more careful than some scholars in this particular area. In his view, at first sight, there appears to be little in 56–66 that betrays acquaintance with 1–39. The only exception would be Isaiah 1:27-31 and 66:17-24, where we may find the work of the final editors.[21] All three of the Isaianic "books," according to Blenkinsopp, are concerned with common themes like the destiny of Jerusalem, judgement and salvation, and the nature of the God of Israel. However, these topics are found "everywhere" in the Hebrew Bible. Blenkinsopp therefore assumes that they are probably too vague to be able to contribute anything significant to the discussion on links between chapters 1-39 and the rest of the Book of Isaiah.

The Literary Character of Isaiah 56–66

Next, Blenkinsopp discusses the literary nature of the Trito-Isaianic corpus.[22] "The Literary Character of Isaiah 56–66" takes its starting point in the issue that "Isaiah 56–66 does not constitute what most people today would recognize as a literary work."[23] When (or if) the modern reader gets a feeling of unity and coherence from reading these texts, this impression is caused by a redactor and not by an author. Blenkinsopp first deals with the structure of the book. "Structure" is here used in a non-technical (or "half-technical") way. One basic question, then, is how structure can convey "meaning." The question is particularly vital in relation to Trito-Isaiah, according to Blenkinsopp. The reason for this is partly that 56–66 is strongly influenced by Deuteronomistic thought.

The last part of this section discusses literary quality, prosody, and genre in 56–66. Again, Blenkinsopp should be praised for not making too many unwarranted positivistic claims. Instead, this part of his book is particularly valuable in the way it shows how intricate problems relating to prosody and genre really are.[24]

Redaction (Oxford: Clarendon Press, 1994). Even if Williamson is primarily dealing with the relationship between 1–39 and 40–55, he has some very useful comments on the "Trito-Isaianic problem" as well. See, *The Book Called Isaiah,* pp. 19-29, and *passim.*

21. *Isaiah 56–66,* p. 35.

22. *Isaiah 56–66,* pp. 37-41.

23. *Isaiah 56–66,* p. 37.

24. *Isaiah 56–66,* pp. 40-41.

The Historical Context of 56–66

Under the heading "Isaiah 56–66 in Its Historical Context," Blenkinsopp discusses dating problems.[25] This essay represents yet another important contribution to the scholarly debate. However, such remarks on the historical context of 56–66 are not restricted to these pages alone. Rather, historical observations permeate the entire commentary.

As one of our foremost experts on the Persian period, Blenkinsopp is eminently qualified for the kind of reading that combines textual analysis with historical issues. After having briefly surveyed some of the difficulties involved in the dating of this text, he tentatively sums up the current consensus:

> Most scholars today would, nevertheless, agree that the bulk of 56–66 reflects the situation in the province of Judah (Yehud) during the first century of Persian rule, corresponding more or less to the reigns of Darius I (522-486), Xerxes I (486-465), and Artaxerxes I (465-424). If we may take this as a reasonable working hypothesis, it will be useful to provide a brief summary of events during this epoch. We may then be in a better position to determine against this background at least the contours of currents and movements within contemporaneous Jewish communities as reflected in these chapters.[26]

Blenkinsopp admits that dating this text is extremely problematic. He nevertheless thinks that it should be attempted. For this reason, he gives first a fine survey of Persian history after the death of Cambyses in 522 B.C.E.[27] Following this broad overview, he discusses historical evidence in the text that may help us with the dating problem. This subsection is entitled "Historical Clues in Chapters 56–66."[28] However, as evidence, he only mentions the reconstructed religious "Trembler" party. Here, Blenkinsopp refers to a thesis that he developed in earlier writings.[29] As for the dating of 56–66, Blenkinsopp himself opts

25. *Isaiah 56–66,* pp. 42-54.

26. *Isaiah 56–66,* p. 43.

27. *Isaiah 56–66,* pp. 44-51.

28. *Isaiah 56–66,* pp. 51-54.

29. This view has in particular been taken up by Lena-Sofia Tiemeyer. It is, however, supported by many: Odil Hannes Steck, *Studien zu Tritojesaja,* Beihefte zur Zeitschrift für die alttestamentliche Wissenschaft 203 (Berlin: de Gruyter, 1991), p. 252, n. 145; Brooks Schramm, *The Opponents of Third Isaiah: Reconstructing the Cultic History of the Restoration,* Journal for the Study of the Old Testament Supplement Series 193 (Sheffield: Sheffield Academic Press, 1995), pp. 113, 169; Paul A. Smith, *Rhetoric and Redaction in Trito-Isaiah: The Structure, Growth*

for the early part of Persian rule. In my view, his own extreme caution when it comes to dating as well as to relating 56–66 to historical events is very wise, indeed. However, it may seem that both some of the details about a "Trembler Party," as well as a dating of 56–66 to the early part of the Achaemenid period, may be problematic in light of the many uncertainties involved.

The Formation of the Book

Above, we saw how Blenkinsopp accepted Duhm's thesis in essence.[30] In a section called "The Formation of Isaiah 56–66," the author elaborates further on this topic.[31] First, he discusses the history of research of the Deutero-Isaianic thesis (and its later Trito-Isaianic developments) from early times till today. He starts out with the twelfth-century Abraham Ibn Ezra, mentions the late-eighteenth-century J. C. Döderlein, and ends up with Bernhard Duhm's predecessors B. Stade, A. Kuenen, and C. H. Cornill. Other names referred to in his survey (mentioned here in the order in which they first occur in Blenkinsopp's volume) are: C. C. Torrey, L. Glahn, F. Maass, J. D. Smart, C. R. Seitz, E. König, E. J. Kissane, P. Volz, W. Zimmerli, T. K. Cheyne, J. Muilenburg, P. D. Hanson, O. H. Steck, W. Lau, H. J. Hermisson, C. Westermann, S. Sekine, K. Koenen, K. Marti, H. Odeberg, W. Kessler, P.-E. Bonnard, A. Zillessen, K. Elliger, J. Vermeylen, and P. A. Smith.

Blenkinsopp concludes that 56–66 does not derive from one hand. Instead, these chapters represent a compound work.[32] He also discusses the composition itself in order to see whether a meaningful structure can be found. Blenkinsopp finds three different redaction units in 56–66: 56–59, 60–62, and 63–66. As the next step, he attempts to deal with the very difficult question of which social realities we may find behind the various texts. He

and Authorship of Isaiah 56–66, Supplements to Vetus Testamentum 62 (Leiden: Brill, 1995), pp. 163, 197, 200-201; Marvin A. Sweeney, "Prophetic Exegesis in Isaiah 65–66," in *Writing and Reading the Scroll of Isaiah: Studies of an Interpretive Tradition,* edited by Craig C. Broyles and Craig A. Evans, Supplements to Vetus Testamentum 70,1 (Leiden: Brill, 1997), p. 473; Leszek Ruszkowski, *Volk und Gemeinde im Wandel: Eine Untersuchung zu Jesaja,* Forschungen zur Religion und Literatur des Alten und Neuen Testaments 191 (Göttingen: Vandenhoeck & Ruprecht, 2000), p. 158; Lena-Sofia Tiemeyer, *Priestly Rites and Prophetic Rage: Post-Exilic Prophetic Critique of the Priesthood,* Forschungen zum Alten Testament 2. Reihe 19 (Tübingen: Mohr Siebeck, 2006), pp. 268-70.

30. *Isaiah 56–66,* pp. 27-29.

31. *Isaiah 56–66,* pp. 54-66.

32. *Isaiah 56–66,* p. 59.

believes (not everyone would agree, of course) that by paying careful attention to prophetic first person speech throughout chapters 40–66 we can detect stages in the development of a prophetic succession. The process, subsequently, led to the emergence of an eschatologically oriented sect within the Persian province of Judah in the mid-fifth century B.C.E. The faction can be traced back to a charismatic individual who is identical with the unknown prophet behind chapters 49–55.

Blenkinsopp refers to the work of Vermeylen, who finds seven stages in Trito-Isaiah. According to Vermeylen, the various layers differ from the sixth century to the time of the finishing editorial make-up in the third century. Blenkinsopp is, and in the present writer's view justly, critical of Vermeylen's extreme redaction criticism. Rather, according to Blenkinsopp, synchronic and diachronic studies should be *combined*. What we are dealing with in texts like the present, is a cumulative process, corresponding to stages in the formation of the book of Isaiah. For practical purposes, the best starting point would be to look for structural elements — clues for meaning — in the way the text is organized. But at the same time, Blenkinsopp points to the difficulties arising from the fact that the text of Isa 56–66 has been expanded, edited, and restructured several times. He finds a pyramidal structure in Trito-Isaiah, with chapters 60–62 as the "central panel."[33] Blenkinsopp finds the following key themes in the text: YHWH as warrior and vindicator (59:15b-20; 63:1-6), communal lament (59:1-15a; 63:7), condemnation of cult (56:9–58:14; 65:1-16), and proselytes and mission (56:1-8; 66:18-24).

Texts and Versions: A Master Class

As is well known, 56–66 has its fair share of textual problems. Textual issues are also dealt with in his exposé "Texts and Ancient Versions."[34] Here, Blenkinsopp deals with the most significant of the ancient versions relating to Isa 56–66 in a more general way. He also describes some of his own principles for dealing with textual issues in the commentary. Blenkinsopp very usefully reminds us that the task of the text critic is not to improve the text. His comments on all the versions are very balanced and should be read by everyone interested in text critical issues in 56–66. All in all, he finds fewer real problems in the text of the MT than some do. In this, he is, in my view, quite correct.

33. *Isaiah 56–66*, p. 61. See also pp. 38-39.
34. *Isaiah 56–66*, pp. 66-71.

From the Early History of Interpretation

One short, but very important part of the commentary has the heading "Chapters from the Early History of the Interpretation of Isaiah 56–66."[35] Here, we find an excellent survey of Isa 56–66 and Jewish-Christian polemic in antiquity. There is also a brief overview on Isa 56–66 in early Christianity. This topic was taken up by Blenkinsopp subsequently and importantly in his book on the early interpretation of the book of Isaiah, *Opening the Sealed Book.*[36] In this study Blenkinsopp examines how the book was understood by early post-biblical Jewish authors as well as early Christian writers and the social movements they represent. As such, the book offers a development and extension of some of the directions he takes in this introductory section of the commentary. Blenkinsopp demonstrates the increasing apocalyptic interpretation of the book, a feature only hinted at in some of the very latest sections of Isaiah itself, including but not limited to Isa 56–66 (see also Isa 24–27, 34–35).

Theology

"Aspects of the Theology of Isaiah 56–66" constitutes the last part of Blenkinsopp's introduction.[37] The word "aspects" is telling as Blenkinsopp already from the start makes it quite clear that Isa 56–66 does not make up a theological unity.

> For those who defend the essential authorial unity of these chapters a certain degree of coherence could perhaps be argued, but for most contemporary scholars it makes better sense to read 56–66 as a deposit of reflection and elaboration on existing prophetic teaching regarded as authoritative — first of all on the preceding section of the book.[38]

Rather, these chapters represent a *Fortschreibung* ("ongoing writing"), based on Isa 40–55. In Blenkinsopp's view, the theology of 56–66 is strongly influenced by Deuteronomistic theology. This would imply that both Deuteronomy and Deutero-Isaiah represent the larger theological framework within which "Trito-Isaiah" has to be understood. Most importantly, 56–66 reflects attempts

35. *Isaiah 56–66,* pp. 71-76.
36. Grand Rapids: Eerdmans, 2006.
37. *Isaiah 56–66,* pp. 77-91.
38. *Isaiah 56–66,* p. 77.

to adjust important theological themes to new demands and altered social and historical situations in the Persian period. Among the main topics, we find questions concerning prayer, fasting, Sabbath, and sacrifice.

Concluding Remarks

In these times of in-depth specialization, it is very rare to find scholars who are able to work in more than one (or maybe two?) areas of research. And, if they do, their work may occasionally appear uneven, revealing that parts of their work are based more on secondary sources and previous commentaries than on solid exegetical work with the Masoretic text. This is certainly not the case with Joseph Blenkinsopp. All of his three volumes in the Anchor Bible series are first rate, based on solid engagement with the Hebrew text, and written in critical dialogue with other prominent Isaiah researchers. For these reasons, his work will forever form a part of that distinguished small group of classical exegetical commentaries that will make a real impact on the scholarly world, not only for today, but also in the future.

"Build up, Pass through" — Isaiah 57:14–62:12 as the Core Composition of Third Isaiah

Andreas Schuele

A Farewell to Third Isaiah?

In recent years, the field of Old Testament studies has seen the departure of some of the grand theories that dominated the discipline over long stretches of the 19th and 20th centuries. The Jahwistic ("J") source of the Pentateuch/ the Torah has been perhaps the most prominent "victim" of this re-evaluation of traditional literary-historical criticism. In many ways, the "J" hypothesis was the flagship of Pentateuch scholarship. With "J," the founding fathers of modern historical criticism thought they had unearthed an author from the (early) days of the monarchy in Israel and Judah who created the master narrative of ancient Israel's national identity as well as its foundational religious beliefs. It seems fair to say that from Julius Wellhausen's *Prolegomena* to Harold Bloom's "The Book of J," scholars and novelists felt drawn to the idea that in and between the lines of the ancient stories of the Pentateuch, one could still hear the voice of great individuals who, not unlike Shakespeare or Goethe, expressed and shaped the *Zeitgeist* of the world in which they lived.

The prophet whom Bernhard Duhm found in Isa 40–55 and whom he called "Deutero-Isaiah" (DI) is another of these great voices in the Hebrew Bible. As a matter of fact, one might say that Duhm's DI is the same defining classic for the exilic and early post-exilic periods that "J" was for the monarchic era. Also, the DI hypothesis seemed a lot less speculative than "J" because there is hardly any disagreement about Isa 40 as the beginning of a new and major section in the overall book that could not have been written before two of its major characters — the personified empire of Babel and Cyrus the Great —

appeared on the stage of world history. However, the DI hypothesis, too, was not as unshakable as one might have thought.[1] The impression of the composite character of these chapters seemed particularly unavoidable with regard to the famous Servant Songs, which many scholars since Duhm have identified as an overlay and, as such, a later addition to Isa 40–55. Another problem with DI was its end. While its powerful introit "Comfort, comfort my people" clearly marks the beginning of something new, there is no equally obvious *conclusio* at the end of ch. 55. The divine speech about the word that comes from and returns to God like rain and water (Isa 55:8-11) could be such a *conclusio* but is certainly less than an obvious case. Also, Duhm himself was quite aware that much of the "sound" of DI continued even in the final eleven chapters of the book and that the only obvious and undeniable "end" was the announcement of the new heaven and the new earth in chs. 65 and 66. Given Duhm's conviction that individual prophets stood behind the three main parts of Isaiah, he concluded that the similarities and differences between Isa 40–55 and 56–66 were best explained if one assumed that the author of 56–66 was a student of DI's, and this student Duhm called Trito-Isaiah (TI).[2]

It comes as no surprise that this imaginative but also quite speculative explanation of TI as a somewhat epigonal figure in the shadow of his grand master[3] did not ultimately pass the test of time, although Duhm's reservations regarding the theological quality of TI still reverberate in some of the discussions about TI's alleged "works righteousness." In contrast to Duhm, scholars today tend to see Isa 56–66 as part of the inner-Isaianic interpretation of tradition that started in Isa 40–55, although this process was now slowing down and reached the point of book closure.[4] In this view, most of the materials gathered in the final eleven chapters of Isaiah were deliberately written as book

1. Cf. Wolfgang Lau, *Schriftgelehrte Prophetie in Jes 56–66: Eine Untersuchung zu den literarischen Bezügen in den letzten elf Kapiteln des Jesajabuches* (BZAW 225; Berlin/New York: De Gruyter, 1994), pp. 3-5.

2. B. Duhm, *Das Buch Jesaia* (Göttingen: Vandenhoeck & Ruprecht, 1903), pp. xviii-xix. For an overview of the history of research on Isa 56-66 see S. Sekine, *Die Tritojesajanische Sammlung (Jes 56–66) redaktionsgeschichtlich untersucht* (BZAW 175; Berlin/New York: De Gruyter, 1989), pp. 3-23; J. Blenkinsopp, *Isaiah 56–66* (AB 19B; New York/London: Doubleday, 2003), pp. 54-60.

3. Duhm, *Jesaia,* p. 380.

4. Cf. Lau, *Schriftgelehrte Prophetie,* pp. 316-25; W. A. Beuken, "Isaiah Chapters LXV-LXVI: Trito-Isaiah and the Closure of the Book of Isaiah," in *Congress Volume Leuven 1989* (ed. J. A. Emerton; VTSup 43; Leiden: Brill, 1991), pp. 204-21; M. Sweeney, "Prophetic Exegesis in Isaiah 65–66," in *Writing and Reading the Scroll of Isaiah: Studies of an Interpretative Tradition* (ed. Craig C. Broyles and Craig A. Evans; VTSup 70/1; Leiden: Brill, 1997), pp. 455-74.

endings. This is most obviously the case in Isa 65 and 66 with the announcement of the new heaven and the new earth, which not only points back to First Isaiah (Isa 65:25; cf. Isa 11:6-9) but also to Gen 1–3 (Isa 65:17; cf. Gen 1:1; Isa 65:20, 23; cf. Gen 3:16-17). The other example of a particularly clear and intentional inner-Isaianic allusion is the speech of the Spirit-bearer in Isa 61:1-3,[5] which, as we shall explore in greater detail below, together with Isa 11:1-5 and 42:1-9 constitutes what one might call an inner axis of the book of Isaiah.

While details about the literary history behind Isa 56-66 remain disputed, there is relative consensus across the scholarly guild that Isa 61 and 65 are two of the defining texts that anchor TI in the Isaianic tradition as recorded in Isa 1–55. It is also worth noticing that these two texts share the same reference point, namely the eschatological vision of Isa 11:1-9. Isaiah 61:1-3 alludes to the announcement of the messianic king in 11:1-5 as the shoot from the stump of Jesse who, guided by the Spirit of God, will correct the political and social order by bringing justice especially to the poor and downtrodden. It seems that Isa 65:25, by drawing on the second part of the same oracle (11:6-9), picks up where 61:1-3 left off. Here it is the re-creation not just of the human world but of the larger natural order that comes into focus — the wolf feeding with the lamb and the lion eating straw like cattle. It is also significant that Isa 11:1-9 is the one text in First (and Second) Isaiah that calls Zion "my holy mountain" (v. 9), which makes it a very likely assumption that TI, with five occurrences of this phrase (56:7; 57:13; 65:11, 25; 66:20[6]), couches its eschatological vision in the language and imagery of the older prophecy.[7]

Regardless of one's opinion about the literary history of TI and its thematic unity or diversity, what permeates the different texts is a particular sense of location. All the events that are envisioned here — the pilgrimage of the nations to Jerusalem (ch. 60), the coming of the Spirit-bearer (ch. 61), even the new heaven and the new earth (chs. 65–66) — are expected to occur at, move towards, or issue forth from the holy mountain.[8] As vast and expansive as TI's

5. Cf. W. A. M. Beuken, "Servant and Herald of Good Tidings: Isaiah 61 as an Interpretation of Isaiah 40–55," in *Book of Isaiah — Le livre d'Isaïe* (ed. J. Vermeylen; BETL 81; Louvain: Leuven University Press, 1989), pp. 411-42; J. Stromberg, "An inner-Isaianic Reading of Isaiah 61:1-3," in *Interpreting Isaiah* (Leicester: IVP Academic, 2009), pp. 261-72 .

6. Additionally, Isa 62:9 mentions "my holy courts" (rather than "the courts of my sanctuary," given that TI does not otherwise use קֹדֶשׁ for "sanctuary").

7. Unless one assumes that Isa 11:1-9, or parts thereof, is a later insertion by some of the same hands that also shaped TI.

8. It has been suggested that TI shows little interest in the temple or is even critcal of the temple as the center of early-Jewish piety. Typically, this judgment correlates with the assump-

prophetic vision presents itself, its actual geographical view is quite narrowly focused on Mount Zion as the *axis mundi.*[9]

Assuming that Isa 61 and 65 are thematic focal points that at the same time link TI with Isa 1–55, what is their function within the Trito-Isaianic corpus itself? Duhm considered the speech of the Spirit-bearer and the announcement of the new heaven and the new earth not only as focal points but, in fact, as the two elliptical poles around which TI revolves. Put in different terms, the coming of the Spirit-bearer in ch. 61 is the beginning of the era of the new heaven and the new earth in chs. 65–66.[10] This view was challenged in the more recent discussion by Claus Westermann and Odil Hannes Steck. The model that Westermann proposed[11] and that Steck developed in great detail and nuance[12] is based on the assumption that there are several redactional layers, the earliest of which remained largely within the horizon of DI's thought world, whereas later additions increasingly moved away from this foundation. The notion that the level of closeness to DI is what determines the dating of different textual layers in TI led Westermann and Steck to a revised view of the literary profile of TI. They no longer regarded Duhm's ellipsis around chs. 61 and 65–66 as the backbone of TI but rather assumed that TI had a core with various concentric circles around it.[13] This core is Isa 60–62, which, due to the

tion that the groups behind TI opposed the Zadokite temple aristocracy and, by extension, the temple itself. However, if at all, then there is only one text in Third Isaiah that one might read as temple-critical: "Thus says YHWH: 'The heaven is my throne and the earth my footstool. So what house is there that you could build for me and what place for my rest?'" (Isa 66:1). In light of the many positive statements about the temple (56:7; 60:7; 63:7; 64:10[11]; 66:20), it is certainly not the case that TI rejects the temple altogether but apparently certain interpretations of its purpose. Blenkinsopp summarizes this aptly: "This is not an outright, ideological rejection of temple worship, since the same sentiments are expressed in Solomon's prayer at the dedication of the First Temple. . . . It could, however, be directed against expectations of miraculous political and social transformation to follow automatically on the rebuilding, expectations of the kind expressed in Hag 2:6-9, 19, 20-23 and no doubt shared by many at the time" (*Isaiah 56–66,* p. 86).

9. Lau, *Schriftgelehrte Prophetie,* pp. 31-34.

10. The theological centrality of Isa 61 and 65-66 is one of the reasons why Duhm even claimed that, originally, the chapter order of Third Isaiah was 61-66, followed by 56-60.

11. C. Westermann, *Isaiah: A Commentary* (trans. David M. G. Stalker; OTL; Philadelphia: Westminster Press, 1969), pp. 306-8.

12. O. H. Steck, "Tritojesaja im Jesajabuch," in *The Book of Isaiah — Le livre d'Isaie,* pp. 361-406. This and other esssays by Steck on TI are brought together in *Studien zu Tritojesaja* (BZAW 203; Berlin/New York: De Gruyter, 1991).

13. Westermann, *Isaiah,* p. 307; Steck, "Tritojesaja," pp. 381-82. The main difference between these two authors, despite their agreement that chs. 60–62 should be seen as the nucleus

motif of the pilgrimage of the nations to Mount Zion, has also been called the "Zion pericope."[14] According to Westermann and Steck, Isa 60–62 was added as a new ending to DI but then also became the nucleus around which other "Trito-Isaianaic" materials clustered. As Steck points out, the Zion-centered message of salvation in chs. 60 and 62 emerged from the seedbed of DI, as did the speech of the Spirit-bearer in ch. 61, which Steck views as a continuation of the Deutero-Isaianic servant songs.

Since this is not the place for a full review, we will fast-forward to the final stage of Steck's analysis, where he argues that the vision of the pilgrimage of the nations to Mount Zion in ch. 66 forms an *inclusio* with the opening section of TI (Isa 56:1-8). In Steck's final analysis, TI is thus characterized by its core (chs. 60–62), the *inclusio* between ch. 66 and 56:1-8 as an outer frame, and several thematically related segments between the core and the frame.[15] While Steck argues from a redaction-critical point of view, he does make eclectic use of compositional criteria as well. For example, he submits that the announcement of the new heaven and the new earth in Isa 65 is a response to the penitential prayer in 63:7–64:11, which leads him to assign these two parts, despite their considerable differences in language and genre, to the same textual layer. Interestingly, Steck does not apply the same logic (prophetic critique/divine response) to the relationship between the Zion pericope in Isa 60:1–62:12 and the Israel-critical prophecies in Isa 58 and 59. While one can certainly see the prophetic critique as building up towards the promises in the Zion chapters, Steck, as others before and after him, concludes that these two sections of TI express mutually exclusive views of salvation as *conditional* on the one hand (58-59) and *unconditional* on the other (60–62).[16] Obviously, this is a theolog-

of TI, lies in their view of the literary status of these chapters. Westermann (*Isaiah*, pp. 295-96) considers them as the message of an individual prophet of the early post-exilic days, whereas, according to Steck, they never were "free" prophecy but intended as an alternate book ending of DI ("Tritojesaja," pp. 373-79).

14. Blenkinsopp, *Isaiah 56–66*, pp. 60-63, proposes a concentric structure to characterize the synchronic text of Isa 56–66, the center of which is Isa 61:1-3. While Blenkinsopp acknowledges that not everything in TI is cut from the same mold, he rightly emphasizes the need for structural and compositional observations as a corrective to exclusively redaction-critical approaches.

15. Steck, "Tritojesaja," p. 397. Recent contributions have even celebrated this model of a core and concentric circles as a new "consensus" among TI scholars; cf. B. Gregory, "The Postexilic Exile in Third Isaiah: Isaiah 61:1-3 in Light of Second Temple Hermeneutics," *JBL* 126 (2007): 478.

16. Westermann, *Isaiah*, pp. 303-4.

ical assessment rather than a literary observation, for which Steck provides strikingly little argumentative support.

In a most recent monograph, Jacob Stromberg takes a similar position and concludes that "What was promised unconditionally in 60–2 is now seen as by 58–9 to depend on the people's behavior — thus illustrating the point that 60–2 as the earlier core is presupposed and developed in new directions by the outer-lying materials in TI."[17] As we shall see below, conditional promise is only one of several different genres. In contrast to 58:8-12 as the most explicit passage in this regard, 59:9-19 emphasizes that there is nothing that Israel can do to turn their own fortunes around, except perhaps confess to their iniquities. This makes it somewhat questionable whether conditional promise is an adequate category to capture the complex picture of prophecy in Isa 58–59.[18] By the same token, one has to question whether "unconditionality" is a key element of Isa 60–62. More characteristic of these chapters are different variations of the motif of "reversal";[19] the oppressed become oppressors (60:1-16), the captives are set free (61:1-3), and the forsaken become the espoused (62:4). There are several competing ideas in Isa 60–62 about why Israel's fortunes will eventually change, ranging from reward (61:7-8; 62:11) and retribution (60:15-16) to forgiveness and mercy (60:10; 62:4).

As Steck's and Stromberg's analyses show, conceptual categories and assumptions matter when it comes to one's assessment of the diachronic profile of a text. Whether one sees differences and tensions in a given text as signs of redactional layers or of intentional composition depends to a major extent on the criteria and categories that one applies to the interpretation of the content of a text.[20] This in particular makes TI a challenging and controversial test case.

17. J. Stromberg, *Isaiah After Exile: The Author of Third Isaiah as Reader and Redactor of the Book* (Oxford: Oxford University Press, 2010), p. 13. For a similar conclusion, cf. already Paul Allen Smith, *Rhetoric and Redaction in Trito-Isaiah: The Structure, Growth, and Authorship of Isaiah 56–66* (VTSup 62; Leiden: Brill 1995), pp. 184-86, who argues that the author of the materials around chs. 60-62 is also the redactor of Isa 40–66 and, to some extent, of the book of Isaiah as a whole. However, in contrast to Stromberg, Smith's redactor/author was responsible for all of 56:1–59:20 and 65:1–66:17. Only the penitential prayer (63:7–64:11) and 66:18-24 are still later additions.

18. Closer to the theological complexity of these chapters is Blenkinsopp's observation of an "alternation of promise and threat, salvation and judgment" (Blenkinsopp, *Isaiah 56–66*, p. 62).

19. Gregory, "Postexilic Exile," p. 493.

20. There are relatively few diachronic analyses of TI that elaborate on the distinct theological profiles of the emerging text. Klaus Koenen, *Ethik und Eschatologie im Tritojesajabuch: Eine literarkritische und redaktionsgeschichtliche Studie* (WMANT 62; Neukirchen-Vluyn:

In the following, we will address these issues with regard to Isa 57:14–62:12. My argument will be that, from a composition-critical point of view, there is no reason or need to assign Isa 60–62 and Isa 57:14–59:21 to separate redactional layers. Whereas passages such as Isa 56:1-8 (inclusion of foreigners and eunuchs in the temple community), 56:9-12 (polemic against the "watchers"), and 57:1-13 (judgment of fertility rituals) appear to be individual segments that were probably added to an already existing core, Isa 57:14–62:12 form an intentionally composed unit with a theological message that one misses if one separates Isa 60–62 from 57:14–59:21.

What one finds in 57:14–62:12 is an understanding of the salvation[21] of Israel that differs from DI in a number of ways. First, in TI, salvation is part of a certain, although yet unfulfilled promise. Whereas in DI the homecoming and restoration of Israel after the dire years of exile *are* the fulfillment of salvation, TI divorces salvation from history; and whereas DI sees God at work in the rise and fall of empires, in historical events like exile and return, or in charismatic individuals like Cyrus the Great, there is next to no mention of any of these in TI.[22] It has always been assumed that much of TI was composed at least one generation after DI when the initial enthusiasm among the Golah after their return had ebbed and given way to a more realistic and even sobering perception of the continued pressure on the Jewish community by external powers, as well as of the political and social injustice both outside and inside this community. However, this perception is not limited to the prophecies in Isa 58–59 that discuss why the redemption of Israel was still incomplete but is also presupposed in Isa 60–62.[23] Salvation does not emerge in or from history but requires a radical make-over of the political as well as natural cosmos, which will be filled, shaped, and ruled by YHWH's glory and spirit alone.

Neukirchener Verlag, 1990), pp. 239-40, argues that TI's eschatological and ethical reflections should be assigned to different textual layers.

21. Note that the term is a leitmotif that is introduced in 56:1 but then connects especially Isa 59 (59:11, 17) with the Zion chapters (60:18; 62:1).

22. On the few historical clues in TI see Blenkinsopp, *Isaiah 56–66*, pp. 51-54.

23. This has been rightly pointed out by Gregory, "Postexilic Exile," pp. 489-92, with regard to Isa 61:1-3: "A prophet in *post*exilic Palestine is preaching as though he were in exile. . . . Isaiah 61:1-3 may represent one of the earliest attestations of the phenomenon of understanding the exile as an ongoing state, that is, understanding the exile theologically rather than just historically." In a similar vein, Koenen, *Ethik und Eschatologie*, p. 156, argues that Isa 58:1–63:8 address the issue of "Heilsverzögerung:" "Er [TI] will . . . die Voraussetzungen für das Kommen des Heils schaffen. Zugleich schildert Tritojesaja in leuchtenden Farben, wie dieses Heil aussieht."

There is a strong sense of the discontinuity between the world that is and the world that shall be.

In a similar vein, TI's expectation of YHWH's salvific deeds clearly exceeds DI's. Not only will the nations stream towards Mount Zion and pay tribute to Israel, the entire cosmos changes around YHWH's holy mountain and YHWH's people: sun and moon will be put out of service because the only source of light in the new world is God's own glory, which radiates forth from Zion into the world of nations that dwell in the dark. It seems that this grandiose and one might even say overwhelming picture of a new creation (Isa 60–62) complements the critical part of the prophetic message in Isa 58–59 and provides an incentive for Israel both to continue to hope for salvation and to aspire to become the covenant people that they are meant to be. Great admonishment towards an even greater promise is how one might characterize the gist of TI's prophecy.

The Composition of Isaiah 57:14–59:21

One of the reasons for separating Isa 60–62 from earlier parts of TI is what some scholars perceive as two diametrically opposed concepts of salvation: whereas in the Zion chapters salvation is an unconditional promise, it appears to be conditional in chs. 58–59. In particular, Isa 58 has earned TI a reputation of advocating for "works righteousness." However, a closer look reveals that the distinction between conditional and unconditional does not capture the diverse and complex picture that presents itself with regard to salvation in Isa 57:14–59:21. This becomes clear if one observes the composition of this part of TI.

57:14-21: Oracle of salvation
- 14: Introduction ("He said: 'Make way, make way . . .'")
- 15-18: Past judgment and healing ("I saw his ways and healed him")
- 19: Salvation oracle for the present ("Peace, peace to the far and the near!")
- 20-21: Judgment on the wicked ("There is no peace for the wicked!")

58:1-14: Conditional salvation[24]
- 1: Introduction "Cry out with full throat . . ."

24. For a more detailed outline of ch. 58 see T. Staubli, "Maat-Imagery in Trito-Isaiah: The Meaning of Offering a Throat in Egypt and in Israel," in *Images and Prophecy in the Ancient Eastern Mediterranean* (ed. M. Nissinen and C. E. Carter; FRLANT 233; Göttingen: Vandenhoeck & Ruprecht, 2009), p. 44.

2-7: Divine oracle about true and false fasting ("Is such the fast that I choose . . . ?")
8-14: Prophetic admonishment and conditional promise ("Then your light shall break forth")

59:1-21: Prophetic critique, confession of sin, promise of deliverance
1-3: Accusation ("*Your* hands are defiled with blood")
4-8: Description ("*Their* feet run to evil")
9-13: Confession ("*Our* transgressions are multiplied before you")
14-19: Description ("YHWH saw it and it displeased *him*")
20-21: Salvation oracle ("And this shall be *my* covenant with them . . .")[25]

The overview shows that Isa 57:14–59:21 include three different prophetic speeches with characteristically different views about God's judgment and Israel's salvation.

1. Isa 57:14-21 focuses on Israel's sins of the past that provoked YHWH's wrath and retribution. However, the end of the exile was also a sign that the time of punishment was over. This presupposes the same understanding of the exile that one also finds in DI (cf. Isa 40:2). The exile was not the final word but only one episode in Israel's covenantal history; it was an episode that was now coming to a close and giving way to a new and restored relationship between YHWH and Israel. Both DI and Isa 57:14-19 share the expectation that this turn from divine wrath to salvation marks Israel's present:

> "For a brief moment I abandoned you, but with great compassion I will gather you. In the overflowing wrath (קֶצֶף) of a moment I hid my face (הִסְתַּרְתִּי פָנַי), but with everlasting (עוֹלָם) kindness I will have compassion on you." (Isa 54:7-8)

25. Isa 59:20-21 has been the subject of much discussion. There is the question of whether v. 21 or both 20 and 21 are a secondary addition to vv. 1-19, either as a conclusion to 56:9–59:19 or a bridge to 60–62. However, there is also general agreement about the composite character of ch. 59, which makes it somewhat speculative to single out one particular piece as not being part of the original composition, unless one follows Blenkinsopp, *Isaiah 56–66*, pp. 184-203, and views ch. 59 as comprising a number of smaller units (1-8, 9-15a, 15b-20, 21). However, separating v. 21 from 20 goes against the grain of the text. The נְאֻם יְהוָה formula at the end of v. 20 requires an actual divine oracle, which one does not find in 15b-20 but only in 21. As a matter of fact, vv. 15b-20 seem to be a very deliberate build-up towards 21, with the נְאֻם יְהוָה as a connecting element.

> I will not contend forever (לְעוֹלָם), nor will I always be angry, but a spirit shall issue forth from me and the breaths that I have made. Because of their sinful greed I was angry (אֶקְצוֹף) and struck him; I hid (my face) (הַסְתֵּר) and was angry (אֶקְצוֹף), and so he went on backsliding in the way of his heart. (Isa 57:16-17)

The passage from TI shows several subtle signs of an allusion to an older text. It repeats the verb (קצף) to rephrase the emphasis on the noun "wrath" (קֶצֶף) in 54:8; it contrasts with God's "eternal" loyalty (54:8) by saying what God will not do "forever," namely contend; and finally, it uses the infinitive הַסְתֵּר apparently as an abbreviation of the full syntagma "hiding the face." However, while the Trito-Isaianic text uses DI's linguistic framework, establishing continuity between the two traditions, there is a different emphasis with regard to theological message: whereas, in DI, God promises eternal covenantal loyalty and mercy, TI views the life-giving spirit as a sign and manifestation of God's unwavering favor.

Another indication of an intentional link between DI and TI is the stylistic similarities between Isa 40:1, 3 and 57:14:

> "'Comfort, comfort my people,' says your God. . . . A voice cries out: 'In the wilderness make a way for YHWH, make straight in the desert a highway for our God.'" (40:1, 3)

The Trito-Isaianic passage imitates the double imperative with words from Isa 40:

> "And he says: 'Build up, build up, prepare a way; remove all obstacles from the way of my people.'" (57:14)

While double imperatives are a stylistic feature that one finds throughout both DI and TI,[26] one would be hard pressed not to view 57:14 as an allusion specifically to 40:1, 3. Both passages include an oracle of salvation for Israel ("my people"), with a number of subtle variations: while the straight passage in 57:14 is to be built for the Israelites, it was reserved for God's own victorious return to Zion in 40:3. Although a more detailed analysis of the intertextual profile of 57:14-21 cannot be offered here,[27] it is safe to say that, with regard to its linguistic and literary shape as well as its general theological

26. Cf. Isa 40:1; 51:9-11, 17; 52:1, 11; 57:14; 62:10-11.

27. Cf. W. Zimmerli, "Zur Sprache Tritojesajas," in *Gottes Offenbarung. Gesammelte Aufsätze zum Alten Testament* (TB 19; Munich: Kaiser 1969), pp. 77-93.

message of Israel's salvation, this passage appears to be modeled after the opening section of DI.[28] This is particularly relevant since 57:14 forms an *inclusio* with 62:10, the concluding passage of the Zion chapters: "Pass through, pass through the gates, prepare the way for the people; build up, build up a highway, clear (it) of stones. Raise an ensign for the nations." As we will discuss below, the *inclusio* between 57:14 and 62:10 establishes the boundaries of a compositional unit and, as such, also distinguishes it from its context.

2. With Isa 58:1-14[29] one enters a different theological discourse, although here, again, one finds language reminiscent of the opening section of DI. The first word of ch. 58, "Speak, announce!", as God's summons to a prophet is only attested in Isa 40:6, 58:1, and Jer 11:6. However, what the prophet is supposed to announce differs from the earlier Isaianic tradition. In Isa 58:2-7, God explains to Israel their social and cultic inequities and why their fasting does not find God's favor. It is interesting to note that God does not threaten any consequences but reminds Israel that justice and mercy are the core values of true worship. The second divine oracle in vv. 13-14 picks up where v. 7 left off: here it is the Sabbath that requires an appropriate inner disposition and not just ritual performance. However, different from vv. 2-7, the divine critique is cast into the form of a conditional promise: "If you refrain from trampling the Sabbath . . . , then you will take delight in YHWH." In contrast to the pre-exilic prophets, this prophecy does not announce destruction and doom if the condition is not met.[30] TI's message emerges from a different intellectual and spiritual atmosphere that one may characterize as disillusionment and perhaps even frustration. While there is no question that God had shown mercy to Israel and brought them home from exile, the renewal of the covenant and a salvific future for Israel among the nations seemed to have come to a halt. The scenario of Isa 58 suggests that Israel sits in the ruins and deserted places that

28. Westermann, *Isaiah,* pp. 327-313; P. D. Hanson, *Isaiah 40–66* (Louisville: Westminster John Knox, 1995), pp. 201-4; Blenkinsopp, *Isaiah 56–66,* pp. 168-73.

29. It is conceivable to separate the Sabbath oracle in vv. 12-14 from the rest of the chapter (Westermann, *Isaiah,* pp. 340-42). However, since it falls in line with the "if/then" pattern of vv. 9b-10b, this is not a necessary assumption.

30. A. Davies, *Double Standards in Isaiah: Re-Evaluating Prophetic Ethics & Divine Justice* (BINS 46; Leiden: Brill, 2000), p. 47 nicely summarizes the divine pedagogy here: "God declares he would rather see freedom than fasting. . . . However, it does seem that Yahweh is not entirely convinced his people will accept this, and he feels the need to tempt them with a list of promises significantly longer than his list of requirements (58:8-12)."

the Babylonians had left behind (58:12). Whether this is a historically accurate picture or reflects felt experience is a matter of much debate. But whatever the answer may be, the sentiment was that the restoration of Israel was yet incomplete and didn't progress as hoped or desired. It is not fear of judgment and divine wrath that fuels the prophetic speech in ch. 58 but an awareness that Israel hadn't fundamentally changed from former days. They had been forgiven their sins of the past but, apparently, that did not make them a new people.[31]

3. Ch. 59 picks up where ch. 58 left off and summarizes the essence of the problem that the previous chapter diagnosed: "See, the arm of YHWH is not too short to save, nor his ear too dull to hear. Rather, your iniquities have been a barrier between you and your God, and your sins have hid (his) face from you so that he will not hear" (59:1). The remarkable phrase here is that it is the sins of the people that "hide" God's face. In Isa 57:17, referencing 54:8, as everywhere else in the Hebrew Bible, the hiding of the face is God's own deliberate reaction to the sins of Israel. Isaiah 59:2, stunningly, changes this perception and suggests that it is not God who does the hiding but that this is an effect that Israel's iniquities have on the relationship between them and YHWH. On the basis of this assumption, ch. 59 unfolds along a carefully crafted movement from judgment to confession and finally to an oracle of salvation.[32] While ch. 59 is harsher and considerably more graphic in its critique of Israel's sins than ch. 58, the critique does not build up to a conditional promise.[33] As a matter of fact, there is no expectation that Israel will fundamentally change or become a new peo-

31. Verse 14 ("riding upon the heights of the earth") may be an allusion to the Song of Moses (Deut 32:13). This could be significant, since the giving of the spirit in Isa 59:21, too, evokes not only Deuteronomic language but seems to allude specifically to the figure of Moses, giving the prophecy of Isa 57–62 the aura of Mosaic authority; cf. Lau, *Schriftgelehrte Prophetie,* pp. 70-71.

32. Karl Elliger, *Die Einheit Tritojesaja (Jesaja 56–66)* (BWANT 45; Stuttgart: Kohlhammer, 1928), p. 15, characterizes the genre of ch. 59 as a "liturgy," which moves from prophetic accusation to lament, petition, and finally divine speech. Westermann, *Isaiah,* p. 344, submits that "the chapter's skeleton is that of a community lament. But it is a lament that has had an answer given it." Both Elliger and Westermann respond to the fact that lament and confession embedded in a prophetic speech with divine oracle make for an unusual literary format. This does, however, point to the fact that in TI's case prophecy includes and perhaps even prepares the ground for the penitential prayer tradition (cf. Isa 63:7–64:12) as a characteristic of postexilic piety.

33. Westermann, *Isaiah,* p. 302.

ple.[34] Rather, the saving activity is solely on YHWH's part: "He saw that there was no one, he realized that there was not one to interfere. So his own arm and his righteousness sustained him" (59:16). There is a very keen sense in ch. 59 that God is the only source of justice that brings order to the world of nations and salvation to Mount Zion and its inhabitants. Israel's response to its past failures and its inability to live up to its role as a covenant people is not a pledge to change its ways but a confession of its sin. This is not the same full-blown penitential prayer that one finds in Isa 63:15–64:11; however, the implicit suggestion that both texts share is that Israel's salvation is a matter of God's favor rather than Israel's own doing.

To summarize our findings, in 57:14–59:21 one finds three characteristically different understandings of Israel's situation after its return to Mount Zion. However, these differences do not suggest that 57:14–59:12 is a mere compilation of texts that, perhaps, date from the same time but have no common denominator otherwise. Isa 58 and 59 both address Israel's role in the completion of its own salvation. While Isa 58 is optimistic that a change of heart and mind on Israel's part will provide a cure, Isa 59 submits that Israel's role is penitence and that nothing short of another powerful intervention of God — as powerful as the one that brought Israel back from exile — will move Israel towards final redemption. It is an open question if one should interpret the difference between chs. 58 and 59 diachronically as a development from an optimistic to a more pessimistic perception of Israel's state after the exile. However, it is equally conceivable that chs. 58 and 59 are contemporaneous voices in the theological discourse of the early Second Temple period, a discourse that either included or presupposed the voice in 57:14-21. As already mentioned, the fact that 57:14 forms an *inclusio* with 62:10 might suggest the latter, which would also indicate that 57:14–62:12 is a composition of different materials embedded in a framework that is indebted to the language and thought world of DI.

34. Cf. A. Rofé, "Isaiah 59:19 and Trito-Isaiah's Vision of Redemption," in *Book of Isaiah — Le livre d'Isaie,* pp. 407-10.

The Inclusio Between Isaiah 57:14 and 62:10

Given the linguistic parallels between these two passages, a closer look at their similarities and differences with regard to content is in order.[35]

> "And he says: 'Build up, build up (סֹלּוּ סֹלּוּ), prepare a way (פַּנּוּ דֶרֶךְ); remove (הָרִימוּ) all obstacles *from the way of my people*.'" (57:14)

> "Pass through, pass through (עִבְרוּ עִבְרוּ) the gates, prepare the way (פַּנּוּ דֶּרֶךְ) *for the people;* build up, build up (סֹלּוּ סֹלּוּ) *a highway,* clear (it) (סַקְּלוּ) of stones. Raise (הָרִימוּ) an ensign *for the nations.*" (62:10)

The comparison shows both verbatim parallels as well as variations within a given pattern. For example, 62:10 adds an object to the imperatives "build up, build up" and a prepositional element to "prepare the way." Isaiah 57:14 mentions that "obstacles" have to be removed from the way of the people, whereas 62:10 talks about "stones." In two places, at its beginning and end, 62:10 adds new elements to the earlier passage. Whereas 57:14 envisions the people approaching Zion from a distance, 62:10 locates them right at the point where they are about to enter the city: "Pass through, pass through the gates." It is almost as if, with 62:10, Israel has completed the journey that began in 57:14. The impression that the summons to "pass through" is, in fact, an addition to the "build up" from 57:14 is further substantiated by the fact that there is an unmarked change of the grammatical subject, which unbalances slightly the syntax of this verse: obviously, the call to enter the city is directed to the returning people, whereas the command to build up a highway for the returnees addresses a different audience.

The other significant addition to the earlier passage is the mention of other nations. The return to Zion is not only a sign for Israel but also a signal to the nations. The phrase "ensign for the nations" occurs at turning points of both First and Second Isaiah (Isa 11:10, 12; 49:22). Together with 62:10, the notion that Israel's restoration will be a witness to other peoples about the power of the God of Israel and his ways of ruling in history is one of the red threads that

35. It is striking that not many commentators assign particular importance to parallel formulations in 57:14 and 62:10. These are typically interpreted as (independent) references to the opening section of DI. As a matter of fact, one has to go back to R. Abramowski, "Zum literarischen Problem von Jesaja 56–66," *TSK* 96/97 (1925): 90-143, who does in fact see the Trito-Isaianic adaptations of Isa 40:3-4 in both 57:14 and 62:10 as compositionally significant.

permeates the final form of the book of Isaiah. And again, there is a subtle play on words and grammatical forms that emphasize the connections between different Isaianic texts: 62:10 uses the phrase הָרִימוּ נֵס "raise an ensign," which is similar to 49:22 ("I will raise an ensign!"). The same imperative, הָרִימוּ, occurs in 57:14 to command that obstacles be "lifted" from Israel's way.

To summarize, as part of the final portion of the Zion chapters in Isa 60–62, 62:10 has a double purpose: first, in expanding on the language and imagery of 57:14, it establishes a framework around what now emerges as an intentionally crafted composition that begins in 57:14 with the summons to prepare the way for the people on their journey home and ends in 62:10-12 with a call to the people to pass through the gates of Jerusalem and take their place as a "holy nation" (62:12). The second purpose is to integrate the turn of Israel's fortune into an overarching vision of a new order of the world of nations. The return to Zion and the passing through the gates are viewed as a sign to the nation that God establishes in order to — as 62:7 phrases it — make Jerusalem "renowned" on earth. This latter aspect requires a closer exploration of Isa 60:1–62:12, where the relationship between Israel and other nations comes into focus.

The Composition of Isaiah 60:1–62:12

As their preceding chapters, Isa 60-62 host a variety of genres as well as theological perspectives on Israel's salvation:

60:1-16 Salvation oracle for Zion (I)
- 1-3: The glory of God will shine forth from Zion and the nation will be drawn to it ("Arise and shine, for your light has come, and YHWH will rise upon you and his glory will appear over you!")
- 4-16a: The nations bring tribute to Jerusalem and its temple ("Your gates shall always be open; they shall not be closed by day or night so that they will bring the wealth of the nations, with their kings led in procession.")
- 16b: Concluding formula ("So that you will know that I am YHWH, your savior and redeemer, the mighty one of Jacob.")

60:17-22 Salvation oracle for Zion (II)[36]

36. Most commentaries see 60:1-22 as one single oracle, although Blenkinsopp, *Isaiah 56–66*, p. 205, notes that there is at least a section break between vv. 16 and 17. The strongest

The reversal of the cosmic order: YHWH will be the only light in the world ("No longer shall the sun be a light by day nor for brightness shall the moon shine for you"); promise of prosperity for Israel in their own land ("They are the shoot of my planting, the work of my hands for the display of [my] splendor.")

61:1-3 First-person speech: self-introduction of the Spirit-bearer ("The Spirit of YHWH is upon me!")

61:4-9 Salvation oracle for Zion (III)[37]
The vindication of Israel ("But you will be called the priests of YHWH and named servants of our God; you will eat the wealth of the nations and in their riches you will boast.")

61:10–62:12 First-person speech: announcement of Zion's restoration and Israel's blossoming

The First-Person Speeches

Isa 60–62 includes two main genres, divine oracles and speeches of the Spirit-bearer (assuming that the first person in 61:1-3 is the same as in 61:10–62:12[38]). Obviously, the outline raises the question of the relationship between the two first-person speeches.[39] In 61:1-3, the Spirit-bearer introduces himself and his mission to proclaim the good news (לְבַשֵּׂר) and to comfort (לְנַחֵם) Israel. Isa

argument for v. 16 as the end of an oracle is the concluding formula ("So that you will know . . ."), which seems to harken back to Isa 49:26. Without exception, this formula marks the end of a prophetic oracle (1 Kgs 20:13; Isa 49:23.26; Ezek 16:62-63) and, as such, is frequently followed by the messenger formula which then introduces a new oracle (cf. Ezek 22:16-17; 25:7-8; Hos 2:22-23[20-21]).

37. Again, there is hardly any consensus about the outline of ch. 61. Some commentators take the entire chapter as one prophetic speech (P. Volz, *Jesaja* II [KAT 9/2; Leipzig: A. Deichartsche Verlagsbuchhandlung D. Werner Scholl, 1932], p. 260; Hanson, *Isaiah 40–66,* pp. 223-26; Lau, *Schriftgelehrte Prophetie,* pp. 66-67); others see vv. 1-7 (Blenkinsopp, *Isaiah 56–66,* pp. 218-27) or 1-9 (Elliger, *Tritojesaja,* pp. 24-25) as a unit.

38. Cf. Volz, *Jesaja* II, p. 260; Lau, *Schriftgelehrte Prophetie,* pp. 86-87.

39. It seems unlikely that 61:10-11 is the response of a community to the prophetic message in vv. 1-9 (Westermann, *Isaiah,* pp. 370-71; Blenkinsopp, *Isaiah 56–66,* pp. 230-31), since one would expect such a response to be given in the first person plural, as in 59:9. One cannot exclude entirely the possibility that the speaker in 61:10-11 is Zion herself (Elliger, *Tritojesaja,* p. 25), although the switch back to the prophet in 62:1 would then be somewhat unexpected.

61:10 picks up where 61:1-3 left off. The background of DI's language is unmistakable in both parts of the Spirit-bearer's speech. The message of comfort is that the time of Israel's hardship has come to a close and that, from now on, they will enjoy peace and prosperity in their own land; and here again one notices close parallels with Isa 57:14-20, especially with regard to the language of comfort and mourning.[40]

Another connection between the two parts of the Spirit-bearer's speech is the use of vegetation and clothing imagery. The combination may seem awkward at first; however, there is a word play in the Hebrew: the terms used for "garment" and "planting" are מַעֲטֵה and מַטַּע (61:3). Both images are first introduced in the first part of the speech and then further developed in the second: the garments become those of a bride and groom in their wedding ceremony, which is also the image used to depict the new relationship between YHWH and Israel (62:5). Intertwined with the clothing imagery is that of Israel's prosperity as a planting of God that grows to impressive size for all the nations around to see. Although there are hardly any linguistic overlaps, one is hard-pressed not to feel reminded of a similar combination of marriage and vegetation imagery in the book of Hosea (Hos 2:18-25[16-23]). The notion that the covenant between YHWH and Israel is modeled after a marriage with the implication of fertility and prosperity is not particularly "Isaianic," so there may be reason to believe that especially Isa 61:1-9 was written with the older Hosea tradition in mind.[41] This may also apply to the motif of reversal and renaming: "Nevermore shall you be called 'Forsaken,' nor shall your land be called 'Desolate'; but you shall be called 'I delight in her', and your land 'Espoused'" (Isa 62:4a; cf. Hos 2:25[23]); and there is also the idea that YHWH will be the "Baal" of the land (Isa 62:4b).

Examining the role of other nations in the speech of the Spirit-bearer, one notices that the nations surrounding Israel are assigned the role of awed witnesses and observers: righteousness and praise will spring forth before the nations (61:11; יַצְמִיחַ צְדָקָה וּתְהִלָּה נֶגֶד כָּל־הַגּוֹיִם) and they will see the righteousness and glory of God (62:2). The language of צְדָקָה is particularly significant in both verses. It seems to be used as a legal term to indicate that the covenantal relationship between God and God's people has been re-established and that Israel has been fully restored to its land and its place among the na-

40. Within the book of Isaiah, the phrase "to comfort the mourning" only occurs in 57:18 and 61:2.

41. For the Isaianic reception of Hosea, cf. B. Sommer, *A Prophet Reads Scripture: Allusion in Isaiah 40–66* (Stanford: Stanford University Press, 1998), p. 256.

tions, which the RSV and NRSV highlight by translating צְדָקָה as "vindication." The same sense of Israel's restoration as a mighty act of God comes across in 62:8: no longer shall strangers and enemies eat the grain and drink the wine of the grapes that grow on Israel's land. While this was possible because, for a time, God had abandoned Israel, the expectation is that Israel will now live under the protection of YHWH again. Thus, the ensign that will be raised when Israel enters the city of Jerusalem (62:10) has the purpose of a protective mark that signals that Israel and its land are no longer "up for grabs."

This leaves the question of Isa 61:4-9, which is positioned between the self-introduction of the Spirit-bearer (61:1-3) and the continuation of the first-person speech in 61:10-11. While there is hardly any doubt that this text presents itself as part of the proclamation of the Spirit-bearer, it is not so clear if this was its original place. As we shall discuss in greater detail below, 61:4-9 has a view of Israel's land and Israel's role among the nations, which is characteristically different from the first-person speeches. There, the message of comfort correlates with a vision of peace and protection for those who mourn in Zion, whereas in 61:4-9 Israel triumphs and in fact rules over its former oppressors.

The Salvation Oracles

Turning to the prophetic oracles of Isa 60–62, one notices a much more aggressive approach to the relationship between Israel and other nations than in the first-person speeches.[42] The ideal scenario is not one of respectful coexistence; rather, the nations are cast in the role of servants to Israel. Isaiah 61:5 depicts them as the ones that tend to Israel's land, flocks, and vineyards, while, by implication, Israel, as YHWH's priests, is in charge of the cult. While this may be seen as a way of including the nations in a priestly worldview, 61:6 goes a step further and suggests that Israel is entitled to the "wealth of the nations." The sentiment here is that, after the dire years of exile, it is now Israel's turn to lord it over others.

The same phrase "wealth of the nations" occurs even twice in the first prophetic speech (Isa 60:5, 11): the doors of Jerusalem shall remain open day and night for a steady inflow of the tributes that the nations and their kings

42. On the conceptual differences especially between chs. 60 and 61 cf. Lau, *Schriftgelehrte Prophetie*, pp. 66-67, although Lau holds that, despite these differences, both chapters should be assigned to the same author.

will offer. The image here is reminiscent of a triumphal parade in which the victorious general returns home with the defeated enemies walking by his chariot. The militant imagery is further emphasized by the threat that kingdoms that fail to serve Israel will be utterly destroyed. There is a barely hidden overtone of triumphalism and even vengeance here. The formerly oppressed picture themselves in the role of the oppressors.

As is the case in Isa 61:3, it seems that Isa 49:22-23 is an important source text also for the first salvation oracle in 60:1-16: the nations will come from afar to Zion, carrying the exiles in their arms and offering tribute (60:4). The corresponding passage in DI pictures the foreign nations as foster parents and wet nurses that carry Israel on their shoulders (49:23aα), an image which is given an aggressive twist in the sentence that follows it: "They shall bow to you in the dust and they will lick your feet" (49:23aβ).

It is striking that 60:1-16 and 61:1-3, two texts from TI, draw on the same Deutero-Isaianic text (49:22-23), although with different emphases and for different purposes: the speech of the Spirit-bearer employs the image of the "ensign" to establish a boundary between Israel and the nations and so to mark off the territory that will never again be taken away from YHWH's people. The concern is for Israel's protection and peace among a potentially dangerous world of nations that have to be kept at bay. The first salvation oracle uses the language of the "ensign" to establish Israel's superior identity as God's priests on earth and, correspondingly, to lay claim to the wealth of the nations. There is a very high level of self-confidence at play as well as a keen sense of entitlement.

These different adaptions of the same Deutero-Isaianic text give one reason to believe that the Zion chapters host more than one point of view about how Israel figures into the world of nations. There is the hope that Israel will enjoy a peaceful and quiet existence around the holy mountain as a protected and safe space for YHWH's people; however, there is also the desire to become a major player in global politics and to inherit the role of those empires under whose influence Israel had found itself since the time of the monarchy.

If one includes the second oracle (60:17-22) in this discourse about Israel's salvation, one notices yet another nuance. This oracle shares the more quietistic tone of the Spirit-bearer's speech and envisions Israel's salvation as the blessed life of a prosperous nation in its own land. However, the announcement of Israel's prosperity is embedded in a vision of a new cosmic order, which is unparalleled in any other text of DI or TI: the natural order of light and dark, night and day will be put out of service because God will be the only light in the world. One notices that, unlike in Isa 60:1-2 and 62:2, this light is not God's *glory* (כבוד) but God "himself." Whereas the כבוד is typically seen as something that shines forth or rises from a particular location (presumably the temple), the notion in 60:19-20 is that God *is* the light in all of creation — a light that, in contrast to Gen 1:2, will not give way to darkness anymore.

While, in contrast to chs. 65–66, the world of 60:17-22 is not called a new heaven and a new earth, it is in fact nothing short of that. The notion is that for justice and righteousness to occur God has to be the light that continually permeates the world. There is a sentiment that violence and injustice can only be eradicated if creation itself changes and God's own presence fills every corner of it. Together with Isa 11:1-10; 24:1-8; and 65:17-25, 60:17-22 is one of the Isaianic texts that does not see Israel's salvation as a merely political matter but as part of and dependent upon a much more profound transformation. The source of hope is not the expectation of a shift in the power arrangements of the political world. Correspondingly, YHWH is not viewed in the first place as a God who acts in history but as one who changes the design of the created sphere so that justice and righteousness can prevail in it.

To summarize, Isa 60–62 host a variety of views about Israel's salvation and the political and cosmological settings in which it will occur. It is quite conceivable that, at some point, oracles I and III as well as the speech of the Spirit-bearer were independent traditions.[43] However, in their current literary location, they show signs of deliberate composition. Taken together, the splicing together of oracle I, the first part of the first-person speech, oracle III, and the second part of the speech suggest that these different elements should be read as a "thick description" of Israel's salvation. As we have noted above, the very same principle of compositional diversity also applies to the Israel-critical prophetic speeches and oracles in Isa 57:14–59:21. Whereas Isa 60–62 form a theological discourse about what salvation is and what it will bring, Isa 57:14–59:12 elaborate on why it has not yet occurred, at least not in its full and final manifestation.

The remaining question is if these two discourses, at the level of the book-composition of Isaiah, should be separated and assigned to different stages of the literary history of Isaiah or whether they should be seen as a unit. Westermann's and Steck's main argument in favor of the latter was the closeness of Isa 60–62 to the language and thought world of DI. As we have seen, this argument is not entirely convincing precisely because these chapters are not nearly as uniform as Westermann and Steck presuppose. Even within the

43. Volz, *Jesaja* II, p. 200, observes that chs. 60 and 62 emphasize the unity of Israel and define its identity in contrast to other nations, whereas ch. 61 conveys a different sentiment: here, Israel is seen as a more inward-oriented "spiritual community."

speech of the Spirit-bearer — Steck's primary example — there are elements that have virtually no connection with DI (the fertility and marriage imagery) but indicate that TI makes broad use of a number of written prophetic traditions. On the other hand, Isa 57:14-21, which is certainly not part of the Zion chapters, shows very deliberate allusions to DI.

As we have demonstrated, the strongest argument in favor of seeing Isa 57:14–62:12 as a compositional unit is its framework in 57:14 and 62:10-12. In the final part of this paper, we will examine other significant links between Isa 57–59 and 60–62 that support this view.

Thematic Connections Between Isa 57–59 and 60–62

Darkness and Light

One of the key imageries in Isa 58, 59, and 60 is that of darkness and light. Isa 58:10 employs it to underline the promise of redemption for Israel, if they change their hearts and minds: "Then your light (אוֹרֶךָ) shall rise (זָרַח, waw-perfect) in the dark (חֹשֶׁךְ), and your gloom (אֲפֵלָתְךָ) shall be like the noonday (צָהֳרָיִם)." The confession in 59:9-10 contrasts this promise by highlighting Israel's inadequacies that keep them entrapped in a dark place: "Therefore, justice is far from us and righteousness doesn't reach us. We hope for light (אוֹר) but there is darkness (חֹשֶׁךְ); for brightness (נְגֹהוֹת) but in gloom (אֲפֵלוֹת) we walk. We grope like the blind along a wall, like people that have no eyes. We stumble at noonday (צָהֳרָיִם) as if in twilight."

While Isa 58 and 59 differ on their views of Israel's redemption, their diagnoses of its current state of corruption are quite similar. Both illustrate the lack of justice and righteousness and, as a consequence, Israel's separation from God through the contrast between the darkness and light. Isa 60 picks up where 58 and 59 left off and uses some of the exact same language to depict the turn of Israel's fortunes: "Arise, shine; for your light (אוֹרֵךְ) has come (בָא) and the glory of YHWH has risen (זָרַח, perfect) upon you" (Isa 60:1). It is worth mentioning that the abstract notion of the "rising of light/glory" (rather than the rising of the sun) is not nearly as common as one might think. As a matter of fact, it only occurs in Isa 58, 60 and Psa 112:4. The same is true for the darkness/light contrast in general, which is one of the characteristic elements specifically of the Isaianic tradition. This also includes the term "brightness" (נֹגַהּ) that connects Isa 59:9 with 60:3: "And the nations shall come to your light (אוֹרֵךְ) and kings to the brightness (נֹגַהּ) of your rising (זַרְחֵךְ)."

With these literary connections in mind, the question of interpretation arises. Is especially Isa 58 a later addition to Isa 60 that turns an unconditional promise into a conditional one, as Steck and Stromberg have suggested? Or should one see Isa 60 as the fulfillment of the promises in Isa 58 and 59? One key factor in this regard is the question of who will be entitled to settle on and around the holy mountain, which is not answered until 60:21: "All of your [Zion's] people who are righteous shall inherit the land forever." One can also translate "All of your people shall be righteous and will inherit the land forever." Either way, the term צַדִּיקִים is used as a criterion to determine membership of the Zion community. There seems to be a very clear sense that not everybody qualifies, which connects with 59:20: "But he will come as a redeemer to Zion and to those who turn back from transgression." There is an ethical imperative built into the Trito-Isaianic message that does not exclude the Zion chapters. One finds a similar parallel between 58:4-5 and 61:8, which both link acceptable cultic performance to proper ethical conduct.

The close connections with regard to light/dark imagery suggests that the judgment prophecy in Isa 58 and 59 and the salvation prophecy in 60 are meant as the two foci of the same ellipse. This assumption receives further support when one compares both these foci with Isa 9:1, a passage that appears to be the seedbed for both Trito-Isaianic texts: "The people who walk in darkness (חֹשֶׁךְ) see a great light (אוֹר); the inhabitants of the valley of the shadow of death — light shines (נָגַהּ) upon them." Here, the people who (still) sit in the dark (already) see the light and experience its radiance. This image is split up in TI: in Isa 58 and 59 the people who sit in the dark do not (yet) see the light, whereas in Isa 60 all darkness has been (permanently) pushed back to the remote corners of the world and the glory of God has risen upon Israel. Put in different words, what First Isaiah sees as one complex event TI assigns to different stages of the process in which Israel's salvation is expected to occur.

Justice, Righteousness, and Salvation

As Rolf Rendtorff has demonstrated, the semantic field of justice, righteousness, and salvation plays a key role for the understanding of the composition of the book of Isaiah.[44] Rendtorff argues that TI intentionally synthesizes the

44. R. Rendtorff, *Canon and Theology: Overtures to an Old Testament Theology* (Minneapolis: Fortress Press, 1993), pp. 181-89; R. Rendtorff, "The Book of Isaiah: A Complex Unity:

notions of righteousness (צְדָקָה) and justice (מִשְׁפָּט) that one finds in First Isaiah and DI with regard to their respective views of salvation (יְשׁוּעָה). Isa 56:1 plays a particularly important role in this regard, since this is the only verse in Isaiah where all three terms not only occur in the same context but form a coherent argument: "Maintain justice and do righteousness, for my salvation is about to come and my (own) righteousness to be revealed." This is an intriguing statement because it introduces a key theme in TI, namely the relationship between God's salvific acts and human conduct.

If one examines the statistical occurrence specifically of מִשְׁפָּט, צְדָקָה, and יְשׁוּעָה, the result confirms Rendtorff's general observation but also calls for a more nuanced account of where and how these terms are used:

justice (מִשְׁפָּט):
56:1; 58:2; 59:4 (verb), 8, 9, 11, 14, 15; 61:8

righteousness (צְדָקָה/צֶדֶק):
56:1; 57:12; 58:2.8; 59:4, 9, 14, 16, 17; 60:17; 61:3, 10, 11; 62:2; 63:1; 64:4-5

salvation (יְשׁוּעָה/יֶשַׁע):
56:1; 58:9 (verb); 59:11, 17; 60:18; 62:11; 63:1 (verb), 8 (participle), 9 (verb); 64:4(5) (verb)

Interestingly, none of these terms appears in the two final chapters of TI with the announcement of the new heaven and the new earth. Most of the "clustering" that Rendtorff observes does in fact occur in chs. 58–62. However, there is certainly no even distribution; rather, one notices that the use of the terms varies within different parts of these chapters. For example, the language of "righteousness" in 61 and 62 falls in line with the speech of the Spirit-bearer (Isa 61:1-3, 10-11; 62:1-12). A combination of "righteousness" and "salvation" occurs precisely in the two opening verses of the second salvation oracle (60:17-22) and a combination of "righteousness" and "justice" in the introduction to the prophetic oracle in ch. 58 (58:2). There are also sections where none of these terms is used, most notably the salvation oracles in 57:14-21 and 60:1-16. Thus it is safe to say that the semantic field of the three terms is in fact "Trito-Isaianic" and characterizes the ethical and theological discourse especially in chs. 58–62, although there is no strict system to the way in which the terms are combined. Rather, it seems to be the specific context of judgment

Synchronic and Diachronic Reading," in *New Visions of Isaiah* (ed. R. F. Melugin and M. Sweeney; JSOT 214; Sheffield: Sheffield Academic Press, 1996), pp. 32-49.

and redemption that orchestrates the mix. It is also important to note that, examining this semantic field, one does not get the impression of a gap between chs. 58–59 and 60–62 that would indicate that these two blocks should be assigned diachronically to different textual layers.

Apart from 56:1, the most striking case of clustering occurs in 59:4-17, comprising the middle segment of this chapter, which marks the transition from the prophetic accusation in vv. 1-3 to the divine announcement of redemption in vv. 20-21.[45] In vv. 9 and 11 the speakers confess that righteousness is far (רָחוֹק) from them. The perspective here is that מִשְׁפָּט and צְדָקָה are not primarily qualities or characteristics of human deeds; however, human deeds can promote, or hamper, the spreading and flourishing of righteousness and justice in the social sphere. As Jan Assmann has shown for Ancient Egypt, justice (Ma'at) was considered to be a web or network that permeates human action and thus provides the texture of the moral world.[46] When the community in ch. 59 confesses that righteousness and justice are "far," then this appears to be a way of saying that the connective dynamic of justice has deteriorated. Isa 60 builds on the same assumption about מִשְׁפָּט and צְדָקָה as spheres or webs that provide order in the social sphere but gives this idea a positive turn: justice and righteousness become "taskmasters" or "overseers" (60:17) and they are associated with the city walls of Jerusalem to create the image of a protective space (60:18). The notion here is that precisely because humans cannot sustain justice and righteousness in their own sphere, it becomes a divine task to appoint these as governing principles.

The Spirit of God

As already indicated above, Isa 61:1-3 is one of three texts in the book of Isaiah about a Spirit-bearer who brings justice to Israel and the nations, and it is a very likely assumption that 61:1-3 is in fact meant as a continuation of Isa 11:1-5 and 42:1-7, although, in contrast to Isa 11 and 42, the Spirit-bearer is not presented to the people but introduces himself: "The Spirit of the Lord YHWH

45. Westermann, *Isaiah,* p. 302, points to the significance of 59:14-19 as the "nucleus of Trito-Isaiah's proclamation." This passage in particular binds TI's prophetic critique and the promise of salvation together. However, this observation does not lead Westermann to the logical conclusion that, with 59:14-19 as its hub, the core composition of TI should then include at least parts of *both* 56:9–59:13 and 60–62.

46. J. Assmann, *Ma'at: Gerechtigkeit und Unsterblichkeit im Alten Ägypten* (Munich: Beck, 2001), pp. 20-42.

is upon me." This may be an intentional variation in TI in order to affirm that God has indeed put God's Spirit on this individual. However, the reworking of older Spirit traditions in TI is not limited to the idea that God will act through an individual to restore the world to what God intends it to be. The giving of spirit as a creative and redemptive act of God is mentioned three times in TI:[47]

> Thus says the high and lofty one, the one who is enthroned forever, whose name is holy: "I dwell in a high and holy place, and also with the contrite and lowly in spirit, reviving the spirit of the humble, reviving the heart of the contrite. I will not contend forever, nor will I always be angry, but a spirit shall issue forth from me and the breaths that I have made. (Isa 57:15-16)

Despite its textual problems, the point of this passage seems to be that by giving spirit/breath God restores the meek and the humble to the fullness of life. As such, the giving of spirit is not just a biological matter but God's way of establishing justice in the world. Isa 59:21 takes this spirit theology even one step further:

> "But as for me, this is my covenant with them," says YHWH, "my spirit which is upon you, and my words which I put in your mouth will not depart from your mouth, or the mouth of your descendants, or your descendants' descendants," says YHWH, "from now, and for all time." (59:21)

Here it is not just spirit and breath that come from God (57:16) but it is God's own Spirit that God places in the mouths of his chosen ones. There is no doubt that this passage references the call of a prophet as recorded in Jer 1:9-10, Ezek 2–3 and Isa 6:4-7. Especially Jeremiah appears to be the template for Isa 59:21, except that the placing of the word in the mouth is complemented by the giving of the Spirit. The other significant modification of the older format of a prophetic call is that, in Isa 59, it refers to a community, which is identified in 59:20 as those in Jacob who turn from their transgression.[48] It has been

47. On the increasing significance of spirit theology in the post-exilic period cf. W. Schoemaker, "The Use of 'Ruach' in the Old Testament and of 'Pneuma' in the New Testament," *JBL* 23 (1904): 13-67; F. Baumgärtel, *Spirit of God* (London: A. & C. Black, 1960); W. Ma, *Until the Spirit Comes: The Spirit of God in the Book of Isaiah* (JSOT 271; Sheffield: Sheffield Academic Press, 1999), pp. 113-57.

48. A point of discussion is the switch from the 3. m. pl. ("with them") to the 2. m. sg. ("upon you"), which some exegetes have taken to indicate that the covenant with Israel is the giving of God's Spirit and word to an individual leader (Volz, *Jesaja* II, p. 238; Blenkinsopp,

debated whether 59:21 should be seen as a conclusion of ch. 59 or as an introduction to ch. 60. From the outline provided above, it is clear that 59:21 is firmly embedded in the structure and flow of ch. 59. However, the call of a particular group to the task of prophecy raises the question of what the prophetic message is, and this is precisely what follows in the speech of the Spirit-bearer. Isa 61:1 presents itself as a direct continuation of 59:21, which means that the speaker is either a particular individual from the group in 59:21 or it is the collective itself that speaks in the first person singular:

> The Spirit of Adonay Elohim is upon me, because YHWH has anointed me to deliver good news to the poor, to bind up the wounded of heart, to proclaim release to the captives and liberty to the ones in prison.

The Spirit-bearer carries out a prophetic task by delivering the message of comfort to the lowly and downtrodden and by announcing the glory of Zion and the restoration of Israel. It is not crucial for our purposes to resolve the tension between the communal and the individual interpretation of the Spirit-bearer, which is reminiscent of the same ambiguity with regard to the figure of the servant in DI.[49] However, it is crucial to recognize that 59:21 is as much of a conclusion to ch. 59 as a preparation for 61:1-3, 9-10 and 62:1-12. The composite text assigns a prophetic identity to those in Israel who are righteous and remain faithful to YHWH. It is worth noticing that this *prophetic* image of the post-exilic community contrasts the notion of Israel as a *priestly* nation in the first and third oracles in chs. 60 and 61. While these two roles are not mutually exclusive, they do represent two characteristically different understandings of Israel's identity, which TI combines within the same literary framework.

In conclusion, the three passages that reference "spirit" move from the more general to the more specific: God is the one who enlivens the meek and humble with spirit and breath, and God is also the one who gives his own Spirit to his servants. The impression of purposeful composition gains further sup-

---

Isaiah 56–66, pp. 200-201). As the outline of ch. 59 indicates, this would be a very sudden and unexpected shift. The collective interpretation of the Spirit-bearer is certainly not a surprise, given that, in TI, also the language of the servant of YHWH is applied to a community (56:6; 63:17; 65:9-15). A close parallel is of course Num 11:17 where God takes from the spirit that rests on Moses and gives it to the seventy elders. Blenkinsopp, *Isaiah 56–66*, p. 203, aptly observes that 59:21 (and its Deutero-Isaianic correlate, 49:8) seems to reference the "prophet like Moses" tradition from Deut 18:16-17. However, within the framework of TI it is very conceivable that the prophet like Moses has turned into a collective.

49. Cf. L. Ruszkowski, *Volk und Gemeinde im Wandel. Eine Untersuchung zu Jesaja 56–66* (FRLANT 191; Göttingen: Vandenhoeck & Ruprecht, 2000).

port from Isa 42:1-7, where "spirit" is characterized as both the breath of life in all the inhabitants of the earth (42:5) and as the unique gift to God's servant. Given the significance of 42:1-7 as a key reference text for TI, the fact that these components are present in the salvation oracle in 57:14-21 and the speech of the Spirit-bearer in Isa 61/62 adds to the impression that these two texts purposefully draw on DI in order to envelop the core composition of TI.[50]

Conclusion

The purpose of this essay has been to show that composition critique is a helpful tool to reconstruct the literary and theological profile of Isa 57:14–62:12. It allows one to see that its two main sections 57:14–59:21 and 60:1–62:12 each host a variety of theological views about Israel's salvation that are organized mostly in individual sections rather than redactional layers. There are significant differences not only about why Israel's salvation did not proceed as expected but also with regard to the promise of salvation itself. Most scholars in recent years have argued that Isa 60–62 are most closely related to DI's message of redemption and comfort, whereas chs. 57–59 show signs of the fading optimism of later generations that faced the reality of a world that had not changed as their predecessor might have expected. Neither had Israel been freed from foreign rule nor had it become a more faithful nation. However, it seems that this is precisely the sentiment also of the Zion chapters.[51] The desire of the formerly oppressed to become the oppressors and to enjoy the wealth of the nations that surfaces in Isa 60:1-16 and 61:4-9 (cf. also 66:12) is hardly a sign of confidence and trust in the present reality but gives witness to an expectation that could only be fulfilled in a radically different world. The same is true for the cosmological scenario in 60:17-22 that envisions a complete makeover of the created order so that all chaos and violence will give way to the all-pervasive presence of God. What one finds here are "Gegenwelten"[52] (counter worlds) that do not deny but actually accentuate and

50. According to Volz, *Jesaja* II, p. 218, chs. 57 and 61/62 in particular express what he calls the "Grundstimmung" (basic mood) of post-exilic piety, which is characterized by the self-perception of the Jewish community as of a humble heart and broken spirit but also by the empowerment of the same group through YHWH's own Spirit and words.

51. Cf. R. P. Carroll, "Eschatological Delay in the Prophetic Tradition," *ZAW* 94 (1982): 47-58.

52. On the notion of "Gegenwelt" cf. F. Stolz, "Paradiese und Gegenwelten," *Zeitschrift für Religionswissenschaft* 1 (1993): 5-23; M. Stausberg, *Faszination Zarathustra: Zoroaster und*

support the critical prophecy of the preceding chapters.[53] As such, Isa 57:14–62:12 appears to be a carefully and purposefully crafted composition with a frame (57:14-15; 62:10-12) and several thematic red threads (darkness/light, justice/righteousness, Spirit of God). The notion of composition acknowledges that behind TI may have stood several originally independent traditions. There is reason to believe that at the time of TI prophetic critique as well as prophetic promise was a vibrant and essential part of early Jewish religion. With regard to the *book* of Isaiah, however, there is no indication that these prophetic voices and their theological views should be assigned to different redactional layers. The more likely assumption is that 57:14–62:12 form the core of what scholars since Duhm have called Trito-Isaiah.

---

die europäische Religionsgeschichte der frühen Neuzeit, part 1 (Berlin: de Gruyter, 1997), pp. 295-98.

53. Gregory, "Postexilic Exile," p. 495, summarizes this as follows: "We see emerging the view that exile persists on account of Israel's sin, which is largely equated with the type of sin during the monarchic period that led to the exile in the first place. The distinctive emphasis in Third Isaiah on the necessity of obedience in order to actualize the program of restoration in chs. 60–62 also finds a counterpart in Ezra's prayer." It is not quite clear, though, why Gregory's apt conclusion about the theology of TI requires a redactional perspective. Why does one have to assume that chs. 58–59 "actualize" the supposedly earlier message in chs. 60–62, rather than conclude that 60–62 is built on the prophecies in 58–59, which makes both sections integral parts of the same textual unit?

Thematic Essays

Major Interchanges in the Book of Isaiah Subservient to Its Umbrella Theme: The Establishment of Yhwh's Sovereign Rule at Mt. Zion (Chs. 12–13; 27–28; 39–40; 55–56)

Willem A. M. Beuken

Introduction

The tripartition of the Book of Isaiah (henceforth BI)[1] has enjoyed general acceptance for more than a century, i.e. since the major commentary of Bernhard Duhm (1892)[2]. During the last forty years, however, the exegesis of this prophetic book has undergone a great development: the strong redactional unity of its sixty-six chapters catches our eyes nowadays. Yet, some real autonomy remains assigned to the three parts within their mutual coherence. In this sense, the idiomatic usage of the terms "Proto-, Deutero-, and Trito-Isaiah" has a right to persist.

Next to the division in three parts, a demarcation in smaller sections has always been agreed to. For example, chs. 1–12 and chs. 28–39 are commonly taken as originally independent collections of prophecies since they have the political situation of Judah and Jerusalem during two different periods of the second half of the eighth century as background (the former the so-called Syro-Ephraimitic war in 734-732, the latter the invasion of Sennacherib in 701).

1. Quotations from the Scriptures according to the Revised Standard Version.

2. B. Duhm, *Das Buch Jesaja*, Göttinger Handkommentar zum Alten Testament (Göttingen: Vandenhoeck & Ruprecht, 1892).

This study elaborates a lecture given at the Lutheran Theological Seminary, Shatin, Hong Kong (October 14, 2011). The comments of the colleagues at the seminary, Francis Borchardt, Ho-Fai Tai and Ting Pong Tsoi, have been incorporated in the article. I am most grateful for their stimulating criticism on substantial points.

Other subsections of Proto-Isaiah, too, have been labelled as belonging to a specific literary and theological milieu: the oracles about the nations (chs. 13–23), the so-called Isaiah Apocalypse (chs. 24–27) and the Hezekiah stories (chs. 36–39). Something similar holds true for Deutero-Isaiah and Trito-Isaiah, although here the demarcation remains a matter of dispute. These two parts of the prophetic book mirror at least different historical situations: the former the return from exile, the latter the restoration of the community around the temple. With regard to chs. 40–55 a sort of gap is presumed between ch. 48 and ch. 49; with regard to chs. 56–66, scholars recognize that chs. 60–62 constitute a sort of unity on their own.

If we respect the pattern of larger compositions in BI, the question arises whether their joints are merely buffers or do they somehow bridge the gaps in a serious, refined way, without detracting from the fundamental differences of vocabulary and literary form between two adjacent text complexes. It is the purpose of this article to take a close look at four major interchanges. The outcome is the following. They do not alleviate the change-over between different areas of thought and language in a rather awkward way, but by means of explicit thematic and verbal effects, they advance the development of the topic of the coming of Yhwh's rule at Mount Zion as a sort of paradigm that dominates and coordinates the prophetic book as a whole.

This study has to avoid two pitfalls. First, it should not create the impression that the coherence between larger sections of BI relies only on the interchanges discussed, as if the sections taken by themselves would not exhibit coherence with the adjacent ones. On the contrary, the sections have coherence, which is enhanced through the interchanges. The exegesis of Isaiah in the last decades has proven that a net of continuous semantic lines unites the book's so-called independent parts. As a consequence, the article wants to show that the "gaps" between them are rather interchanges.

Second, recognizing the autonomy of the various adjacent, but connected sections does not involve assuming two quite distinct writing activities: the authorial process by which the sections came into being and the redactional process of their being connected. The distinction between "author(s)" and "redactor(s)" is somehow abstract, and, moreover, mistaken if redactors are considered as second-rate writers. For not only do we know little about the scribes who carried out these activities, but both categories were rooted, too, in the same cultural memory of their people. The experience of the exile, the threat of it and its aftermath, affected the whole nation, literate and illiterate, and crystallized in the icons "Babylon" and "Zion." It ranged over centuries, and so did the production of BI. The writing activity developed and changed with the progress of the book in the making. The scribes of prophetic books considered themselves to be authentic successors of the prophets, whether their contribution was more at the level of an author or a redactor. (It was the exegesis of the nineteenth and twentieth century that set up a contrast between the two groups.) All of them, prophets and scribes, created BI as a testimony of Israel's religious view of its history and future. In that light, the term "redactor/ redactional" will be used here.

The article profits from Joseph Blenkinsopp's three-volume commentary on BI.[3] One of its many qualities is its particular interest in the phenomenon of "serial editing." The author has defined it as "the creation of new prophecy out of old, which is the central feature of the editorial history of the book."[4] This procedure originates from the fundamental belief that "the prophetic word spoken in the past retains its validity but that the past must be continually revisioned and reassimilated in the light of each successive present. By being recontextualized or viewed from a different vantage point or plane of observation it can take on different forms and meanings with the changing circumstances of the present."[5] Attention to this phenomenon undermines the idea of rough clefts between the various parts of the prophetic book and helps to discover their connections. It is, of course, impossible to discuss here all the interchanges concerned. I intend to describe the most explicit ones.

I. Ch. 12 vs. Chs. 13–14: Prophecies with a Song about a City and Its Sovereign

The new title of chs. 13–14, "The oracle concerning Babylon which Isaiah the son of Amoz saw" (13:1), implies a break with ch. 12 but shows some likeness with the title of 2:1-5: "The word which Isaiah the son of Amoz saw concerning Judah and Jerusalem" (2:1). Thus an antithesis between Zion and Babylon presents itself, more specifically between Yhwh's powerful presence in Zion (12:3-5), even for the nations (2:1-5), and his intervention against Babylon (ch. 13) which ends in the ruin of its king (ch. 14). The antithesis consists of several data.

3. J. Blenkinsopp, *Isaiah 1 39; Isaiah 40–55; Isaiah 56–66,* Anchor Bible 19, 19A, 19B (New York: Doubleday, 2000, 2002, 2003).

4. Blenkinsopp, *Isaiah 1–39,* p. 273.

5. Blenkinsopp, *Isaiah 1–39,* p. 172.

(a) A Song of a City (Ch. 12) versus a Prophecy about a City (Ch. 13)

First of all, there is a contrast between the end of the prophet's call: "Shout and sing for joy, O inhabitants (ישבת) of Zion" (12:6), and that of the verdict on Babylon: "Babylon, the glory of all kingdoms . . . It will never be inhabited (לא תשב) or dwelt in for all generations" (13:19-20). Zion regains its habitation through God's judgment (cf. 1:7-8; 5:3; 6:11; 8:14; 10:24), Babylon loses it forever. This contrast is raised in relief by the fact that the land of Babylon will not be searched, not even by nomads, only by wild animals, even by "satyrs" who elsewhere are representative of vain idols (13:20-22; cf. Lev. 17:7; 2 Chr. 11:15), while Yhwh will reside and be active in the midst of Zion (12:6; cf. the root שכן in 8:18 and 13:21).

This contrast between ch. 12 and ch. 13 is in line with two different views on Zion's position in ch. 1 and ch. 4. We are set on this track by 13:19 which contains a combined allusion to texts about Zion in the introduction to BI:

> 13:19-20 Babylon, the beauty (צבי) of kingdoms,
> the splendor and loftiness (תפארת גאון) of the Chaldeans,
> will be like Sodom and Gomorrah when God overthrew them
> (כמהפכת אלהים את סדם ואת עמרה).
> It will never be inhabited or dwelt in for all generations . . . (theme: no people left)
>
> 1:9 If Yhwh Sebaoth had not left us a scanty remnant
> (הותיר לנו שריד כמעט),
> we should have been like Sodom, and become like Gomorrah
> (כסדם היינו לעמרה דמינו).
>
> 4:2-3 On that day the sprout (צמח) of Yhwh
> shall be for beauty and glory (לצבי ולכבוד),
> and the fruit of the land shall be the loftiness and splendor
> (לגאון ולתפארת)
> of the survivors of Israel (פליטת ישראל).
> And who remain (הנשאר) in Zion and are left (הנותר) in Jerusalem . . .

These texts create a particular opposition between Zion and Babylon. Zion will succeed to Babylon in "beauty," "splendor and loftiness," but along no other road than that she will narrowly escape the destiny that is prepared for Babylon: to be overthrown like Sodom and Gomorrah. In other words, when Babylon will be devastated, Zion will recognize as in a mirror that what she had called down upon herself because of her wickedness had been prevented only by Yhwh's plan to save a remnant.

Against this background, other analogies between Zion and Babylon in ch. 13 and chs. 1–12 come to the fore:

(1) Both visions are connected to "the day of Yhwh" (2:12; cf. vv. 11, 17, 20; 13:6, 9). This is directed against "the earth" (2:19, 21; 13:5), i.e. "against all that is proud and lofty" (2:12-17; cf. 13;7: "all hands / every human heart"), and causes panic and fear of Yhwh's power (2:10-21; 13:7-8, 14).

(2) In both visions foreigners go up: "nations / many peoples" (2:2-3, 4) to Zion, "a great multitude" and "kingdoms / nations" to Babylon (13:4-5). The former go up to the house of Yhwh in order to receive instruction in the torah and to break the habit of warfare whereas the latter go up to Babylon in order to wage war and execute Yhwh's judgment. In both prophecies Yhwh is the primary actant: the nations gather because of what he initiates. With regard to the nations in Zion: "He may teach us his ways . . . He shall judge between the nations, and shall arbitrate for many peoples" (2:3-4). With regard to Babylon: "I myself have commanded my consecrated ones, have summoned my mighty men. . . . Yhwh Sebaoth is mustering an army for battle . . . the weapons of his wrath" (13:3-5).

(3) The point of assembly in both stages is a mountain amidst mountains. With regard to Zion: "The mountain of the house of Yhwh shall be established as the highest of the mountains" (2:2). With regard to Babylon, the prophet urges to raise an ensign "on a bare hill" (13:2), while he draws attention to "the rumble on the mountains . . . the noise of kingdoms, nations assembled" (13:4).

(4) The march of the nations to Zion means "light of Yhwh" for the house of Jacob, a metaphor of divine presence (2:5), yet on the day of Yhwh against Babylon, the astral light is obscured, which is a metaphor for divine wrath (13:10).

These analogies between ch. 13 and chs. 1–2 (with ch. 2 and ch. 4 in the background) take a significant place in the total structure of BI: ch. 12 is the conclusion of the first section of the book, ch. 13 the beginning of the series of oracles against the nations, while ch. 2 forms a part of the introduction. Therefore, it can be concluded that they owe their function as opposing counterparts to the book's redaction, which is responsible for the joining together of chs. 1–12 and chs. 13–23. Counterpart, however, does not mean antithesis in all aspects. Zion in her sinfulness is the image of Sodom and Gomorrah, and she could become the same by God's judgment (ch. 1), exactly as will happen to

Babylon (ch. 13). Still, Zion will end up as the reverse of Babylon, for Yhwh has decided to redeem her by justice (1:27). ". . . the linkage serves to emphasize once again how the reflection on the experience of Judah faced with direct and potentially terminal threat from the Assyrians informed the interpretation of events during the rise, heyday and decline of the Neo-Babylonian Empire."[6]

(b) A Song on the Holy One of Israel (Ch. 12) and a Dirge on the King Masqué of Babylon (Ch. 14)

The songs of ch. 12 and ch. 14 are opposed, not only as literary genres — a hymn and a taunt in the form of a dirge — but also in their content. The following interconnected antinomies between Yhwh and the king of Babylon can be established:

(1) The hymn praises Yhwh for his pre-eminence: "His name is exalted (נשגב) . . . He has done high things (גאות) . . . "He is great (גדול) in your midst" (12:4-6). It is exactly the topic of "highness" and its reverse that determines the song on Babylon's king: the staging of his fall from self-conceited height down to the grave and Sheol (14:9-20). The passage culminates in the embedded lament of the kings there with the quotation of the Assyrian's self-praise (vv. 11-15):

> 11 Your loftiness (גאון) is brought down to Sheol . . .
> 12 How are you fallen from heaven, O shining one, son of dawn!
> How are you cut down to the ground, you who laid the nations down!
> 13 You who said in your heart: "I will ascend to heaven;
> above the stars of God, I will set my throne on high.
> 14 I will ascend above the heights of the clouds, I will make myself like the Most High."
> 15 But you are brought down to sheol, to the depths of the pit.

There is a preview on this topic in ch. 13 by means of the opposition between Yhwh's "highness" (v. 3: גאוה) and the "haughtiness / pride" (גאון / גאות) of the "arrogant / ruthless" (vv. 11, 19). The topic has, moreover, a basis in the *magna carta* of 2:6-22. This passage opposes the "loftiness" (2:10: גאון) of Yhwh against the "haughty looks of man / upstart of men" (2:11: עיני גבהות / רום אנשים) and elaborates the theme by means of several terms for "high" and "low" (2:12-19). The motto "Yhwh alone will be exalted (נשגב) on that day" (vv. 11, 17) is even programmatic for BI as a whole (cf. 12:4; 26:5; 33:5).

6. Blenkinsopp, *Isaiah 1–39*, p. 270.

(2) The accusation against the king of Babylon runs: "he smites the peoples in wrath . . . / he beats down the nations in anger" (14:6). Preceding this passage in BI, the terms "wrath" (עברה) and "anger" (אף) occur exclusively within the scope of Yhwh's judgment: separately with regard to Israel ("wrath": 9:18[19]; 10:6; "anger": 5:25; 9:11, 16, 20[12, 17, 21]; 10:4; 12:1; in 13:3 against Babel) together with regard to Babylon (13:9, 13). From their use in 14:6 it appears that the king of Babylon has appropriated a prerogative of Yhwh Judge (cf. the behaviour of the king of Assyria in 10:5-7).

(3) The term "to rise / to stand" (קום) for Yhwh's exclusive dominance plays a comparable role. The *magna carta* of Yhwh's exalted position above all human beings (2:6-22) has the refrain that people will hide themselves "from before the terror of Yhwh, and from the glory of his loftiness (גאון), when he rises (בקומו) to terrify the earth" (vv. 19, 21). Therefore, the conspiracy of earthly powers against Yhwh is warned as follows: "It shall not stand" (7:7: לא תקום; 8:10: לא יקום). The king of Babylon and his progeny, too, are destined to fall "lest they rise (בל יקמו) and possess the earth" (14:21). For Yhwh himself announces: "I will rise up (וקמתי) against them and will cut off from Babylon name and remnant, offspring and posterity" (14:22). Only Yhwh's plan persists: "As I have planned, so shall it be, and as I have purposed, so shall it stand" (14:24: תקום; cf. vv. 26-27).

From all this, it may be clear that ch. 14 elaborates on chs. 1–12, especially on the declaration of Yhwh's transcendence above all human might and wealth (2:6-22) and on Zion's anticipated hymn on Yhwh's great works among the nations (ch. 12). By virtue of this supremacy, the prophet can promise to "Jacob/Israel" that "on the day of Yhwh," they will raise a taunt against the king of Babylon (14:4). "It seems likely that the Babylonian poems in 13:1–14:23 were at some point in the editorial process placed where they are to make the point that the prophetic history about Judah and Assyria recorded in chs. 1–12 provides the essential clues to interpret the course of events during the time, much closer to the reader, of Neo-Babylonian ascendancy."[7]

II. Ch. 27 and Ch. 28: Two Icons of Zion

As opposed to earlier hypotheses, yet in agreement with a good number of recent authors, I do not assume that chs. 13–23 and chs. 24–27 are two strange sections in the overall structure of BI. On the contrary, they are interconnected

7. Blenkinsopp, *Isaiah 1–39*, p. 272.

in many ways. In my view, they present an indispensable forward movement in the sequence of actions as this continues into chs. 28–39.[8]

(a) The Connection of the Oracles about the Nations (Chs. 13–23) with the Apocalypse of Isaiah (Chs. 24–27) and the Integral Position of Both Segments in Proto-Isaiah

Older exegesis considered the collection of oracles about the nations (chs. 13–23) and the so-called Isaiah Apocalypse (chs. 24–27) as erratic blocks. They would interrupt the chronological sequence of chs. 1–12 and chs. 28–39 which have their background in two Assyrian military campaigns: the former segment in that of Tiglath-pileser III in 734-732 (the so-called Syro-Ephraimitic war), the latter segment in that of Sennacherib in 705-701. It was argued, moreover, that chs. 13–23 and chs. 24–27 have different literary-historical and theological views, the latter collection being the youngest part of the book.

Recent exegesis is willing to admit that the many similarities between chs. 28–32 and chs. 1–12 make them interdependent, not only historically (both have an Assyrian attack as background), but also editorially (failing acceptance of these prophecies was the beginning of their recording: 8:16-22; 30:8-14).[9] It has been argued, moreover, that the two collections chs. 13–23 and chs. 24–27 do not interrupt chs. 1–12 and chs. 28–39 but form a combined composition in the first part of BI.[10] Their language, style and theology show affinity with the supposedly "original" collections of Isaiah ben Amoz.

This does not imply that the oracles about the nations and the Isaiah Apocalypse stem from the same "author." Rather, their unity is the product of redactional arrangement at a later time which was based on the development of reinterpretation and application of prophetic material. The oracles about the nations (chs. 13–23) passed through a threefold process of focalization on Babylon, Zion and the topic of "the separation of the pious and wicked" which brings them on one line with important topics in BI. Together, the nations mentioned stand for all evil world powers that oppose Yhwh's reign on Zion. They will be subdued by God's universal judgment on the world, as a result of which the righteous are rescued and the wicked perish (chs. 24–27). The coun-

8. W. A. M. Beuken, *Jesaja 13–27*, Herders Theologischer Kommentar zum Alten Testament (Freiburg: Herder Verlag, 2010), pp. 310-14.

9. Blenkinsopp, *Isaiah 1–39*, pp. 381-82.

10. J. Kreuch, *Unheil und Heil bei Jesaja: Studien zur Entstehung des Assur-Zyklus Jesaja 28–31*, Wissenschaftliche Monographien zum Alten und Neuen Testament 130 (Neukirchen-Vluyn: Neukirchener Verlagsgesellschaft, 2011).

terpoint of 24:23 with 27:13 (Yhwh will be king on Zion — the returnees, back in Zion, will worship him) is the second landmark after 12:6 in the continuous sequence of actions in the book. Some specific points deserve attention:

(1) The position of Babylon in chs. 13–23, at the beginning of the two subsections chs. 13–19 and chs. 21–23, characterizes this metropolis as the high point of arrogant might. The land of Israel with Zion as a place of refuge for the poor is slowly brought to the fore in these chapters and becomes the counterpart of the nations and cities that will perish (14:32; 16:1-5; 17:10; 18:7; 23:18). Yhwh's exalted mountain (2:2-5; 11:9-10) will surpass the bare hill of Babylon (13:1-2) and become the center of the cosmos when Yhwh establishes his rule there (24:23) and carries his plans into effect (25:6-7, 10; 27:13).

(2) Yhwh's judgment has less the antinomy between Israel and the nations in view and more the discrepancy between wicked rulers and suppressed people (13:9-11; 14:5-6, 16-17, 20, 30; 16:4; 17:12-14; 19:20; 21:9-10; 23:8-9). In this way, the announcement in the introduction to BI that all arrogant haughtiness will fall before the majesty of Yhwh (2:6-22) is realized in the destruction of single nations (13:11, 19; 15:6; 23:9; 26:5-6), exemplified by the ruin of Babylon's king (14:4-21).

(3) Chs. 24–27 contain a continuous interaction. Within the future foretold by the prophetic agent, some figures react to his statements while the time carries on. Milestones in this development are the hymn to Yhwh by nameless people from the ends of the earth (24:14-16a), the prophet's reaction at the sight of the calamity (24:16b-20), his thankgiving for the establishment of Yhwh's kingship (25:1-5) together with the anticipated song of the redeemed (25:9-10a), the alternating voices in the song of Judah (ch. 26), and the prophet's invitation to concur with Yhwh's canticle on his vineyard (27:2-5).

(b) The Connection between Ch. 27 and Ch. 28: Is Zion Prepared to Host Yhwh's Kingship?

The sequence of actions in BI as a whole strongly depends on the connection between ch. 28 and chs. 24–27. In the prophetic perspective, the enforcement of Yhwh's kingship on his holy mountain in Jerusalem (24:23) and his adoration there by the gathered returnees (27:13) is an interconnected final point. The vision asks for a sequel with regard to the acceptance of Yhwh's reign in Zion, for recalcitrant, later miserable Jerusalem/Zion forms an obstacle. Consequently, the moral reform of this city becomes the encompassing theme of chs. 28–39. It is at stake in varying constellations of addressees. Only ch. 39 does not explicitly speak of Zion/Jerusalem.

At first sight, ch. 27 and ch. 28 are connected by the contrast between two localities: "the holy mountain at Jerusalem" (27:13) and "the proud crown of the drunkards of Ephraim . . . on the head of the rich valley" (28:1). The last expression refers to the elevated capital Samaria. In vv. 1-3, one reads of "Ephraim," but this changes into "Jerusalem" in 28:14; the carousing priests and prophets of vv. 7-10 form a sequel to the boozers of vv. 1-3. The real opposition between ch. 27 and ch. 28 is evident in the two appearances of Jerusalem, i.e. "the holy mountain at Jerusalem" (27:13) and "the proud crown of Ephraim" (28:1), which anticipates rebellious Jerusalem dominated by its reckless dominating class (28:1-3, 14).

The level of the acting persons, i.e. Yhwh and the persons addressed, mirrors the continuity and the contrast between the two chapters. With regard to God, there is continuity of intention: compare "Behold, Yhwh is coming forth out of his place to punish the inhabitants of the earth for their iniquity" (26:21) and "Behold, the Lord has one who is mighty and strong. Like a storm of hail, a destroying tempest . . . he will cast down to the earth with violence the proud crown of the drunkards of Ephraim" (28:2-3). With regard to the people, there is the difference between the people who convert to Yhwh, and those who persevere in wickedness: compare "Come, my people, enter your chambers . . . until the wrath is past" (26:20) and "Hear the word of Yhwh, you scoffers, who rule this people in Jerusalem" (28:14).

Some preeminent topics in ch. 27 and ch. 28 support their contrast. Opposite Yhwh's care for his vineyard and Israel's fertility (27:2-6) stands the abuse of wine among the leaders of Ephraim and Jerusalem (28:1-10), and the loss of Ephraim's harvest (28:1-4). Contrary to the worship of Yhwh by the returnees (27:13) is the covenant of Jerusalem's leadership with death (28:14-15). That covenant, however, will not hold out. For Yhwh, not the leaders, has laid the foundation stone of Zion and he will maintain justice there (28:16-17).

Some secondary analogies support the contrast between ch. 28 and ch. 27 (as part of chs. 24–27):

- The adjunct "proud" (28:1: גאות) integrates the metaphor "crown" in the theme of Yhwh's "highness" (גאון). This theme starts in the opening of BI: "before the terror of Yhwh, and from the glory of his highness" (2:10, 19, 21), and is resumed in the programmatic conclusion of Isaiah's call to Zion to praise Yhwh: "Sing praises to Yhwh, for he has done gloriously" (גאות, 12:5). In the Isaiah Apocalypse, this call finds a hearing: "They shout over the highness of Yhwh" (24:14). The theme situates Ephraim in 28:1 among the powers that pay no attention to Yhwh's judgment: "The wicked . . . does not see the majesty (highness) of Yhwh. . . . Thy hand is lifted up, but they see it not" (26:10-11).

- Ephraim's "fading flower" (28:1, 4: ציץ נבל) is a part of "the earth mourns and withers" (24:4: נבל) and stands opposite Israel which "shall blossom and put forth shoots and fill the whole earth with fruit" (27:6: יציץ).
- Ephraim's fall, as announced in: "He will cast down to earth (הניח לארץ) . . . The proud crown of Ephraim will be trodden under foot" (28:2-3: ברגלים תרמסנה), which corresponds to Judah's song of confidence: "He lays it low to the ground (ישפילה עד ארץ), casts it to the dust. The foot tramples it, the foot of the poor, the step of the needy" (26:5-6: תרמסנה רגל רגלי עני).
- In the sequence of actions in ch. 26, people in Judah ask for admittance to Yhwh's city: "Open the gates (שערים), that a righteous nation (גוי צדיק) which keeps faith may enter" (v. 2). Subsequently, they express their hope in the coming of Yhwh's "judgments" (vv. 8-9: משפטים). Against this background, 28:5-6 can be understood. In the same way as the capital of Ephraim passed for the crown of its drunkards (vv. 1, 3), so is Yhwh in the city which he prepares (26:1) a crown for the rest of his people (28:5). Consequently, he guarantees "a spirit of justice (משפט) to him who sits in judgment (משפטים), and strength to those who turn back the battle at the gate" (28:6: שערה).
- In this connection, the reversal in the concept "rest" (28:5: שאר) draws our attention. According to the Isaiah Apocalypse, the outcome of the judgment will be: "Desolation is left in the city" (24:12: נשאר; cf. v. 6). This clause summarizes the destiny of the nations mentioned earlier (cf. שאר or שארית in 14:22: Babylon; 14:30: Philistia; 15:9; 16:14: Moab; 17:3: Aram; 21:17: Kedar). Opposite this overall ruin, the prophet foresees a blessed existence for "the remnant of his (Yhwh's) people" (28:5). This will be situated, at the end of this part of BI, in Jerusalem (37:4, 32; cf. 4:3).

In this way, ch. 28 is connected to chs. 24–27 by means of semantic analogies. The proud capital of Ephraim's drunkards (28:1-6) metaphorically becomes a debauchery, like obstinate Jerusalem with its drinking to excess (28:7-15); both places belong to "the city of chaos" with its careless drinking (24:7-10). This city will simply disappear in front of the holy mountain at Jerusalem where Yhwh reigns (24:23) and is worshipped by the exiles (27:13).

III. Chs. 36–39 and Ch. 40: Survival from Exile Adumbrated and Coming True

The classical theory holds that chs. 36–39 have been taken over from 2 Kgs 18–20. It does not pay enough attention to the position of these chapters within the structure of BI. There is a broad consensus now that whatever their separate origin may have been, the form and meaning of the present triptych are strongly determined by its function in the book.

(a) The Open End of the Three Stories about King Hezekiah, the Son of David, in Chs. 36–39

The purpose of these narratives is likely to prove that Isaiah's prophecies recorded in chs. 1–35 are reliable.[11] Yhwh has shown to be determined and able to rescue Jerusalem and its king from foreign oppressors (chs. 36–37) and, moreover, to save the king from death as separation from God (ch. 38) if they and he only trust in Him. Even the consequences of the misfortune that will come in the future to the Davidic dynasty should be left to Yhwh's providence (ch. 39). The three stories are open-ended. Chs. 36–37 speak in light of the population: "Out of Jerusalem shall go forth a remnant, and out of Mount Zion a band of survivors" (37:32); ch. 38 speaks in light of the access to the temple: "What is the sign that I shall go up to the house of Yhwh?" (vv. 21-22); ch. 39 speaks in light of the promise to David's dynasty: "There will be peace and security in my days" (v. 8).

Two issues in this regard should be noted. First, in the story of Hezekiah's recovery from a deadly disease, the king represents his people (ch. 38). He describes his illness in his prayer (vv. 9-20) by means of metaphors for the exile which is the consequence of Israel's sins, and reports his recovery not with a view to its physical aspects but to its religious meaning. It symbolizes the revival of the community and the restoration of the temple which will enable the people to praise Yhwh again in his house (vv. 19-20).

Second, the very last clause of the third story which also concludes the first part of BI, "There will be peace and security in my days" (39:8b), need not be interpreted as evidence of Hezekiah's narrow-minded, self-satisfied lack of interest in the future of his dynasty but, against the background of 38:19-20

11. W. A. M. Beuken, "The King Diseased and Healed (Isaiah 38), the King Embarrassed and Comforted (Isaiah 39): What Do These Figures Add to the King Beleaguered and Rescued (Isaiah 36–37)?" *Ephemerides Theologicae Lovanienses* 86 (2010): 379-91.

and especially the prophecy of Nathan (2 Sam 7:12-17, 25-29), as an act of entrusting the future to Yhwh. The deportation of Hezekiah's progeny to Babylon seems to take the edge off Yhwh's promise to the house of David but the king remains confident with regard to the validity of Yhwh's oath for his own lifetime, and by silently accepting the announcement of future calamity, he leaves it to Yhwh to be faithful, even when his days will have come to an end.

(b) Retrospect from the Call to Comfort Jerusalem (40:1-11) on the First Part of the Book of Isaiah (chs. 1–39)

The opening of the second part of BI, the comfort of Jerusalem (40:1-11), makes full sense, even if one does not consider the passage intertextually connected to the first part of the book. However, the dialogical structure of ch. 40 induces readers to look back on chs. 1–39 for an answer to questions which it raises, such as: Who are the speaker and the person(s) addressed? Who is "your God"? and How "has Jerusalem received double for all her sins"? At first sight the following facts are striking (they regard acting persons and the message):

(1) The command "comfort my people / speak tenderly to Jerusalem" opens a new perspective (40:1) after the dominating theme of Yhwh's judgment on the city in chs. 1–39, yet the prophet himself has been challenged to anticipate this positive experience of Yhwh (12:1: "You will say [sing.] on that day: 'Your anger turned away, and you did comfort me' ") and to call upon Zion to endorse his praise of Yhwh (12:4: "You will say [plur.] on that day: 'Give thanks [plur.] to Yhwh' ").

(2) The transformation of Jerusalem/Zion from subject of discussion (40:1-2) to active speaker (40:9-10) is comparable to her changing position in chs. 36–37: from object of conquest (36:20: ". . . that Yhwh should deliver Jerusalem out of my hand") to her assuredly taking the floor as "the daughter of Zion" in order to defend Yhwh's supremacy (37:23).

(3) The short dialogue about the dissemination of some message: "Cry! . . . What shall I cry?" (40:6) reminds one of the commissioning vision of Isaiah (with due respect for all the differences): "Whom shall I send? . . . Here am I! Send me!" (6:8).

(4) There are many points of connection between 40:1-11 and ch. 35, the prophecy about the return through the desert to Zion (cf. the topics of desert, Yhwh's glory, strength/might, shepherd, no fear). The most important is certainly that of Yhwh's "glory" (35:2; 40:5) because it evokes two texts that play a role in the structure of BI (6:3; 24:23; apart from 3:8, there are no other occur-

rences of this theologoumenon in chs. 1–39). Another correspondence between these chapters forms the extension of the revelation of Yhwh's "glory," i.e. from "the whole earth" (6:3) over "the ransomed of Yhwh" (35:10) to "all flesh" (40:5).

It may be concluded that the opening of Second Isaiah (40:1-11) is aimed at bridging the two parts of BI by referring to some important junctions in chs. 1–39.

IV. Ch. 55 and Ch. 56: The Everlasting Covenant: Admittance for All People but Evildoers

The coherence of Trito-Isaiah with Deutero-Isaiah, both diachronically and synchronically, is still a subject of discussion. The question regards, apart from various forms of continuity, the meeting point of ch. 55 and ch. 56. On the one hand, it seems to be that "ch. 55 was created as a transition between chs. 40–54 and chs. 56–66, a hinge on which these major sections of the book turn."[12] On the other hand, "the many points of linguistic and thematic similarity between 56:1-8 and 66:15-24 suggest a deliberate intent at creating a framework for these last 11 chapters."[13] This frame deals with the question which inevitably arises and is left over from 54:17: Who are "the servants of Yhwh" and what is their "heritage / vindication" from Yhwh?

The explicit answer comes only in the beginning of ch. 56. Being servants of Yhwh is defined here as "to minister to him, to love the name of Yhwh . . . everyone who keeps the sabbath, and does not profane it, and holds fast my covenant" (56:6). Moreover, their "heritage / vindication" by Yhwh is defined here as follows: "These I will bring to my holy mountain, and make them joyful in my house of prayer; their burnt offerings and their sacrifices will be accepted on my altar" (56:7). This means that sinners have no access to Yhwh's salvific presence (56:1-2: "profaning the sabbath / doing evil"; 65:13-16; 66:15-16), while disabled people and even foreigners and nations are welcomed (56:3-8[9]; 66:18-21).

Although ch. 55 does not explicitly elaborate on 54:17, it leads over to chs. 56–66 in as far as the universal perspective in the frame surrounding these chapters, particularly in 56:1-8, is somehow prepared by the broad invitation to life in abundance and covenant with Yhwh, directed to all people on the sole condition that they take heed: "Everyone who thirsts, come to the waters; he who has no money, come, buy and eat! (55:1) . . . Incline your ear, and come

12. Blenkinsopp, *Isaiah 40–55*, p. 369.
13. Blenkinsopp, *Isaiah 56–66*, p. 132.

to me; hear, that your soul may live; and I will make with you an everlasting covenant" (55:3). In this context, the topic of "covenant" is important, although it occurs under the different points of view of the two covenant partners: "I will make with you an everlasting covenant" (55:3) and "everyone who holds fast my covenant" (56:6). Finally, the promise of an everlasting token forms a link between the two passages, remarkably enough under the same difference of angle: "a name for Yhwh, an everlasting sign which shall not be cut off" (55:13b) and "a monument and a name . . . an everlasting name which shall not be cut off" (56:5b). While the the literary genres of ch. 55 and 56:1-8 greatly differ, these eye-catching connections make it likely that a redactional process has attuned the chapters.

These data, and many others, have given rise to various literary-historical theories about earlier phases of the chapters the details of which need not be discussed here. While the evidence proves that 56:1-8 and ch. 66 form a strong redactional frame around "Trito-Isaiah,"[14] it would be pushing things too far to state that 56:1-8 was composed with 55:1-13 in mind.[15] Just the same, the present text form of these passages seems to be the result of a deliberate effort to facilitate the transition from one larger composition to another, both of which were shaped in different historical and religious circumstances. As a consequence, readers are invited to move over the gap while taking the development of form and content into account.

(a) The View of Ch. 55 as the Absolute End of Deutero Isaiah (Chs. 40–55) Is Inadequate

The theme of Yhwh's effective word in 55:11 aptly concludes chs. 40–55 (cf. 40:8). The next promise of an exodus (55:12: "You shall go out in joy, and be led forth in peace") catches one's eye on account of its vagueness with regard to the point of departure and the destination of the journey. In this way, it can refer to the call to "depart, go out thence" (55:11-12) in connection with Yhwh's entry as king in Jerusalem (52:8-10), but it can also anticipate Yhwh's remarkable initiative to bring his servants to his house on his mountain (56:1-8). Moreover, the first part of ch. 55 is determined by three groups of imperatives (and jussives): "come, buy, eat, come, buy" (v. 1); "hear, eat, incline your ear,

14. J. Gärtner, *Jesaja 66 und Sacharja 14 als Summe der Prophetie: Eine traditions- und redaktionsgeschichtliche Untersuchung zum Abschluss des Jesaja und des Zwölfprophetenbuches*, Wissenschaftliche Monographien zum Alten und Neuen Testament 114 (Neukirchen-Vluyn: Neukirchener Verlagsgesellschaft, 2006).

15. Blenkinsopp, *Isaiah 56–66*, p. 132.

come, hear" (vv. 2b-3); and "seek, call, forsake, return" (vv. 6-7) which reveal a dominance of the topic to set off for Yhwh. The second half of the chapter continues the theme of a way (to be) traversed by someone, however not in imperatives but in indicatives: first the "thoughts / ways" of Yhwh (vv. 8-9) and of "my word that goes forth from my mouth" (vv. 10-11), next of the people addressed: "You shall go out in joy, and be led forth in peace" (v. 12). The parallelism between v. 11 and v. 12 (the verb "to go out," יצא) contains an important contrast: v. 11 mentions a destination for the word of Yhwh (v. 11: "that which I purpose / the thing for which I sent it") but the destination for "you shall go out" (v. 12) is not mentioned. This concealment *(aposiopesis)* prepares for the next passage which reveals that Yhwh "will bring" (בוא *hiphil*) people to his house on the mountain (56:1-8).

(b) The View of 56:1-8(9) as the Absolute Beginning of Trito-Isaiah (Chs. 56–66) Is Inadequate

There are grounds for not considering the opening passage of Trito-Isaiah, 56:1-8, as the abrupt beginning of Trito-Isaiah but as intended to smooth the transit between the second and third sections of the book.

A preliminary question which bears upon the connecting function of the opening passage is: How far does it extend? Does it include v. 9 or is this the beginning of the next passage (56:9–57:21)? The Masoretic text has a *s*^{e}*tûmā*ʾ after v. 9, and this delimitation is supported by the Qumran scrolls, the versions and several codices.[16] If v. 9, according to the majority of the commentaries, opens the next passage, it has a cynical purport: the animals would bear upon the leaders of Israel who devour their people. On the contrary, if v. 9 concludes vv. 1-8, it would extend the salvation, promised there, to the animals: "All you beasts of the field, come to eat" (somehow in line with Isa 11:6-8; 65:25; not "to devour," בלע [Isa 28:4] or טרף [Gen 49:27; Mic 5:7(8); Ps 22:14(13)]). In any case, the plus reading of the Targum in v. 9a shows that this scribe had some problems with the transition of the two passages ("All the kings of the peoples which gather together to oppress thee, O Jerusalem, shall be cast down in thy midst; they shall be food for the beasts of the field, the beasts of the forest shall be sated with them"[17]).

From the point of view of content, it can indeed be argued that 56:1-8 ends

16. R. de Hoop, "The Interpretation of Isaiah 56:1-9: Comfort or Criticism?" *Journal of Biblical Literature* 127 (2008): 671-95, especially pp. 674-76.

17. J. F. Stenning, *The Targum of Isaiah* (Oxford: Clarendon Press, 1949), p. 188.

in v. 9 although the arguments in favour of the other interpretation, i.e., that v. 9 opens the next passage, do not lose their value, especially if v. 9 is seen in relation to v. 1: "The dogs have a mighty appetite; they never have enough." It seems therefore reasonable to combine the two ways of reading v. 9 and to attribute a double function to the verse: it concludes vv. 1-8 and it opens 56:9–57:21.[18] (In this case, ch. 55 together with 56:1-9 would constitute a planned literary composition.[19]) It would be enclosed by two invitations to come and eat, one directed to needy people (55:1: לכו . . . ואכלו) and one to the animals (56:9: אתיו . . . לאכל).[20] The gathering of disqualified people and even foreigners into Yhwh's house (56:1-8) would symbolically be broadened to a welcome to the animals in v. 9, as a metaphor for the overabundance of salvation. Moreover, the transformation of the fauna in 56:9 would suit the transformation of the flora in 55:12-13. In this way, the bridging of ch. 55 with 56:1-9 would not fill up the crack between Deutero-Isaiah and Trito-Isaiah but soften it.

(c) Connective Literary Data Between Ch. 55 and 56:1-8(9)

(1) **The Invitation** The direction of speech may corroborate the coherence of the two chapters. Generally, Yhwh is envisaged as the speaking person in 55:1-2: thus he would continue his utterance from 54:16-17 and introduce his call in 55:3-5. Yet, some scholars suggest that Zion is the speaking person in 55:1-2 (or even in v. 3a). In this way, she would perform the role which the unnamed woman of ch. 54 is challenged to take up. This woman is confirmed there as wife of Yhwh. Moreover, she is promised a large progeny (54:2-8) and a secure, prosperous position amidst the nations (54:11-17). The promise would suit as the background of the supposed woman's broad call to "water, food and life" (55:1-3) and of Yhwh's unrestricted invitation to his mountain (56:1-9).

The question who is speaking in 55:1-3 has been discussed by many authors, most recently by Oosting[21] in reaction to Paganini.[22] Oosting seems

18. de Hoop, "The Interpretation of Isaiah 56:1-9," speaks of a "Janus-text, looking backward and forward" (p. 678).

19. S. Paganini, "Osservazioni su Is 56,9," *Rivista Biblica Italiana* 54 (2006): 202-206.

20. W. G. E. Watson, *Classical Hebrew Poetry: A Guide to Its Techniques,* Journal for the Study of the Old Testament Supplement Series 26 (Sheffield: JSOT Press, 1984), pp. 282-83: "envelope figure."

21. R. Oosting, "Walls of Zion and Ruins of Jerusalem: A Corpus-Linguistic View on the Participant Zion/ Jerusalem in Isaiah 40–55" (Ph.D. diss., VU University Amsterdam, 2011), pp. 222-32.

22. S. Paganini, *Der Weg zur Frau Zion, Ziel unserer Hoffnung. Aufbau, Kontext, Sprache,*

to have convincingly shown that a change of speaking person cannot occur in the middle of v. 3, in thc sense that Zion would start speaking in v. 1 and continue up to v. 3a: "Incline your ear, and come to me; hear, that your soul may live," while Yhwh would take over from v. 3b: "and I will make with you an everlasting covenant." However, the conclusion that vv. 1-2 cannot be ascribed to Zion if Yhwh starts speaking in v. 3a, does not follow logically. It is feasible that the two calls to listen in v. 2b and v. 3a do not originate from the same speaker. First, they are followed by different verbs connoting the result of listening (in v. 2b "eat . . . and delight yourselves," in v. 3a: "that your soul may live"). Second, v. 3a opens with a special call for attention, "incline your ear,"[23] which is worked out by "come to me" before the imperative "hear" from v. 2b is repeated. In this way, Zion could utter the invitation to foods of vv. 1-2 while Yhwh would elaborate this with the promise of "life / covenant" in v. 3.[24] The change of speaker would not be indicated by a conventional formula, but this absence is not a rare phenomenon in prophetic oracles.

Seen in this way, the two calls of Zion and Yhwh form a climax, from "water . . . wine and milk" (55:1) and "good / fatness" (55:2) to "life" and "everlasting covenant" (55:3). The climax concerns also the people invited, for it does not hold any ethnic limitation as is still the case in ch. 54 (v. 13: "your sons"; v. 17: "the heritage of the servants of Yhwh"). Indeed, the call is directed to people who live the human condition as such ("every one who thirsts") and it annuls any social-economic restriction ("come . . . who have no money"), for one can profit from the abundance of foods "without money, without price" (55:1). The only restraint of persons is almost imaginary: people who spend their money and efforts for something that does not satisfy (55:2). If it is here Zion who, in agreement with her vocation (ch. 54), speaks and broadens the access to happiness in life unimpeded (55:2: "Delight yourself in fatness") while Yhwh confirms this with an "everlasting covenant" (55:3), it follows that in ch. 56, Yhwh permits access to his house to ". . . every one who holds fast to my covenant — these I will bring to my holy mountain" (56:6-7). In this perspective, disqualifying characteristics like being an alien or sterilized are no longer valid (vv. 3-6).

Kommunikationsstruktur und theologische Motive in Jes 55,1-13, Stuttgarter biblische Beiträge 49 (Stuttgart: Katholisches Bibelwerk, 2002), pp. 35-55.

23. H. Ringgren, "נטה," *Theologisches Wörterbuch zum Alten Testament*, 5:413.

24. M. C. A. Korpel and J. C. de Moor, *The Structure of Classical Hebrew Poetry: Isaiah 40–55*, Oudtestamentische Studiën 41 (Leiden: Brill, 1998), p. 625: v. 2 and v. 3 are separate strophes, vv. 1-3 are one canticle.

(2) **The Exodus Leads into Yhwh's House** At the end of ch. 55, in v. 12, the exodus theme is at stake in the form of an indicative only: "You shall go out (תצאו) in joy, and be led forth (תובלון) in peace," not in the form of an imperative as in 48:20: "Go forth (צאו) from Babylon," or in the combined form of an imperative and an indicative as in 52:11-12: "Depart, go out thence (סורו צאו) ... You shall not go out (תצאו) in haste, and you shall not go (תלכון) in flight, for Yhwh will go (הלך) before you." In the reading model of a coherent series of actions in chs. 40–52 (resulting in Yhwh's return to Zion), these texts prepare, first of all, for 55:12, and ultimately for 56:1-9, where Yhwh announces "these I will bring (והביאותים) to my holy mountain" (v. 7). In 55:12, the exodus is stripped from its geographical components: the issues "from where?" and "where to?" are not discussed. This incompleteness prepares for the surprising destination where Yhwh will lead his servants: "to my holy mountain" (56:7). The bare announcement of a successful exodus and the supplementary mention of the destiny agree in the fact that departure and arrival will happen in "joy" (55:12; 56:7: שמחה).

The exodus is mentioned as an established fact, the result of Yhwh's word which is as effective as the rain which brings fertility and thereby bread (55:10-11). The comparison with the cosmic process forms an appropriate, later background for Zion's wide invitation to the meal of Yhwh's covenant (55:1-3). Moreover, it paves the way to Yhwh's declaration that the entry into his house is open to all mankind but on the condition that people serve him in righteousness (56:4-7). Seen in this connection, ch. 55 and 56:1-9 arrive at a similar end: the landscape with its vegetation (55:12-13) and the animal realm (56:9) are involved in Yhwh's salvation. This pursues a topic of Deutero-Isaiah (41:15-16, 18-19; 42:10-11, 15; 43:20; 44:2, 16, 23; 49:13; 51:3) and anticipates the transformation of the cosmos (58:10-11; 60 *passim;* 61:11; 63:12; 64:1; 65:25) by the creation of new heavens and a new earth (65:17-20; 66:22).

Conclusion

In the four interchanges between major sections of BI that we have discussed, the agent Zion plays a varying role with respect to Yhwh's reign. In this way, larger passages and sections are bridged. Chapter 12 and chs. 13–14 form a diptych: Zion's mission to proclaim Yhwh's height is set against the king of Babylon's pretension to be equal to God. Chapters 27 and 28 are connected by the contrast between the holy mountain at Jerusalem where the returnees will worship Yhwh (27:13), and "the crown of Ephraim" together with Jerusalem

(28:1, 14) where priests and prophets, leaders and people hold Yhwh's covenant in contempt (28:15). In chs. 36–39, Zion's confession of Yhwh's supremacy (37:23) and the city's rescue (37:35-37) prepare for Jerusalem's consolation (40:1-2) and Zion's mission to proclaim Yhwh's arrival (40:9-11). The transit from ch. 55 to ch. 56 is characterized by the resemblant performances of Zion and Yhwh. The former invites all needy people to the banquet of Yhwh's salvation (55:1-2), the latter indiscriminately ushers all human beings who keep his covenant into his house on his holy mountain (56:7).

This study of interchanges in BI raises but does not answer the question of who was responsible for them. Do they stem from individual scribes over time or from the guild that produced Third Isaiah, or are they to be ascribed to later recipients of the Isaianic heritage who created the so-called final form of the prophetic book? Moreover, how far is a distinction between authors of larger parts of BI and redactors of interchanges appropriate? For the moment, however, it is not audacious to state that the interchanges support the integrating paradigm of the book of Isaiah: The establishment of Yhwh's sovereign rule on Mt. Zion.

Little Highs, Little Lows: Tracing Key Themes in Isaiah

Hyun Chul Paul Kim

Introduction

One of the key themes occurring quite consistently in the Hebrew Bible is the divine intention to look upon the lowly ones. God in the majestic height comes down to the earth to rescue the oppressed (Exod 3:8). Likewise, God is also depicted as coming down to deter the haughty and sinful endeavors of humanity (Gen 11:5; 18:21). That YHWH the sovereign Lord is deeply involved with the humbling of the arrogant and the lifting up of the weak recurs in the song of Hannah: "The bows of the mighty are broken, but the feeble gird on strength" (1 Sam 2:4; cf. 2 Sam 1:19; 22:18).[1] Indeed, the psalmists testify to such notions of subversive hope in light of numerous historical situations of ebb and flow (Pss 37:17; cf. 49:3 [Eng 49:2]; 72:4; 113:7-8; 140:13-14 [Eng 140:12-13]).

Accordingly, this theme of the "universal dominion" of God in divine majesty and might is intricately intertwined with the divine care and intervention for "justice and righteousness" in the daily affairs of human world.[2] This perspective continues in the prophetic traditions, thus, it is no surprise that it

1. Unless otherwise noted, all translations are from the NRSV.

2. Rolf P. Knierim, *The Task of Old Testament Theology: Substance, Method, and Cases* (Grand Rapids: Eerdmans, 1995), pp. 1-56.

It is a great honor to contribute to this volume honoring Joseph Blenkinsopp, from whom I have learned so much about Isaiah the prophet, the book, and their subsequent interpretation.

stands as one of the key themes in the book of Isaiah. In Isaiah, we thus find distinctive contrasts between highs and lows.[3] Most evidently, first of all, there is the competition between the incomparable, living God and the chaotic forces, often illustrated in fabricated idols. Second, there is the contrast between the holy, almighty God and the seemingly formidable foreign oppressors; this contrast is mirrored by another confrontation between the pompous foreign ruler and the vulnerable people of the Levant. Third, in the dynamic dichotomy, we find the contrasts within Israel, i.e., between the haughty leaders and the most marginalized poor. Fourth, this contrast is intricately entangled with the dichotomous tension between the insiders and the outsiders, with which the complex issues of identity become interwoven. Fifth, these contrasts further encompass the more abstract yet persistently occurring dichotomy between the righteous and the wicked in the book of Isaiah.

This study intends to analyze the key linguistic and metaphorical theme of the dichotomous contrasts between the exalted/haughty/highs and the exiled/contrite/lows that connect and proceed throughout the book of Isaiah.[4] Recent Isaiah scholarship has made significant contributions to reading the unified themes of the book of Isaiah as a whole, as well as to reconstructing the redactional development in its composition history.[5] This study is an attempt to build on those scholarly insights: so as to examine how this theme of contrasts portrays the ongoing sociopolitical tensions in monarchic and postmonarchic Israel; how this theme grows, evolves, and is redefined in key sections of the book of Isaiah; and how this theme ultimately shapes the formation of the book of Isaiah into a holistic unity.

3. Admittedly, the title of this essay borrows the theme motto of the family of Little in the children's novel by E. B. White, *Stuart Little* (New York: Harper, 1945). In the film versions (Columbia Pictures, 1999 and 2002), the family sing together, "Little high, little low," as if confidently — and subversively — reminding themselves that those little ones, the *lowly* underdogs, can indeed do the great, *highly* powerful things.

4. James Muilenburg, "The Book of Isaiah: Chapters 40–66," in *The Interpreter's Bible,* vol. 5 (New York: Abingdon, 1956), p. 388: "Similes, metaphors, apostrophes and personifications, hyperbole — all appear in great profusion. We see [YHWH] seated high above the firmament, looking down upon his creature far below (40:22)."

5. Marvin E. Tate, "The Book of Isaiah in Recent Study," in *Forming Prophetic Literature: Essays on Isaiah and the Twelve in Honor of John D. W. Watts* (ed. J. W. Watts and P. R. House; JSOTSup 235; Sheffield: Sheffield Academic Press, 1996), pp. 22-56; Roy F. Melugin, "Isaiah 40–66 in Recent Research: The 'Unity' Movement," in *Recent Research on the Major Prophets* (ed. Alan J. Hauser; Sheffield: Sheffield Phoenix Press, 2008), pp. 142-94; Mark E. Biddle, "Teaching Isaiah Today," *Perspectives in Religious Studies* 36 (2009): 257-72.

1. Isaiah 1–12

The theme of polar opposites in the first section of Isaiah (chs. 1–12) mainly deals with the chastisement of the injustice wrought within the kingdoms of Israel and Judah. This motif hits home in the realm of the monarchy, as the prophet vehemently accuses the royal leaders of corruption and exposes their oppression of socially, economically, and politically marginalized groups.

The initial chapter is a prologue that opens its vehement social criticism in light of the contrasts between the high-ranking officials and the lowly, oppressed groups:

> Learn to do good; seek justice, rescue the *oppressed,* defend the *orphan,* plead for the *widow.* (1:17)

> Your *princes* are rebels and companions of thieves. Everyone loves a bribe and runs after gifts. They do not defend the *orphan,* and the *widow*'s cause does not come before them. (1:23; cf. 10:1-2)

The princes are directly accused of being sinful oppressors, whereas the oppressed are delineated as the orphans and the widows. In this dichotomy of opposite social classes, the prophet cries out for the practices of goodness and justice, reminiscent of Amos's social criticism, but eventually laments the rampant practices of bribery and injustice.[6] In fact, the opening chapter starts with the metaphorical contrasts of the faithful ox and donkey over against the obdurate Israel (1:3). Likewise, this sin-saturated society is depicted as corrupt from the feet to the head (1:6). Ultimately, Israel is identified with Sodom and Gomorrah, starting with the "rulers of Sodom" affecting the whole "people of Gomorrah" (1:10).

Similar motifs of the highs and lows consistently occur in subsequent chapters, depicting the stark contrast between haughty rulers and the lowly weak, whose fate will be reversed by YHWH — as though presenting a thesis statement. It is interesting that the metaphors of mountains and hills (cf. 40:4) function similarly in depicting the extreme contrasts between divine majesty and human ephemerality:

6. Joseph Blenkinsopp, *Isaiah 1–39,* AB 19 (New York: Doubleday, 2000), pp. 106-7: "Isaiah's debt to Amos is nevertheless not difficult to detect. . . . In these and similar respects the relevant sections of Isaiah read like an application to Judah of Amos's threats directed at the sister-kingdom to the north."

> In days to come the mountain of the LORD's house shall be established as the *highest* of the mountains, and shall be *raised* above the hills; all the nations shall stream to it. (2:2)[7]

> And so people are *humbled*, and everyone is *brought low* — do not *forgive* (literally, *"raise up,"* נשׂא)[8] them! . . . The *haughty* eyes of people shall be brought *low*, and the *pride* of everyone shall be *humbled;* and the Lord alone will be *exalted* in that day. (2:9, 11; cf. 2:17)

> For the LORD of hosts has a day against all that is *proud* and *lofty*, against all that is *lifted up* and *high;* against all the cedars of Lebanon, *lofty* and *lifted up;* and against all the oaks of Bashan; against all the *high* mountains, and against all the *lofty* hills; against every *high* tower, and against every *fortified* wall. (2:12-15)

This contrary motif recurs with the message of subversion.[9] YHWH will put down the haughtiness of the abusive rulers: "The LORD enters into judgment with the *elders* and *princes* of his people: It is you who have devoured the vineyard; the spoil of the *poor* is in your houses" (3:14; cf. 3:15-16).[10] Coupled with this motif of the divine lowering of the haughty, readers learn that YHWH alone will then be exalted: "People are *bowed down,* everyone is brought *low,* and the eyes of the *haughty* are *humbled.* But the LORD of hosts

7. On the significance of this motif, consider Hans Wildberger, *Isaiah 1–12* (trans. Thomas H. Trapp; Minneapolis: Fortress, 1991), pp. 88-89: "It is quite obvious that the overarching height of the temple mount is mentioned very seldom in the OT . . . which is only to be expected, since Zion is not even as high in elevation as the surrounding hills. But, in the ancient Near East, the temple mount was equated with the mountain of the gods. . . . But, for Isaiah, the actual height of the mount does not play any central role. Kerygmatically, he employs this concept only to characterize the great importance of the sanctuary on Zion as a place where [YHWH] will reveal himself to the nations of the world."

8. Blenkinsopp, *Isaiah 1–39*, p. 194.

9. Walter Brueggemann, *Isaiah 1–39* (Louisville: Westminster John Knox, 1998), pp. 29-30: "In the extended section of [2:11-18], the poet meditates on the theme of 'humbling.' . . . [YHWH] is elevated while all others are lowered." See also Marvin A. Sweeney, *Isaiah 1–39*, FOTL 16 (Grand Rapids: Eerdmans, 1996), p. 89: "This is frequently expressed through metaphorical use of the imagery of height and depth. . . . The Day of YHWH will therefore correct this situation by stripping away all symbols of human pride so that YHWH's exalted status will be manifested."

10. Christopher R. Seitz, *Isaiah 1–39* (Louisville: Westminster John Knox, 1993), p. 41: "The next section (3:1-5) also speaks of a reversal of rank: all honored and revered offices will be undone, as boys, and babes, and youth take charge, insolent and base to their 'elders.' "

is *exalted* by justice, and the Holy God shows himself holy by righteousness" (5:15-16).[11]

It is noteworthy that this section highlights the thematic contrast between YHWH the divine King and the human kings. For example, over against the death of King Uzziah, the prophet witnesses the divine King "sitting on a throne, *high* and *lofty*" (6:1). Likewise, the would-be kings of Syria and Ephraim, together with Ahaz the king of Judah, are described as a mere *"head"* that "shall not stand at all" (7:8-9; cf. 9:8, 13-14 [Eng 9:9, 14-15]). Additionally, even the atrocious king of Assyria is ultimately declared to be brought down from his vain arrogance: "When the Lord has finished all his work on Mount Zion and on Jerusalem, he will punish the *arrogant boasting* of the king of Assyria and his *haughty pride*" (10:12). Eventually, toward the end of this section, we learn that the haughty ones will be cut down by YHWH who alone is the Most High: "Look, the Sovereign, the Lord of hosts, will lop the boughs with terrifying power; the *tallest* trees will be *cut down,* and the *lofty* will be brought *low*" (10:33).

In the concluding chapters of this section, we find similar motifs, except with somewhat reversed depictions. It is as if chapter 11 builds an inclusio with chapters 1–2 in this regard, forming a progression from the negative critiques of the reality to the climactic positive hopes of ideals:

> But with righteousness he shall judge the *poor,* and decide with equity for the *meek* of the earth; he shall strike the earth with the rod of his mouth, and with the breath of his lips he shall kill the *wicked.* (11:4; cf. 3:14-15; 10:2)[12]

Contrary to the present reality of social injustice in the stinging accusations of the initial chapters, here in chapter 11 the prophet envisions an era of a peaceable kingdom in which the righteous king will protect the poor and meek with uprightness and equity. In this text, therefore, the comparable motif of the poor and disenfranchised versus the oppressive rulers recurs in

11. For the similar combination of the motifs of the "righteous" with the "poor," "oppressed," "needy," and "lowly" over against the "wicked" with the "insolent" foes as the central theology in the Psalter, see Jerome F. D. Creach, "The Destiny of the Righteous and the Theology of the Psalms," in *Soundings in the Theology of Psalms: Perspectives and Methods in Contemporary Scholarship* (ed. Rolf A. Jacobson; Minneapolis: Fortress, 2011), pp. 49-61.

12. On a similar linguistic and thematic correlation between 3:14-15 and 10:2 (as though forming another bracket within chs. 1–2 and 11), note Wildberger, *Isaiah 1–12,* p. 214: "Just as the עניים *(poor)* are clearly identified in 3:15 as the people of God [*'my people'*], so in this passage [10:2] they are called the עניי עמי (*poor* among *my people*)."

a reversed message of hope. In this utopian kingdom, even other opposite components are depicted as cohabiting with peace and trust instead of hatred and war:

> The wolf shall live with the lamb, the leopard shall lie down with the kid, the calf and the lion and the fatling together, and a little child shall lead them. The cow and the bear shall graze, their young shall lie down together; and the lion shall eat straw like the ox. The nursing child shall play over the hole of the asp, and the weaned child shall put its hand on the adder's den. (11:6-8)[13]

2. *Isaiah 13–23*

This section is a composite whole held together by the unique superscription called משא ("oracle"; literally, "burden"). Read sequentially, this section addresses YHWH's subjugation and humbling of the daunting neighbors, from Babylon to Moab, from Egypt to Tyre. Just as the haughty rulers of Israel are said to be brought down in chapters 1–12, so here the arrogant tyrants of the neighboring empires are confirmed to be brought low. As expected, in this Oracles Against the Nations (OAN) section, the emphasis on practicing justice and righteousness for the sake of the "poor" and "needy" (14:30, 32) occurs far less frequently in comparison with chapters 1–12. Instead, the announcement of drastic mortification of the towering empires resounds emphatically, evoking a dangerous "fantasy of the oppressed" by the extremely vulnerable and powerless petty kingdoms of Israel and Judah.[14]

Hence the metaphor of highs and lows functions to underscore the downfall of the oppressive nations. It is noticeable that these pertinent words occur most frequently in the oracles against Babylon:

> I will punish the world for its evil, and the *wicked* for their iniquity; I will put an end to the *pride* of the *arrogant,* and lay *low* the *insolence* of tyrants. (13:11)

13. Wildberger considers this motif of peace among the animals as Isaiah's reinterpretation of the ancient mythological imagery. Note his comments on the thematic correlation between 2:2-4 and 11:6-8 (as if forming a bracket): "The problem [on 11:6-8] is similar to the one which was raised in the exposition of 2:2, namely, the elevation of Zion over all of the other mountains was meant in a physical or symbolic sense" (*Isaiah 1–12,* p. 480).

14. Joseph Blenkinsopp, *Isaiah 1–39,* p. 311. Note also Seitz, *Isaiah 1–39,* p. 137.

> You will take up this taunt against the king of Babylon: How the oppressor has ceased! How his *insolence* has ceased! (14:4)
>
> Sheol beneath is stirred up to meet you when you come; it *rouses* the shades to greet you, all who were leaders of the earth; it *raises* from their thrones all who were kings of the nations. . . . Your pomp is *brought down* to Sheol, and the sound of your harps; maggots are the bed beneath you, and worms are your covering. How you are *fallen* from heaven, O Day Star, son of Dawn! How you are *cut down* to the ground, you who *laid* the nations *low*! (14:9, 11-12; cf. 2 Sam 1:19, 25, 27)
>
> Prepare slaughter for his sons because of the guilt of their father. Let them *never rise* to possess the earth or cover the face of the world with cities. I will *rise up* against them, says the LORD of hosts, and will cut off from Babylon name and remnant, offspring and posterity, says the LORD. (14:21-22)

In this taunt against an anonymous king of Babylon, Blenkinsopp highlights the sharp contrast between "the sons" who are "not to rise up [בל־יקמו] to take possession of the earth" (14:21) and YHWH who will "rise up [וקמתי] against them" (14:22).[15] Similarly, the haughtiness of this king is cited but only to be refuted by the divine scorn against such a vain aspiration:

> You said in your heart, "I will *ascend* to heaven; I will *raise* my *throne above* the stars of God; I will sit on the mount of assembly on the *heights* of Zaphon; I will *ascend* to the *tops* of the clouds, I will make myself like the Most High." But you are *brought down* to Sheol, to the depths of the Pit. (14:13-15)[16]

Indeed, the Babylonian king's claim to "ascend to heaven" and "sit on the mount" is reminiscent of the common ancient Near Eastern motifs of the deity.

15. Blenkinsopp, *Isaiah 1–39*, p. 286: "It may be assumed that poems originally composed subsequent to, or in anticipation of, the death of one of the great Assyrian kings could have been 'recycled' for a different occasion during the Neo-Babylonian era or later. . . . Some of these particulars would fit practically any prominent Mesopotamian ruler." Similarly, note Göran Eidevall, *Prophecy and Propaganda: Images of Enemies in the Book of Isaiah* (Winona Lake, Ind.: Eisenbrauns, 2009), p. 72.

16. Hans Wildberger, *Isaiah 13–27* (trans. Thomas H. Trapp; Minneapolis: Fortress, 1997), p. 75: "The central theme, a common wisdom topic, is about the judgment against the hubris of human beings who reach for the stars and break into a world reserved for God alone."

Such a pompous claim makes a stark contrast with YHWH's assertion as the only Lord of the divine council, the theme of which occurs frequently in the Psalter (e.g., Pss 2:4; 76:10 [Eng 76:9]; 82:1).

Other nations, such as Moab, Ethiopia, and Egypt, are informed of their humiliation as well. In the case of Moab, the similar language of highs versus lows abounds, with the graphic depictions of the Moabites' going up and down the high places of their capital Dibon only to lament and weep:

> Dibon has *gone up* to the temple, to the *high places* to weep; over Nebo and over Medeba Moab wails. On every *head* is baldness, every beard is shorn; in the streets they bind on sackcloth; on the housetops and in the squares everyone wails and melts in tears (literally, "*going down* in weeping").[17]. . . For at the *ascent* of Luhith they *go up* weeping; on the road to Horonaim they raise a cry of destruction. (15:2-3, 5)

Thus, the empty pride of Moab is foretold to be brought down and laid low, in a sharp contrast with the "tent of David" whose throne "shall be established in steadfast love" (16:5):

> We have heard of the *pride* of Moab — how *proud* he is! — of his *arrogance,* his *pride,* and his *insolence;* his *boasts* are false. (16:6; cf. 25:10-12)[18]

Whether literal or metaphorical, the *tall* — or "anomalously elongated in height"[19] — stature of the Ethiopians and the Egyptians symbolizes their insurmountable forces which remain as mere threat (18:2, 7), as unreliable and insecure as "palm branch" and "reed" in actuality (19:6, 15; cf. 36:6). Following these oracles, this section in one dimension culminates with the oracle against Babylon, which builds a nice inclusio, with a climactic denouncement. This oracle vividly describes the destroyer's attack against Babylon, whose demise is solemnly declared:

17. Blenkinsopp, *Isaiah 1–39,* p. 296; note also p. 364: "It is this that may have prompted or justified the addition of the anti-Moabite saying that follows, especially in view of the mountainous nature of that country."

18. Brian C. Jones, *Howling over Moab: Irony and Rhetoric in Isaiah 15–16* (SBLDS 157; Atlanta: Scholars Press, 1996), p. 263: "The response given in 16:6 is the turning point in the rhetoric of the poem. . . . The response makes explicit what has been implicit throughout the first two sections of the speech: Moab is suffering the just punishment for its arrogance."

19. Blenkinsopp, *Isaiah 1–39,* p. 309.

> A stern vision is told to me; the betrayer betrays, and the destroyer destroys. *Go up,* O Elam, lay siege, O Media; all the sighing she has caused I bring to an end. (21:2)

> "Look, there they come, riders, horsemen in pairs!" Then he responded, "*Fallen, fallen* is Babylon; and all the images of her gods lie shattered on the ground." (21:9)

Following this inclusio framework (chs. 13–21),[20] readers find a strange oracle identified as the oracle against "the valley of the vision" in ch. 22. It is unclear whether the addressee is Judah, Jerusalem, or an unknown nation. But if we take the addressee as the people of Judah, then the taunt seems to be directed at the callous leaders who are unaffected — or became more obdurate — even by the downfalls of the more powerful surrounding nations. Interestingly, Jerusalem on an elevated hill is depicted as a steep, withdrawn valley:[21]

> The oracle concerning the *valley* of vision. What do you mean that you have *gone up,* all of you, to the *housetops,* you that are full of shoutings, tumultuous city, exultant town? Your slain are not slain by the sword, nor are they dead in battle. . . . For the LORD GOD of hosts has a day of tumult and trampling and confusion in the *valley* of vision, a battering down of walls and a cry for help to the *mountains.* (22:1-2, 5)

This inclusion of the unrepentant leaders of Judah becomes more apparent, as the warning is issued against an abusive palace superintendent named Shebna:

> What right do you have here? Who are your relatives here, that you have cut out a tomb here for yourself, cutting a tomb on the *height,* and carving a habitation for yourself in the *rock?* The LORD is about to hurl you away violently, my fellow. He will seize firm hold on you." (22:16-17)

By reading sequentially, the stripping of Shebna's office after the death of Ahaz (14:28) may symbolize the forces of ongoing oppressors within Judah and Jeru-

20. Blenkinsopp, *Isaiah 1–39,* p. 272.

21. Sweeney's insights on the word play are noteworthy: "But this view fails to account for the above indications of a setting in the Kidron Valley and Isaiah's well-known penchant for wordplay. . . . Both terms ['vision' and 'Kidron'] employ the nominative ending -*ôn* attached to the main root so that they rhyme. Furthermore, the meaning of the verbal root *qdr* is 'to be dark.' . . . Although the name of the Kidron suggests YHWH's actions are hidden from normal view, the prophet has revealed the true significance of the siege through prophetic vision" (*Isaiah 1–39,* p. 300).

salem, who are proclaimed to be brought down: "I will thrust you from your office, and you will be *pulled down* from your post" (22:19; cf. 17:4). Regardless of the historical settings of this text, in light of the thread of the motif of highs and lows, readers can find a mirror effect in that just as the king of Assyria is predicted to be brought down (10:12) in the preceding section, so here in ch. 22 amid the oracles against the neighboring nations, the recalcitrant leaders of Jerusalem are informed of the downfall of their own oppressive governance and false security.

3. *Isaiah 24–35*

This third section is probably the least cohesive segment, containing various units that appear to be more disjointed than coherent. Apart from the middle portion (chs. 28–33), which is held together by the superscriptions of הוי and thus commonly called the woe-oracles, other sections do not flow in distinctly correlated sequences. However, due to the next unit (chs. 36–39), which is very likely an excerpt from 2 Kgs 18–20 and thus "clearly a section apart,"[22] we treat this section together in its given form.

As commentators have cogently argued, chs. 24–27 can be taken as an extension of chapters 13–23.[23] Read together, the divine subjugation of numerous foreign nations (chs. 13–23) continues on now with the divine control of the chaotic, mythological forces of the whole universe. What is unique in this so-called Isaiah Apocalypse (chs. 24–27) is the lack of certain target enemies like Assyria, Babylon, or human kings.[24] Yet the thematic continuity signals the same motif of YHWH's humbling of the chaotic forces from highs to lows:

22. H. G. M. Williamson, *The Book Called Isaiah: Deutero-Isaiah's Role in Composition and Redaction* (Oxford: Clarendon, 1994), p. 184.

23. Seitz, *Isaiah 1–39*, pp. 115-27; Sweeney, *Isaiah 1–39*, pp. 312, 316; Blenkinsopp, *Isaiah 1–39*, pp. 346-48; Patricia K. Tull, *Isaiah 1–39* (Macon, Ga.: Smyth & Helwys, 2010), pp. 258-60, 368-70.

24. Blenkinsopp, *Isaiah 1–39*, pp. 346-47: "We saw that in these poems historical acts of judgment adumbrate a more universal and cosmic doom. . . . we would be led to suspect that the anonymity of the doomed city often referred to in this section (24:10, 12; 25:2-3; 26:5; 27:10) is deliberate and that it represents a kind of composite of the named cities in the previous section or a symbolic Babylon as the embodiment of opposition and hostility to [YHWH's] purposes."

> For he has *brought low* the inhabitants of the *height;*[25] the *lofty* city he *lays low.* He *lays* it *low* to the ground, casts it to the dust. The *foot* tramples it, the *feet* of the poor, the *steps* of the needy. (26:5-6)

Just as "heavens" and "earth" are summoned to witness the divine accusation at the overture (1:2), so now YHWH announces the takeover of the entire cosmic realm: "On that day the LORD will punish the *host of heaven* in heaven, and on earth the *kings of the earth*" (24:21; cf. 24:4). The target is indeed the mythological chaotic force in the ancient Near East: "he will swallow up death forever" (25:8).

Furthermore, in the unit of the woe-oracles (chs. 28–33), we find the motif of the downfall of the unrighteous leaders of Jerusalem over against the poor and needy. Initially, Ephraim's pride is announced to fall and be trampled:

> [Woe to] the proud garland of the drunkards of Ephraim, and the fading flower of its glorious beauty, which is on the *head* of those bloated with rich food, of those overcome with wine! See, the Lord has one who is mighty and strong. . . . with his hand he will *hurl* them *down* to the earth. *Trampled under foot* will be the proud garland of the drunkards of Ephraim. (28:1-3)

Likewise, Ariel, another name of Jerusalem, would meet the same fate of abject humiliation:

> And like David I will encamp against you; I will besiege you with towers and *raise* siegeworks against you. Then *deep* (literally, "low") from the earth you shall speak, *from low in the dust* your words shall come; your voice shall come from the ground like the voice of a ghost, and your speech shall whisper out of the dust. (29:3-4; cf. 30:13-14)

Jerusalem's leaders, who only rely on Egypt, are chided by YHWH in whom they should put their trust: "Alas for those who *go down* to Egypt for help and who rely on horses. . . . When the LORD stretches out his hand, the helper will *stumble*, and the one helped will *fall*" (31:1-3). Ultimately, however, YHWH's eventual restoration of this city with steadfast love makes an equally resounding sound: "For the LORD will *rise up*" (28:21; cf. 29:5-8; 30:25; 31:4, 8). Thus, in a sharp contrast, YHWH reaffirms the divine protection of the poor and needy, recapitulating the central theme in the first section (chs. 1–12):

25. Wildberger, *Isaiah 13–27*, p. 548: "מרום (heights) was used earlier (24:4, 18, 21) as an alternate way to refer to the heavens; here it simply describes a city that was established on high ground, though 'heights' serves at the same time as a symbolic expression to describe the pride of its inhabitants."

> The *meek* shall obtain fresh joy in the LORD, and the *neediest* people shall exult in the Holy One of Israel. For the tyrant shall be no more, and the scoffer shall cease to be; all those alert to do evil shall be cut off. (29:19-20; cf. 25:4-5; 26:5-6; 32:7)

This theme of the divine uplifting of the downtrodden is to be further implemented by the spirit of God as the agent of the cosmic transformation: "Until a spirit from on *high* is poured out on us, and the wilderness becomes a fruitful field, and the fruitful field is deemed a forest. . . . My people will abide in a peaceful habitation, in secure dwellings, and in quiet resting places. The forest will disappear completely, and the city will be utterly *laid low*" (32:15, 18-19).[26] Eventually, these motifs of highs and lows again point to YHWH who alone will be exalted above any treacherous destroyers and nations: "The LORD is *exalted* (נשׂגב), he dwells on *high;* he filled Zion with justice and righteousness" (33:5; cf. 2:11, 17). At the dawn of the triumphant theophany, YHWH claims to be glorified again: "'Now I will *arise,*' says the LORD, 'now I will *lift* myself *up* (ארומם); now I will be *exalted* (אנשׂא)'" (33:10).

In consequence, the prophet warns the people not to be swayed by the "sinners" and "godless" (33:14; cf. 33:12) but instead be cautious to hold onto the divine moral order of justice and righteousness:

> Those who walk righteously and speak uprightly, who despise the gain of oppression, who wave away a bribe instead of accepting it, who stop their ears from hearing of bloodshed and shut their eyes from looking on evil, they will live on the *heights;* their refuge will be the fortresses of rocks; their food will be supplied, their water assured. (33:15-16)

Therefore, it is in acknowledging YHWH as the truly exalted One, and not succumbing to the false and lofty forces in the world, that the oppressed people can rediscover their hope and honor: "For the LORD is our judge, the LORD is our ruler, the LORD is our king; he will save us" (33:22). Similarly, and continuously, the contrary depictions of the haughty and the humble are most vividly portrayed in the diptych in chs. 34–35, where the dismal demise of the oppressors, exemplified in the fate of Edom, is contrasted with the dawn of a new era for Zion.[27]

26. Blenkinsopp, *Isaiah 1–39*, p. 434.

27. Bo H. Lim, *The "Way of the LORD" in the Book of Isaiah* (LHB/OTS 522; New York: T&T Clark, 2010), pp. 131-57.

4. Isaiah 36–39

This section is an isolated and odd portion within the book of Isaiah, which obviously has caused much debate, particularly with its compositional relationship with 2 Kgs 18–20.[28] Yet, whatever the redactional rationales, most scholars agree that this section is placed deliberately for its literary and thematic functions. Indeed, just like a magnetic marble that connects two larger metal balls, chs. 36–39 function not merely as a hinge that joins the two preceding and following parts but rather as the center of the entire book of Isaiah with significant messages and implications.[29]

Such central messages include the contrast between Ahaz the faithless king and Hezekiah the faithful king (though this generalized dichotomous depiction is not without a theological problem),[30] as well as the overall contrast between the human imperial kings and the divine universal King YHWH. Ultimately, this bridge, or core, section functions to convey the messages of trust in YHWH the true living God to the people in socially, politically, and religiously dire situations.[31]

28. Peter R. Ackroyd, *Studies in the Religious Tradition of the Old Testament* (London: SCM, 1987), pp. 105-20; Christopher R. Seitz, *Zion's Final Destiny: The Development of the Book of Isaiah* (Minneapolis: Fortress, 1991); Edgar W. Conrad, *Reading Isaiah* (Minneapolis: Fortress, 1991), pp. 49-51; K. A. D. Smelik, "King Hezekiah Advocates True Prophecy: Remarks on Isaiah xxxvi and xxxvii/II Kings xviii and xiv," *OTS* 28 (1992): 93-128; Williamson, *The Book Called Isaiah*, pp. 189-211; Brevard S. Childs, *Isaiah* (OTL; Louisville: Westminster John Knox, 2001), pp. 260-66.

29. Ulrich F. Berges, *The Book of Isaiah: Its Composition and Final Form* (trans. Millard C. Lind; Sheffield: Sheffield Phoenix Press, 2012 [German edition, 1998]), pp. 245-99; idem, *Isaiah: The Prophet and His Book* (Sheffield: Sheffield Phoenix Press, 2012), pp. 24 and 42-47; Hyun Chul Paul Kim, "The Spider-Poet: Signs and Symbols in Isaiah 41," in *The Desert Will Bloom: Poetic Visions in Isaiah* (ed. A. Joseph Everson and Hyun Chul Paul Kim; Atlanta: Society of Biblical Literature, 2009), pp. 159-80.

30. Marvin A. Sweeney, *Reading the Hebrew Bible after the Shoah: Engaging Holocaust Theology* (Minneapolis: Fortress, 2008), pp. 84-103.

31. Blenkinsopp, *Isaiah 1–39*, p. 459: "The theme of trust in God and his instructions communicated through the prophet recurs throughout the book and also, with different emphases, in the Rabshakeh's harangue (different forms of the verbal stem [בטח], 'trust,' occur nine times in the two speeches)." Consider also W. A. M. Beuken, *Isaiah II: Chapters 28–39* (Leuven: Peeters, 2000), p. 340: "The motif-word which opens chs. 36–37 and connects them with chs. 28–32, is 'to trust' (בטח). . . . We already noted that, besides 'to trust' the topic 'to deliver' (נצל *hiphil*) and 'to save' (ישׁע *hiphil*) also govern the narrative"; John N. Oswalt, *The Book of Isaiah: Chapters 1–39* (NICOT; Grand Rapids: Eerdmans, 1986), p. 57: "A more detailed analysis of chs. 7–39 shows a recurrence of the theme of trust." We should further note that the name Hezekiah, which connotes "to strengthen (one's faith)" (חזק), occurs in a condensed way within this section.

Strikingly and fascinatingly, this section insinuates these conceptual contrasts by way of subtle puns and figurative portrayals of the fallings of the pompous and the risings of the penitent. Thus, in the face of the national crisis, Hezekiah beseeches the prophet Isaiah to "*lift up* your prayer for the remnant that is left" (37:4). Assuredly, Isaiah delivers the divine answer, "I will cause him to *fall* by the sword in his own land" (37:7). Likewise, in the second perilous context, Hezekiah "*went up* to the house of the Lord" (37:14; cf. 2:3; 38:22; 2 Chr 36:23) and offered his earnest prayer to YHWH. Here the divine assurance to Hezekiah and his people resonates with the scorn and taunt against the futile pride of Sennacherib king of Assyria:

> Whom have you mocked and reviled? Against whom have you *raised* (הרימות) your voice and haughtily *lifted* (ותשׂא) your eyes? Against the Holy One of Israel! By your servants you have mocked the Lord, and you have said, "With my many chariots I have *gone up* the *heights of the mountains,* to the far recesses of Lebanon; I felled its tallest cedars, its choicest cypresses; I came to its *remotest height,* its densest forest. I dug wells and drank waters, I dried up with the *sole of my foot* all the streams of Egypt." (37:23-25; cf. 10:12-14; 14:12-15)

In depicting this Assyrian king's flaunting jabber, the usage of the phrase "raising" (רום) the voice and "lifting" (נשׂא) the eyes is unique and noteworthy. This combination of words, though idiomatic, occurs in pivotal places in the book of Isaiah (2:12-15; 6:1; 52:13; 57:15; cf. 30:25; 33:10), referring to YHWH the divine King as well as the humiliated but soon-to-be-exalted servant of YHWH. If these literary expressions are deliberate, the effect is stunning.[32] Sennacherib's boast has reached its highest point,[33] except that his haughtiness was aimed at none other than the "Holy One of Israel" (37:23), who will unfailingly defeat and mortify this pompous ruler. In fact, God rebukes Sennacherib as if taming and controlling Leviathan in the YHWH speech from the book of Job:

32. Arguing for the literary dependence of the following references on 6:1, H. G. M. Williamson (*The Book Called Isaiah,* pp. 38-41) judiciously delineates the unique occurrences of this phrase (רום + נשׂא): "This particular combination of words occurs only twice in the Old Testament outside the book of Isaiah [Prov. 30:13; Dan. 11:12]. . . . Occurrences of the phrase elsewhere in the book of Isaiah are thus likely to be of significance for our purpose" (p. 39).

33. Beuken, *Isaiah II: Chapters 28–39,* p. 366: "Sennacherib's boasting, however, exhibits one single binding theme. The speaker has literally exceeded everything considered 'high': he has penetrated to the highest places of the highest mountains and has cut down the highest trees (cf. 14:8)."

> I know your *rising up* and your *sitting down,* your going out and coming in, and your raging against me. Because you have raged against me and your arrogance has come to my ears,[34] I will put *my hook* in your nose and *my bit* in your mouth; I will turn you back on the way by which you came. (37:28-29; cf. Job 41:1-2)

To the contrary, God promises to the trusting remnants that "the surviving remnant of the house of Judah shall again take root *downward,* and bear fruit *upward*" (37:31). Therefore, this core section conjoins the preceding and following parts of the book of Isaiah, with the literary correlations that mock the seemingly formidable imperial rulers while accentuating the incomparability of YHWH. These thematic contrasts flow in the continuity of the overall message throughout the book of Isaiah, with the theme of the divine salvation hinted in the very name of this prophet (ישעיהו): "So now, O LORD our God, save (ישע) us from his hand, so that all the kingdoms of the earth may know that you alone are the LORD" (37:20; cf. 1:3; 2:3; 19:21; 41:20; 45:6; 49:26).

5. *Isaiah 40–48*

In the second half of the book of Isaiah, readers find both continuity of vocabulary and motif, as well as a shift or expansion (*Fortschreibung* or *relecture*) of such conceptuality in a new way. In the first section (chs. 40–48),[35] we learn not only of the dominant messages of the divine consolation but also of the concentrated reference about the servant of YHWH. First of all, even though

34. Beuken, *Isaiah II: Chapters 28–39,* p. 368: "In the clause: 'Your arrogance has gone up to my ears', which suggests *distance* between YHWH and Sennacherib, one can read a correction of the king's boastful words in [37:24]" (emphasis added).

35. Following the doxology patterns of the five books of the Psalms, I propose to divide Isaiah 40–66 into three sections. The attention to the threefold endings goes back at least to 1831, quoted by James Muilenburg in his seminal commentary: "The German poet Friedrich Rückert, in his work on the Hebrew prophets, articulated the poems of Isa. 40–66 into three divisions of nine chapters each, and he called attention to the similarity of the rubrics which mark each section (48:22; 57:21; 66:24)" ("The Book of Isaiah: Chapters 40–66," p. 384). Recently, Shalom M. Paul proposed a single authorship of Isaiah 40–66, which he divides into two parts: chapters 40–48 and chapters 49–66 (*Isaiah 40–66* [Grand Rapids: Eerdmans, 2012]), p. 11: "If one draws a line between two sections of [chapters 40–66], the line should be drawn between the prophecies delivered in Babylonia (chaps. 40–48) and those delivered in Jerusalem (chaps. 49–66). One should not speak of two different personalities, but of a change in locus following the prophet's return to Israel." My proposal then is to subdivide chapters 49–66 into two: i.e., chapters 49–57 and chapters 58–66.

the rhetorical contrasts or reversals between the haughty and the lowly do not occur as explicitly as in the previous sections, the opening chapters do contain the comparable metaphors of the highs and lows: "Every valley shall be *lifted up,* and every mountain and hill be *made low;* the uneven ground shall become level, and the rough places a plain" (40:4). This metaphor does not appear to have any direct designations about rulers or leaders per se; yet it expressly serves the function of continuing the theme of the divine intention and capability in working miracles of subversion in the world.[36]

Accordingly, Zion is admonished to be a messenger amid exilic despair, proclaiming: "Get you up to a *high* mountain, O Zion, herald of good tidings; *lift up* your voice with strength, O Jerusalem, herald of good tidings, *lift it up,* do not fear; say to the cities of Judah, 'Here is your God!'" (40:9; cf. 52:7). As a polemic against the Babylonian claim that "Marduk is king!" in *Enuma Elish,* the prophet affirms YHWH as the universal King.[37] Thus, the would-be rulers are ridiculed for their frailty in a sharp contrast with YHWH who gives real strength, "who brings *princes* to naught, and makes the *rulers* of the earth as nothing" (40:23); "Even youths will faint and be weary, and the young will fall exhausted; but those who wait for the LORD shall renew their strength, they shall *mount up* with wings like eagles, they shall run and not be weary, they shall walk and not faint" (40:30-31).

Moreover, the theme of rhetorical accusation against the imperial oppressors in contrast with the poor and needy (41:17) is effectively dramatized. In the derisive scenes against the false deities of Babylon, the similar language of their mortification recurs:

> Bel *bows down,* Nebo *stoops,* their idols are on beasts and cattle; these things you carry are loaded as burdens on weary animals. They *stoop,* they *bow down* together; they cannot save the burden, but themselves go into captivity. (46:1-2; cf. 1 Sam 5:1-5)

It is intriguing that the word משׂא ("burden") occurs only in this text in Isaiah, except in chs. 13–23 (cf. 30:6). In the OAN, the key target is Babylon, which frames the inner sections by chapters 13–14 and 21. Interestingly, this word

36. Muilenburg, "The Book of Isaiah: Chapters 40–66," p. 426: "Valleys and hills, uneven and rough places, represent difficulties — political, physical, psychological — which are filling their minds with forebodings. These will disappear as their wonder-working God marches to them and with them."

37. Joseph Blenkinsopp, *Isaiah 40–55* (AB 19A; New York: Doubleday, 2002), pp. 106-8 (note also pp. 342-43).

recurs here in the oracles of the similar motif against Babylon. In this case, it seems possible that the word משא might have a double meaning. On the one hand, it does mean "burdens" which are heavy idols that make the false deities stoop and bow down.[38] On the other hand, it can echo the "oracles" which had already been announced against Babylon (chs. 13–14; 21), now reaffirmed equally loudly, if not more.

Furthermore, readers may hear a pun in the verbs of bowing down (כרע) and stooping (קרס). Especially, the verb to "stoop" (קרס) sounds strikingly similar to the name "Cyrus" (כורש; cf. Judg 12:6). This pun seems a deliberate derision of Babylon's fall by Cyrus, YHWH's anointed ruler (45:1).[39] The effect is that now the audiences are reminded of the mighty acts of YHWH which were announced previously in the OAN: this divine king will lower the arrogant Babylon and lift up the downtrodden Jacob/Israel. Such a theme of dramatic reversal culminates in the utter humiliation of daughter Babylon: "*Come down* and *sit* in the dust, virgin daughter Babylon! *Sit* on the ground without a throne, daughter Chaldea! For you shall no more be called tender and delicate" (47:1).[40]

Here we should note that God's exalted status and incomparable might are further accentuated by the instrumentality of the superpower rulers. For example, just as YHWH was "exalting" a stronger nation against the arrogant Ephraim (9:10 [Eng 9:11]) and "stirring up" the Medes against the haughty Babylon (13:17), so this time another ruler from the north is "stirred up" to fulfill the divine salvific plan (41:25; cf. 41:2). Such instrumentality depicts, on the one hand, those imperial rulers in a positive note. Unlike the Babylonian king, who is hardly depicted favorably in the book of Isaiah (but cf. Jer 25:9; 27:6), Cyrus the Persian king is not only "aroused" by YHWH (Isa 45:13) but

38. Blenkinsopp, *Isaiah 40–55,* p. 75: "There is . . . a deliberate contrast between the Babylonian gods who have to be transported on animals and [YHWH] who carries Israel (46:1-4)."

39. Note the chiasm within 46:1-2: "Verse 2 increases the picture of helplessness by a skillful literary use of chiasm between the verbs of 'bow down' and 'cower,' which highlights the shame" (Childs, *Isaiah,* p. 359). Also, in a roughly chiastic pattern of chs. 40–55, Cyrus stands at the central place (Blenkinsopp, *Isaiah 40–55,* p. 92).

40. Chris Franke, "Reversals of Fortune in the Ancient Near East: A Study of the Babylon Oracles in the Book of Isaiah," in *New Visions of Isaiah* (ed. R. F. Melugin and M. A. Sweeney; JSOTSup 214; Sheffield: Sheffield Academic Press, 1996), pp. 119-20: "Chapter 47 is the key to the reversal of fortune of Daughter Zion. It functions as a pivot for Second Isaiah in that it is the point in the book where Judah/Israel changes places with the oppressor, Babylon. . . . Everything that Judah once was, Babylon becomes; all that Babylon thought she was is given to Zion."

also called YHWH's "shepherd" (44:28) and "anointed," i.e., messiah (45:1). Cyrus the liberator of the exilic Judeans clearly assumes an honorable role. On the other hand, however, these notions ultimately intensify YHWH's unrivaled power over against any imperial ruler or deity. It is God who whistles (5:26; 7:18), uplifts, and wields those rulers as mere tools. No matter how glorious or menacing they may appear, the prophet asserts that the foreign conquerors are tools at best, e.g., "rod," "staff" (10:5), and "shepherd" (44:28). They are to carry out the commissioned tasks. The Assyrian king is thus sternly reminded of his mere instrumentality: "as if a rod should raise the one who *lifts* it *up*, or as if a staff should *lift* the one who is not wood" (10:15). Likewise, the Persian king Cyrus is repeatedly depicted in his ignorance: "though you do not know me" (45:4, 5; cf. 44:25). In the Psalter, the notion of not knowing God is often an expression tantamount to being foolish (e.g., Pss 14:1, 4; 53:1, 5; 73:11; 79:6; 82:5; cf. Isa 6:9; 44:19; 45:20). By reminding of Cyrus's ignorance, and by replacing Marduk with YHWH vis-à-vis the Cyrus Cylinder (45:1-3), the prophet ingeniously achieves a double purpose of both supplanting the foreign deity, plus rulers, and uplifting YHWH alone.[41]

Additionally, the theme of contrast is recapitulated by the rhetorical jeers at the idol-fabricators and also by the introduction of the new concept of Jacob/Israel as the "servant" (עבד) of YHWH. In chapters 40–48, the anti-idol passages occur quite frequently, filled with rhetorical taunt and accusation.[42] Both the idols and the idol-makers are declared meaningless and powerless:

> All who make idols are *nothing*, and the things they delight in do not profit; their witnesses neither see nor know. And so they will be put to shame. (44:9)

41. R. N. Whybray, *Isaiah 40–66* (NCB; Grand Rapids: Eerdmans, 1975), p. 106: "[Cyrus] is merely [YHWH's] instrument in carrying out a task whose real purpose is the liberation of Israel and the universal honouring of God's name." Note also Antti Laato, *The Servant of YHWH and Cyrus: A Reinterpretation of the Exilic Messianic Programme in Isaiah 40–55* (Stockholm: Almqvist & Wiksell, 1992), pp. 47-68 and 177-87. For the Cyrus Cylinder, see Amélie Kuhrt, *The Persian Empire* (London: Routledge, 2007), pp. 49 and 70-74.

42. Also, from the similar phrases of anti-Babylonian polemic (e.g., "Fear not . . . I am your God" in 41:10), Claus Westermann trenchantly remarks: "Deutero-Isaiah therefore adopted the form deliberately for purposes of polemic. By putting self-glorification into the mouth of the God who alone is God, he reduces the self-glorification found in the Babylonian pantheon to absurdity" (*Isaiah 40–66* [trans. David M. G. Stalker; OTL; London: SCM, 1969], pp. 72-73). See also Knut Holter, *Second Isaiah's Idol-Fabrication Passages* (Frankfurt am Main: Peter Lang, 1995).

> Those who lavish gold from the purse, and weigh out silver in the scales — they hire a goldsmith, who makes it into a god; then they *fall down* and worship! (46:6)

In contrast, the people of Israel are identified as YHWH's servant, to whom YHWH vows enduring loyalty: "Because you are precious in my sight, and honored, and I love you" (43:4; cf. 43:1). Here, with the issue of ambiguity and multiplicity of the identity of the servant aside,[43] it is still interesting that Israel, God's chosen people, is called "servant" of YHWH. This word might denote the role of the loyal delegates, as servants of the Israelite kings or deity.[44] However, etymologically, the word can also mean "slave" (note "the *slave* [עבד] of rulers" in 49:7). It is no wonder that Jacob/Israel is called "worm" and "insect": "Do not fear, you *worm* Jacob, you *insect* Israel! I will help you, says the LORD; your Redeemer is the Holy One of Israel" (41:14; cf. 14:11; 66:24).[45] In this section, where the motif of the second Exodus rings loudly, readers might hear the divine command to Pharaoh through Moses: "Say to him, The LORD, the God of the Hebrews, sent me to you to say, 'Let my people go, so that they may worship [literally, *"serve"*] me in the wilderness'" (Exod 7:16; cf. Exod 1:13-14). This motif is relevant to our theme of the highs and lows in that the idols and idol-fabricators are sternly warned of their impending utter shame, while the imprisoned, worm-like Israel is now exhorted to fulfill the grand mission as YHWH's servant — no longer the servile subject of Babylon but the delightful agent of the divine King:

> Here is my servant, whom I *uphold,* my chosen, in whom my soul delights; I have put my spirit upon him; he will bring forth justice to the nations. He will *not* cry or *lift up* his voice, or make it heard in the street. . . . It is too

43. Hyun Chul Paul Kim, *Ambiguity, Tension, and Multiplicity in Deutero-Isaiah* (New York: Peter Lang, 2003), pp. 73-88.

44. For the Deuteronomic significance of the meaning of the "servant," see Blenkinsopp, *Isaiah 40–55,* p. 200. Note also Westermann, *Isaiah 40–66,* pp. 69-70: "The Hebrew word for 'servant' *('ebed)* expresses something like a balance between the idea of belonging to someone who protects and gives security and that of standing under someone, being subordinate to him"; Muilenburg, "The Book of Isaiah: Chapters 40–66," p. 464.

45. Walter Brueggemann, *Isaiah 40–66* (Louisville: Westminster John Knox, 1998), pp. 34-35: "Perhaps these derogatory terms reflect Israel's expressed self-evaluation as unimportant and hopeless (see Psalm 22:6 [MT 22:7]). If this is correct, then the salvation oracle takes Israel as it is and as it perceives itself — lowly, ignoble, without hope. All of that, however, is immediately countered by the speech and promised intervention of [YHWH]." Consider also Klaus Baltzer, *Deutero-Isaiah* (trans. Margaret Kohl; Hermeneia; Minneapolis: Fortress, 2001), p. 103: "It is the most extreme contrast possible when [YHWH], 'the Holy One of Israel,' addresses this 'worm Jacob' and promises him his help."

light a thing that you should be my servant to *raise up* the tribes of Jacob and to restore the survivors of Israel; I will give you as a light to the nations. (Isa 42:1-2; 49:6; cf. 32:15)

6. Isaiah 49–57

As a counterpart to the servant Jacob/Israel in chapters 40–48, we now find daughter Zion taking an equally central role in this section (chs. 49–57).[46] As if Jacob (the northern Israel) and Zion (the capital of the southern Judah) form a unified whole, the laments of both characters occur in parallel modes and motifs in the transitional chapter 49:

> But I [Israel] said, "I have labored in vain, I have spent my strength for nothing and vanity; yet surely my cause is with the LORD, and my reward with my God." . . .
>
> But Zion said, "The LORD has forsaken me, my Lord has forgotten me." (49:4, 14)

Against these dual complaints, YHWH assures the restoration of Israel's glory and honor: "Kings shall see and stand up [literally, '*rise up*'], princes, and they shall prostrate [literally, '*bow down*'] themselves, because of the LORD, who is faithful, the Holy One of Israel, who has chosen you" (49:7). Likewise, Zion's complaint is refuted by the divine reassertion of her offspring who will return home gloriously from all corners of the earth:

> Thus says the Lord GOD: I will soon *lift up* my hand to the nations, and *raise* my signal to the peoples; and they shall bring your sons in their bosom, and your daughters shall be carried on their shoulders. Kings shall be your foster fathers, and their queens your nursing mothers. With their faces to the ground they shall *bow down* to you, and lick the dust of your *feet*. Then you will know that I am the LORD; those who wait for me shall not be put to shame. (49:22-23; cf. 26:5-6)

Furthermore, in the subsequent passages, both the servant and Zion are distinctly assured of their vindication and exaltation. What is intriguing in

46. Blenkinsopp, *Isaiah 40–55*, p. 114: "In the first section [chs. 40–48], Jacob/Israel is center-stage. . . . In the second section (49–55), the name *Jacob* occurs only once. . . . In chs. 49–55, therefore, Zion enters the stage as a participant in the dialogue" (note also p. 80).

both accounts is the language and motif which echo the theme of highs and lows. For example, in the case of the servant, despite humiliation and defeat, this servant, "the righteous one" (53:11), is depicted ultimately to be vindicated: "See, my servant shall prosper; he shall be *exalted* and *lifted up*, and shall be *very high*" (52:13). Significantly, this phrase (ירום ונשא) may echo the same occurrence in 6:1, where YHWH was depicted as "high and lofty" (רם ונשא) on the throne of the temple. Also, in the case of Zion, though the exact phrases may not be found, its thematic allusion is noticeable:

> Sing, O barren one who did not bear; burst into song and shout, you who have not been in labor! For the children of the desolate woman will be *more* than the children of her that is married, says the LORD. (54:1; cf. 54:14-15, 17)[47]

In the anxious anticipation of the triumphant homecoming, this section then introduces another new concept as to who those descendants of the servant Jacob (53:10) and daughter Zion (54:1, 3) shall be. This new concept in a way extends or redefines the dichotomy of highs and lows: this new concept signifies (a) the insiders versus the outsiders, as well as (b) the wicked versus the righteous.

In the first half of the book of Isaiah, we have noted how God intends extra care for the poor and needy, i.e., the lows over against the highs. This theme recurs in the invitation to the whole community — especially the poor and needy: "Ho, everyone who thirsts, come to the waters; and you that have *no money*, come, buy and eat! Come, buy wine and milk *without money* and *without price*" (55:1). This invitation is intertwined with a condemnation to the wicked, who are yet given a chance to repent and return, albeit with a warning: "Let the *wicked* forsake their way, and the *unrighteous* their thoughts; let them return to the LORD, that he may have mercy on them, and to our God, for he will abundantly pardon" (55:7; cf. 57:1, 20). Precisely here, we hear the premise of the radical concept in the definition of the identity of YHWH's people, Israel's and Zion's offspring, using the metaphor of highs and lows: "For as the heavens are *higher* than the earth, so are my ways *higher* than your ways and my thoughts than your thoughts" (55:9; cf. 28:21).

47. This invitation to sing echoes subtly but evidently the similar motif in Hannah's song: "My heart exults in the LORD; my strength is exalted in my God. . . . Talk no more so very *proudly*, let not *arrogance* come from your mouth. . . . The barren has borne seven, but she who has many children is forlorn" (1 Sam 2:1, 3, 5).

What then is this radical concept for the identity of a new community? It has direct relationship with justice and righteousness (55:1). And this invitation is radically directed to the outsiders: none other than the foreigners and eunuchs (56:3; cf. Deut 23:1-6). Just like the "preferential option for the poor,"[48] it is to these outsiders that YHWH offers the emphatic promise to bring them in. Note the repeated uses of the preposition "in" in the divine promise to the "out" groups:

> I will give, *in* my house and *within* my walls, a monument and a name better than sons and daughters; I will give them an everlasting name that shall not be cut off. . . . these I will bring to my holy mountain, and make them joyful *in* my house of prayer; their burnt offerings and their sacrifices will be accepted on my altar; for my house shall be called a house of prayer for all peoples. (56:5, 7; cf. 66:18-24)[49]

This divine acceptance of the outsiders creates a sharp contrast with the obdurate and self-righteous attitudes of the wicked and haughty insiders. They are the people of "transgression" and "deceit" (57:3-4): "Upon a *high* and *lofty* mountain you have set your bed, and there you went up to offer sacrifice. . . . for, in deserting me, you have uncovered your bed, you have *gone up* to it, you have made it wide" (57:7-8). This dire situation is portrayed by a reversed echo of Psalm 1, in that instead of the wicked who should perish (Ps 1:6, רשׁעים תאבד), the righteous one perished (57:1, הצדיק אבד). Nevertheless, against these pursuers of vain idols and wickedness, for whom there is no peace (57:21), YHWH reiterates who the truly lofty One is, as well as whom this Holy One desires to accept:

> For thus says the *high* and *lofty* [רם ונשׂא] one who inhabits eternity, whose name is Holy: I dwell in the *high* and holy place, and also with those who are *contrite* and *humble* in spirit, to revive the spirit of the *humble*, and to revive the heart of the *contrite*. (57:15; cf. 6:1)

48. Joseph Blenkinsopp, *Isaiah 56–66* (AB 19B; New York: Doubleday, 2003), p. 223.

49. Westermann, *Isaiah 40–66*, p. 313: "This brought about a fundamental change on the form that the community had had in pre-exilic times, and it required to be made known by changing regulations about its membership"; Blenkinsopp, *Isaiah 56–66*, p. 139: "What this implies is membership in good standing in the Jerusalem cult community ('in my house'), with which civic status — that is, status 'within the walls,' meaning, in the city — was at that time inseparably united."

7. Isaiah 58–66

In this final section, the dichotomy between outsiders and insiders is intricately entwined with the "contrast" between the righteous and the wicked, or to use Blenkinsopp's definitions, between the "Tremblers" (66:2, 5; cf. Ezra 9:4; 10:3) or "Servants" (54:17; 56:6; 63:17; 65:9, 13-15; 66:14) and the reprobate "opponents" from the temple priesthood (50:10-11; 51:7-8; 65:11-12).[50] As cited near the end of the preceding section (57:15; cf. 66:1-2), YHWH the truly exalted One regards the "humble" and "contrite" as the righteous ones. To put this another way, it is not the ritualistic cultus that sets up the standard for righteousness, but rather the social ethos that satisfies divine approval.[51] A case is provided as an illustration in this section on the issue of the fasting that YHWH would accept:

> Look, you fast only to quarrel and to fight and to strike with a *wicked* fist. Such fasting as you do today will not make your voice heard on *high*. (58:4)

> Is it not to share your bread with the *hungry,* and bring the homeless *poor* into your house; when you see the *naked,* to cover them, and not to hide yourself from your own kin? (58:7; cf. 58:10-14)

This subversive ideology, in the sense of "lay exegesis,"[52] is a reaffirmation of the divine intention to reverse the present realities of humiliation and hardship by the glorious, grand homecoming of Zion's new offspring. Here, in particular, echoing the "despoiling of the Egyptians" theme, Zion's fortune is to be exchanged with that of her oppressors, underscoring the glorious rise and eternal radiance of YHWH:[53]

> *Arise,* shine; for your light has come, and the glory of the LORD *has risen* upon you. . . . The descendants of those who oppressed you shall come

50. Blenkinsopp, *Isaiah 56–66,* pp. 51-54, 133, and 150-62.

51. Blenkinsopp, *Isaiah 56–66,* p. 171: "Yet it would be wrong to minimize the force and originality of the prophetic redefinition of religious priorities, according to which ceremony, and even the sacrificial cult, take second place to the option for the poor and oppressed."

52. Michael Fishbane, *Biblical Interpretation in Ancient Israel* (Oxford: Clarendon, 1985), p. 128.

53. Blenkinsopp, *Isaiah 56–66,* p. 226.

> *bending low* to you, and all who despised you shall *bow down* at your feet; they shall call you the City of the LORD, the Zion of the Holy One of Israel." (60:1, 14; cf. 60:4-7, 10-11, 19-20)

This radical topsy-turvy perspective provides a model of the divine purpose for the lowly, downtrodden, and oppressed ones: "The spirit of the Lord GOD is upon me, because the LORD has anointed me; he has sent me to bring good news to the *oppressed,* to bind up the *brokenhearted,* to proclaim liberty to the *captives,* and release to the *prisoners*" (61:1). YHWH declares once again that heaven and earth, i.e., the entire universe, are under the divine control and governance of justice and righteousness: "Thus says the LORD: Heaven is my *throne* and the earth is my *footstool;* what is the house that you would build for me, and what is my resting place?" (66:1; cf. 60:13; 66:22).[54] To this divine, righteous YHWH, what is deemed righteous is neither haughtiness nor in-group privilege, but rather being the "humble and contrite" and those who are committed to care for the poor and the outgroups: "All these things my hand has made, and so all these things are mine, says the LORD. But this is the one to whom I will look, to the *humble* and *contrite* in spirit, who trembles at my word" (66:2).

Conclusion

In light of the examination above, what contributions and implications can we find in reading and interpreting the book of Isaiah? A few resultant observations may be iterated. First, this reading strategy of tracing the key themes throughout the book of Isaiah as a unified whole can enable a better understanding and appreciation of the overall messages of the entire book on the synchronic level. Admittedly, the scroll of Isaiah is so bulky that reading it holistically and sequentially cannot be the only reading strategy. Nevertheless, with the recent contribution of Isaiah scholarship toward the unity approach and also with respect to the importance of the final form of the entire text, it is worthwhile to read it by tracing the pertinent and recurrent themes. In doing so, we the "little" readers might discover some "great" insights.

Second, admittedly, even if this theme of exalting of the humble/lows and

54. Blenkinsopp, *Isaiah 56–66,* p. 215: "Where the Solomonic temple is referred to, YHVH's footstool is the ark originally located in Shiloh and then transferred to Jerusalem (Ps 132:7; 1 Chr 28:2). With the destruction of the first temple . . . God's residence is relocated in the heavens and the temple becomes his footstool (66:1; Ezek 43:7)."

crushing the haughty/highs is a keythread, this is not the only major theme in the book of Isaiah. Scholars have astutely discovered other key themes, such as the Holy One of Israel,[55] light versus darkness,[56] seeing/hearing/understanding,[57] justice and righteousness,[58] and so on. What is fascinating and humbling is that the book of Isaiah consists of such complexity amid continuity. It is replete with key themes that are correlated and intertwined in multifaceted fashions, like a tapestry of numerous threads. Such multifaceted complexity can cause readers to consider the various compositional layers and developments in diachronic investigation. Or it may invite readers to analyze how each theme functions uniquely in various sections, how those themes interrelate with one another, and how they may interact, overlap, or even counter with others. Eventually, attention to these interrelations should coincide with the intertextual correlations in the rest of the Hebrew Bible.

Third, retrieving and tracing these key themes can help illuminate the possible cultural, social, and religious backgrounds of the texts. For example, although in some sections the theme of highs and lows occurs more explicitly than in other sections, it is interesting that this dichotomy occurs rather consistently and, significantly, throughout the entire book of Isaiah. This perspective of two polar opposites may have been influenced by the Zoroastrian worldview of the Persian empire.[59] If so, Isaiah's intention may be both a rhe-

55. J. J. M. Roberts, "Isaiah in Old Testament Theology," *Int* 36 (1982): 130-43; Baltzer, *Deutero-Isaiah*, pp. 33-44.

56. Ronald E. Clements, "A Light to the Nations: A Central Theme of the Book of Isaiah," in *Forming Prophetic Literature: Essays on Isaiah and the Twelve in Honor of John D. W. Watts* (ed. J. W. Watts and P. R. House; JSOTSup, 235; Sheffield: Sheffield Academic Press, 1996), pp. 57-69; Ronald E. Clements, "'Arise, Shine; For Your Light Has Come': A Basic Theme of the Isaianic Tradition," in *Writing and Reading the Scroll of Isaiah: Studies of an Interpretive Tradition* (ed. C. C. Broyles and C. A. Evans; vol. 1; Leiden: Brill, 1997), pp. 441-54.

57. Robert P. Carroll, "Blindsight and the Vision Thing: Blindness and Insight in the Book of Isaiah," in *Writing and Reading the Scroll of Isaiah: Studies of an Interpretive Tradition* (vol. 1; ed. Craig C. Broyles and Craig A. Evans; Leiden: Brill, 1997), pp. 79-93.

58. Thomas L. Leclerc, *Yahweh is Exalted in Justice: Solidarity and Conflict in Isaiah* (Minneapolis: Fortress, 2001); H. G. M. Williamson, *Variations on a Theme: King, Messiah and Servant in the Book of Isaiah* (Carlisle: Paternoster, 1998).

59. Wildberger, *Isaiah 13–27*, p. 507: "Even Gesenius suggested that this [24:21] could have been an assimilation of ideas that originated in Zoroastrianism." Note also James Barr, "The Question of Religious Influence: The Case of Zoroastrianism, Judaism and Christianity," *JAAR* 53 (1985): 201; Brent A. Strawn, "'A World under Control': Isaiah 60 and the Apadana Reliefs from Persepolis," in *Approaching Yehud: New Approaches to the Study of the Persian Period* (ed. Jon L. Berquist; Leiden: Brill, 2008), pp. 85-116; Joseph Blenkinsopp, "The Cosmological and Protological Language of Deutero-Isaiah," *CBQ* 73 (2011): 493-510.

torical importation of such popular cultural conventions and a theological reaction to the dualistic religiosity. On the one hand, Isaiah's rhetorical use of the binary opposites may demonstrate the subversive perspectives of the people struggling with their survival and identity amid exilic and postexilic hardships under the dominant empires.[60] Wildberger insightfully observes the wisdom influence on the opposites between the righteous and the wicked (e.g., Prov 8:22-31; 15:25; 16:18; 29:23).[61] Just as the book of Psalms starts with the clear dichotomy between the righteous and the wicked as a reality (Ps 1), so the second half of the book of Isaiah concludes each section with similar phrases, reinforcing the stern warning that the wicked are still everywhere, that they will not find true peace, and that the righteous will be vindicated by the faithful God some day:

> "There is no peace," says the LORD, "for the wicked." (48:22)
>
> "There is no peace," says my God, "for the wicked." (57:21)
>
> And they shall go out and look at the dead bodies of the people who have rebelled against me; for their worm shall not die, their fire shall not be quenched, and they shall be an abhorrence to all flesh. (66:24)[62]

On the other hand, over against the realities of the unequivocally dualistic world, Isaiah casts a theological counterclaim that there is only one God, who is the sole creator of all things in this universe and who will ultimately bring about righteousness over corruption, justice over oppression, and peace over war:

> The grass withers, the flower fades, when the breath of the LORD blows upon it; surely the people are grass. The grass withers, the flower *fades* (literally, "sinks," נבל); but the word of our God will *stand* (יקום) forever. (40:7-8)

60. Wildberger, *Isaiah 1–12,* p. 477: "When brutality is present, it pairs up with haughtiness, the hubris which brings such disastrous consequences, which Isaiah never grows tired of depicting."

61. Wildberger, *Isaiah 13–27,* pp. 75-76.

62. Muilenburg, "The Book of Isaiah: Chapters 40–66," p. 773: "Christian readers of the book of Isaiah wish that v. 23, rather than v. 24, had been its conclusion. But the parables of our Lord contemplate a similar ultimate separation: . . . the Judge dividing sheep from goats, with his 'Come ye' and his 'Depart ye.' . . . The book of Isaiah ends by facing its readers with this momentous and inevitable choice."

Kingship and Servanthood in the Book of Isaiah

Ulrich Berges

I. Introduction

Over the past few decades there have not been many exegetes who have worked as intensively on the book of Isaiah as the one we are celebrating. His Isaiah commentaries, which comprehend the entire book,[1] are a benchmark and reference point for all further attempts to grapple with the composition and intentions of this complex prophetic scroll. In this celebratory volume I would like to answer a question that has often been raised but which, in my opinion, has never been fully grasped in all its significance and profundity: What is the relationship between the motifs of "king/kingship" and "servant/servants" in the final form of the book of Isaiah? Do they have a genuine connection with each other or do they come from different contexts?

The connection between "king" and "servant" has been on the agenda of Isaiah research at least since Otto Kaiser's post-doctoral research, completed in 1957 in Tübingen and published in 1959. The sub-title indicates the perspective within which the answer is sought: "*The Royal Servant:* A Tradition-Historical Exegetical Study of the Ebed-Yahweh-Songs in Deutero-Isaiah." For Kaiser, the way in which the themes of "king" and "servant" come together is that the servant is in possession of royal characteristics.[2] He argues that the

1. Joseph Blenkinsopp, *Isaiah 1–39; Isaiah 40–55; Isaiah 56–66,* Anchor Bible 19; 19A; 19B (New York: Doubleday, 2000/ 2002/ 2003).

2. The honorific title "servant" is applied, inter alios, to Abraham, Isaac, Isaiah — the prophet modelled on Moses, but also Zerubbabel, even Nebuchadnezzar (Jer 25:9; 27:6). Interestingly, the designation "servant" is never used for priests!

servant in the so-called Ebed-Yahweh Songs is a collective identity, namely the people of Israel. In other words, the people who had been exiled to Babylon are being presented as a *royal* servant. Regarding the controversial Isa 49:6a ("It is too little that you should be my servant in order to raise up the tribes of Jacob and to bring back the preserved of Israel"), Kaiser has the following to say: "In my analysis of the first song I indicated that Israel itself had taken over the role of the monarchy and that the entire book did not contain a proper expectation of the renewal of the monarchy. If we bear this insight in mind, it is clear that our prophet is referring back to the ideal of the pre-monarchial period in order to give expression to his hope for the restoration of the ancient sacral amphictyony."[3] Although Otto Kaiser does not specifically treat the relationship between the expectation of a king in Proto-Isaiah and the Servant Songs in Deutero-Isaiah, it appears that he assumes that the servant texts are a continuation of the royal expectations, albeit in a different context.[4] But is it really the case that in Deutero-Isaiah "Israel itself takes over the role of the monarchy"?

Kaiser sticks to his collective interpretation in his analysis of the fourth Servant Song (Isa 52:13–53:12): "Israel is the guilt-offering for the unwitting sins committed by the multitudes who do not know the living God and his will. . . . The ancient promise to the patriarchs that all the nations would be blessed through the seed of Abraham is thereby fulfilled. Salvation history has arrived at its destination."[5] In this interpretation, the ancient expectations of the Davidic monarchy were transferred to Israel as a collectivity: "In 55:3 the promise of חסדי דוד הנאמנים which may have meant the renewal of the ancient promises given in 2 Samuel 7 and Psalms 89 and 132, shows very clearly that [Israel's] future expectations were ultimately synonymous with the ideal of the Davidic period. Indeed, Ezekiel even expected a David *redivivus,* cf. Ezekiel 34:23ff. Israel should once again take over the leadership of the nations."[6] This statement, however, is qualified by what Kaiser says directly after-

3. Otto Kaiser, *Der Königliche Knecht: Eine traditionsgeschichtlich-exegetische Studie über die Ebed-Jahwe-Lieder bei Deuterojesaja,* Forschungen zur Religion und Literatur des Alten und Neuen Testaments 70 (Göttingen: Vandenhoeck & Ruprecht, 1959), p. 63.

4. Hugh G. M. Williamson also follows a similar direction. See *Variations on a Theme: King, Messiah and Servant in the Book of Isaiah* (Carlisle, UK: Paternoster Press, 1998), especially with a view to Isaiah 55:3 (see pp. 5, 117-19, 140, 166, 205-6).

5. Kaiser, *Knecht,* p. 118. Concerning the term *'āshām* in Isaiah 53:10, which Kaiser understands to be a "sin offering for the unintended sins of the nations," he goes on to argue on p. 127 that here ". . . the prophet [shows] that he has been influenced by priestly thought."

6. Kaiser, *Knecht,* p. 125.

wards: "It is nevertheless striking that although our prophet evokes the memory of the ancient promises to David, at no point does he expressly state the hope that a new David would arise. He already solemnly proclaimed Cyrus to be the anointed one of Yahweh in 45:1. The political royal office has thereby already been allocated."[7] According to Kaiser, Isa 55:1-5 is not concerned with the political restoration of the Davidic claim to power along with the privileges that this entailed, "but rather Israel's calling to be a continual witness to the nations."[8] This is indeed correct, but how does the royal idiom in this passage relate to the express monarchy of Yhwh in 52:7-10?

In order to answer this question the servants need to be accorded more significance than has been the case with Otto Kaiser. From Isa 54:17 until the end of the book, they are the ones who take over from the "servant." Joseph Blenkinsopp has repeatedly expressed his views on the servants within the book of Isaiah.[9] It will not be possible to explain the connection between "king" and "servant" in Isaiah without making reference to this Jerusalem-based post-exilic group. It will not suffice, however, to note that in Isa 55:1-5 the servants have simply appropriated for themselves a certain Davidic "flair," for this tells us nothing about the nature of the connection between the "king" (Proto-Isaiah) and the "servant" (Deutero-Isaiah). Why is "David" named in Isa 55:3 despite the fact that, in contrast to Isa 1–39, chapters 40–66 do not otherwise mention him?[10] There is no trace of a Davidic restoration along the lines of Jer 23:5 and Ezek 34:23-24 in Isa 40–66, and this includes Isa 55:3. This is all the more surprising because the "messianic" texts of Isa 7, 9, and 11 are ideally suited for being connected into a chain of neo-Davidic expectation. Indeed, in light of Ezek 37:24-26, where David is expected to return as king, shepherd, and prince, Isa 55:1-5 reads like a counter-proposal. Here "my servant David" is not expected to return as king *(melek)* and prince *(nāśî');* on the other hand, Jacob will dwell as "my servant" (!) in the land of the Patriarchs. In contrast to Ezek 37:26, Isa 55:3 portrays Yhwh as establishing an eternal covenant — one in accordance with the faithfulness promised to David

7. Kaiser, *Knecht,* p. 125.

8. Kaiser, *Knecht,* p. 126.

9. *Inter alia* Joseph Blenkinsopp, "The 'Servants of the Lord,'" *Proceedings of the Irish Biblical Association* 7 (1983): 1-23; Joseph Blenkinsopp, "A Jewish Sect of the Persian Period," *Catholic Biblical Quarterly* 52 (1990): 5-20; Joseph Blenkinsopp, "The Servant and the Servants in Isaiah and the Formation of the Book," in Craig C. Broyles and Craig A. Evans, eds., *Writing and Reading the Scroll of Isaiah: Studies of an Interpretative Tradition,* Vetus Testamentum Supplements 70/1 (Leiden: Brill, 1997), pp. 155-75.

10. David in Isa 1–39: 7:2, 13; 9:6(7); 16:5; 22:9, 22; 29:1; 37:35; 38:5.

— with the servants, the true descendants of Jacob. The question thus becomes even more unavoidable: How can the Servant Songs in Deutero-Isaiah be reconciled with the expectation of a ruler or king in Proto-Isaiah?[11] Do both motifs have their roots in one and the same circle of tradents or is their juxtaposition a result of post-exilic redactional work? Ultimately, this matter of detail raises the greater question of what is the most adequate paradigm for explaining the development of the scroll of Isaiah: was it through literary extension *(Fortschreibung)* or supplementation?[12]

II. King and Kings in Isaiah 1–39

In order to examine the relationship between "kingship" and "servant figure" it is necessary to point out the contexts in Proto-Isaiah in which the terms "kingship"/"king" are used.[13] The superscription to the entire book, which was probably added during the time of the Chronicler, already provides us with an important note: "The vision of Isaiah, son of Amoz, which he saw concerning Judah and Jerusalem during the days of Uzziah, Jotham, Ahaz, and Hezekiah, the kings of Judah." Isaiah's vision took place during the last third of the eighth century B.C.E. when these four kings ruled over Judah. This statement is particularly meaningful, as the end of Isaiah's prophetic activity coincides with the end of Hezekiah's political career. The reader is given the impression that the period of the monarchy after Hezekiah was no longer under prophetic auspices — indeed, the monarchy after the son of Ahaz appears to be already doomed to destruction (cf. Isa 39).

Isaiah's vision within the Jerusalem temple of Yhwh as universal king (Isa 6) functions as a counter-image to the kings of Judah who, according to chapters 1–5, do not implement social or cultic law. Significantly, this vision is dated

11. For the theme of "power," see Konrad Schmid, ed., *Prophetische Heils- und Herrschererwartungen,* Stuttgarter Bibelstudien 194 (Stuttgart: Verlag Katholisches Bibelwerk, 2005).

12. See the important but, in English-language exegesis, little-noticed article by Rüdiger Feuerstein, "Weshalb gibt es 'Deuterojesaja'?," in Friedrich Diedrich, and Bernd Willmes, eds., *Ich bewirke das Heil und erschaffe das Unheil (Jes 45,7): Studien zur Botschaft der Propheten,* Forschung zur Bibel 88 (Würzburg: Echter Verlag, 1998), pp. 93-134.

13. Concerning the distribution of the terms in the book of Isaiah: *melek* 80x (66x Proto-Isaiah; 8x Deutero-Isaiah; 6x Trito-Isaiah); *mal'ak* 5x (4x Proto-Isaiah; 1x Deutero-Isaiah); *mamlākâ* 14x (12x Proto-Isaiah; 1x Deutero-Isaiah; 1x Trito-Isaiah), according to Francis I. Andersen and A. Dean Forbes, *The Vocabulary of the Old Testament* (Rome: Editrice Pontificio Istituo Biblico, 1992), pp. 360-61.

to the "year of King Uzziah's death" (6:1; cf. 14:28 [the year of King Ahaz's death]). Regardless of whether this information refers to the sickness-ridden years of the second half of Uzziah's long reign (cf. 2 Chron 26), "the provision of this piece of chronological information within the context of Isaiah's commissioning creates a contrast between the transience of the worldly king and 'the king, Yhwh Sebaoth' (v. 5)."[14] The date is also a clear indication that divine and earthly kingship ought to be perceived and analysed "in tandem" in the book of Isaiah.[15]

Incidentally, the book of Isaiah does not report the years of the reign of Jotham, son of Uzziah and father of Ahaz (in contrast to 2 Kgs 15:32-38). This lacuna could possibly function to create the impression that the vision of the divine council took place at a time when Yhwh and Yhwh alone was the king in Jerusalem. In support of this interpretation is the fact that Isa 6:5 conspicuously talks of "*the* king (המלך יהוה) Yhwh Sebaoth,"[16] just as he is portrayed as sitting upon a "high and lofty throne" (6:1; ישב על כסא רם ונשא). This expression is more significant than appears at first glance, for 2:12-14 uses the expression "high and lofty" to characterize everything that Yhwh will bring low "on his day." Yhwh's occupation of a high and lofty throne signifies the deprivation of all earthly kings — including Jewish ones — of their power. The lofty monarchy of God in Isa 6, therefore, is a critique rather than a legitimation of human claims to power. The elevation of the servant in 52:13 also points in this direction, for he will be high and lofty and kings will shut their mouths. The last time Yhwh is called the high and lofty One is in Isa 57:15. It is as such that he turns to help those who are broken in spirit.

The critical undertone in the book of Isaiah against earthly "kings" is further substantiated when the promised heir to the throne in Isa 7, 9, and 11 is nowhere called a "king." Political machinations do indeed play an important role in Isa 7, for the *kings* of Aram and Israel go to fight against the *king* of Judah in order to install the son of Tabeel as *king* in Jerusalem (Isa 7:1, 6). Yet

14. Willem A. M. Beuken, *Jesaja 1–12,* Herders Theologischer Kommentar zum Alten Testament (Freiburg i.Br.: Herder, 2003), p. 168; cf. Williamson, *Variations,* p. 3.

15. Hugh G. M. Williamson, "The Messianic Texts in Isaiah 1–39," in John Day, ed., *King and Messiah in Israel and the Ancient Near East, Proceedings of the Oxford Old Testament Seminar,* Journal for the Study of the Old Testament Supplement Series 270 (Sheffield: Sheffield Academic Press, 1998), pp. 238-70: ". . . it points us to the wisdom of examining the themes of divine and human kingship in tandem in the book of Isaiah" (p. 238).

16. Cf. Hubert Irsigler, "Gott als König in Berufung und Verkündigung Jesajas," in Friedrich V. Reiterer, ed., *Ein Gott — eine Offenbarung. Beiträge zur biblischen Exegese, Theologie und Spiritualität* (Würzburg: Echter Verlag, 1991), pp. 127-54 (here p. 129 and p. 154).

standing behind all this activity is the author of history who has summoned the king of Assyria (7:17, 20; 8:4, 7) in order to test Ahaz's faith. Assyria, however, exalts itself against Yhwh, for it intends to annihilate Israel rather than punish it in accordance with Yhwh's standards (10:5-7). It acts as if it is something great and declares that all of its princes are "kings" (10:8). Moreover, it has captured the "kingdoms of the idols," including Samaria (10:10). As such, it believes it will be able to do the same thing to Jerusalem and its graven images (10:11). Yhwh, however, makes sure that its plans fail, for he will punish the fruit of the boastful heart of the king of Assyria; he will destroy the arrogant pride in his eyes (10:12).

In the first part of the book of Isaiah, the rise and fall of Assyria constitutes the literary context for those chapters that are concerned with correct exercise of power: Isa 7, 9, and 11. This is not the place to analyze the vast amount of literature that has been dedicated to these texts and their interpretation.[17] Blenkinsopp's own treatment of this subject in his commentary on Isa 1–39 is characterized by great care and clarity. He considers Hezekiah to be the most likely referent of Isa 7:14, not least due to the inner-biblical interpretation in Isa 8:8, 10.[18] He also believes that Hezekiah is the best candidate for Isa 9:1-6, although Josiah could be another possibility.[19] Blenkinsopp dates Isa 11:1-9 with good reason to the post-exilic period, a time in which thoughts of a Davidic renaissance find expression in other prophetic books (cf. Jer 23:5-6; 33:14-22; Ezek 34:23-31; 37:24-28; Amos 9:11-15; Mic 5:1-3).[20] A glance at the "messi-

17. See, for example, Ursula Struppe, eds., *Studien zum Messiasbild im Alten Testament,* Stuttgarter Biblische Aufsatzbände 6 (Stuttgart: Verlag Katholisches Bibelwerk, 1989). Horst Seebass, *Herrscherverheißungen im Alten Testament,* Biblisch-Theologische Studien 19 (Neukirchen-Vluyn: Neukirchener Verlag, 1992). James H. Charlesworth, ed., *The Messiah: Developments in Earliest Judaism and Christianity* (Minneapolis: Fortress Press, 1992). Gerbern S. Oegema, *The Anointed and His People: Messianic Expectations from the Maccabees to Bar Kochba,* Journal for the Study of the Pseudepigrapha Supplement Series 27 (Sheffield: Sheffield Academic Press, 1998).

18. Blenkinsopp, *Isaiah 1–39,* p. 234.

19. Blenkinsopp, *Isaiah 1–39,* pp. 248-49. For a different view, see Paul D. Wegner, "A Re-Examination of Isaiah IX 1-6," *Vetus Testamentum* 42 (1992): 103-12: "We believe that Isaiah expected a coming deliverer who would fulfil the ideas expressed in this name" (p. 112).

20. Blenkinsopp, *Isaiah 1–39,* pp. 264-65; for a different view, see Williamson, *Variations,* pp. 53-56, who believes in the "Isaianic authorship of the opening verses of chapter 11" (p. 53); Isa 11:10-16, on the other hand, are post-exilic; see Hugh G. M. Williamson, "Isaiah XI 11-16 and the Redaction of Isaiah I–XII," in John Adney Emerton, *Congress Volume Paris 1992,* Vetus Testamentum Supplement 61 (Leiden: Brill, 1995), pp. 343-57 (especially p. 355).

anic triptych"[21] of Isa 7-9-11 reveals a development from a concrete expectation within the period of the Syrian-Ephraimite crisis (Isa 7: Hezekiah), via the idea of an ideal ruler (Isa 9: Hezekiah or Josiah), to pure idealization (Isa 11).[22] However one identifies the exact referents of these texts, one thing is certain: In the book of Isaiah redemption is not achieved by a single individual.[23] The figure of the servant does not bring about redemption either, for firstly it does not intend an individual with a personal biography[24] and secondly it is only a complementary actor alongside Yhwh as the one true sovereign.[25]

Over and against this divine king all earthly rulers must, sooner or later, fall silent. Thus Isa 14:4 intones the great satirical song against the king of Babylon who, as a paradigm for the great rulers, must go down to the underworld. There he meets *all* the kings who have fallen before him, who now rise up to feebly greet him as one of their own (14:9). In the lowest part of the underworld the shades ask themselves in wonder if this is really the man who had once struck fear into kingdoms and who had caused the earth to tremble (14:16).

"Kings/kingdoms" are mentioned once again at the end of the first series of oracles against the nations. Here Yhwh announces that he will stir up the Egyptians against each other, give them over into the hands of a strict ruler, and that a hard king will rule over them (19:4). Egypt's advisors are powerless; when one of them told Pharaoh he was a son of royal descendants he made a mockery

21. For this expression see Erich Zenger, "Jesus von Nazaret und die messianischen Hoffnungen des alttestamentlichen Israel," in Walter Kasper, ed., *Christologische Schwerpunkte* (Düsseldorf: Patmos, 1980), pp. 37-78 (here: p. 58).

22. Cf. Shemaryahu Talmon, "The Concept of Messiah and Messianism in Early Judaism," in James H. Charlesworth, ed., *The Messiah* (Minneapolis: Fortress Press, 1992), pp. 79-115. Picked up in Daniel Schibler, "Messianism and Messianic Prophecy in Isaiah 1–12 and 28–33," in Philip E. Satterthwaite et al., eds., *The Lord's Anointed: Interpretation of Old Testament Messianic Texts* (Carlisle, UK: Paternoster Press, 1995), p. 102.

23. Ernst-Joachim Waschke, "Die Stellung der Königstexte im Jesajabuch im Vergleich zu den Königspsalmen 2, 72 und 89," *Zeitschrift für die alttestamentliche Wissenschaft* 110 (1998): 348-64 draws our attention to the compositional function of these royal texts in the book of Isaiah and the Psalter.

24. Ulrich Berges, "Farewell to Deutero-Isaiah or Prophecy Without a Prophet," in André Lemaire, ed., *Congress Volume Ljubljana 2007,* Vetus Testamentum Supplement 133 (Leiden: Brill, 2010), pp. 575-95. Ulrich Berges, "The Literary Construction of the Servant in Isaiah 40–55: A Discussion about Individual and Collective Identities," *Scandinavian Journal of the Old Testament* 24, no. 1 (2010): 28-38.

25. Cf. Richard Schultz, "The King in the Book of Isaiah," in Satterthwaite et al., eds., *The Lord's Anointed,* pp. 141-65: "Thus the 'Servant' of Isaiah 40ff. can be understood as a complementary portrait of Yahweh's agent, which corresponds to the king of Isaiah 1–39" (p. 159).

of himself and his wisdom (19:11). The question of the identity of the hard king has opened the door to a multitude of hypotheses. Possible candidates stretch from Sargon II or the Ethiopian Piye (25th "Nubian" dynasty) in the 8th century to Antiochus II in the 2nd century, with Esarhaddon, Cambyses, Artaxerxes II and the Macedonian Alexander the Great in between.[26] Alexander seems to be the most likely candidate, for the following passage mentions the road between Egypt and Assyria (Isa 19:16-25), which indicates the Hellenistic period.[27]

Isaiah 20 is set exactly in the middle of the oracles against the nations and is the only place where the prophet does a symbolic act. In this chapter Sargon, the king of Assyria, does battle against Ashdod, which he succeeded in conquering in 711. This functions as a warning to all those in Israel and Jerusalem who would turn to Egypt for protection from the king of Assyria (20:1; 20:6). Without doubt, within the context of the book this oracle functions to point the reader towards the Sennacherib-Hezekiah narrative in chapters 36–39.

Whether it is a coincidence or not it is astounding that, following the first oracle against Babylon (13–14) and Isaiah's central symbolic act in chapter 20, the theme of king/kingdom only reappears in the final oracle against Tyre in Isa 23. Whereas Babylon represents the military power of the nations which Yhwh, the true king, had broken, Tyre represents the economic potential to be found in international trade. Yhwh's stretched-out hand had destabilized kingdoms (23:11). The prophecy in v. 15 that Tyre would be forgotten for seventy years — the years of a single king (כימי מלך אחד) — transfers the motif of the seventy-year exile to this port-city in the eastern Mediterranean (Jer 25:12; 29:10; Zech 1:12; Dan 9:24; 2 Chron 36:21).[28] In contrast to Babylon, which opened the list of nations and went down with them, Tyre will have a future after this seventy-year period (v. 17). This future will consist in the fact that the profit that Tyre acquires from its whoring with all the kingdoms of the earth will be holy to Yhwh. The trade surplus, however, should not be stored (in the temple treasury in Jerusalem); rather, it should finance the nourishment and clothing of those who dwell before Yhwh (23:18). This no doubt reveals something of the identity of those who authored and composed the final form of the book of Isaiah. They are to be found in non-priestly circles of the Jerusalem temple establishment.

26. Blenkinsopp, *Isaiah 1–39*, p. 314.

27. Cf. Blenkinsopp, *Isaiah 1–39*, p. 319: "Babylon is referred to here and in other late texts as 'Assyria' (Isa 11:16; Zech 10:10), and when linked with Egypt we may suspect a coded allusion to the Seleucid and Ptolemaic Empires respectively."

28. W. A. M. Beuken, *Jesaja 13–27*, Herders Theologischer Kommentar zum Alten Testament (Freiburg: Herder, 2010), p. 293 and p. 302.

The so-called Isaiah Apocalypse (24–27) universalizes the programme of the oracles against the nations (13–23), something that chapter 24 underscores with its sixteen-fold mention of the "earth" (ארץ). Once again the term "king(s)" is placed at the climax of the chapter: "On that day it will happen: Yhwh will punish the host of the heights in the heights and the kings of the earth on the earth" (24:21). This verse betrays a strong similarity to the formulation found in 23:17: "with all the kingdoms of the earth upon the face of the earth."

The climax of this section is found shortly afterwards in 24:23: "Then the moon will be abashed and the sun will be ashamed, for Yhwh Sebaoth rules as king upon Mount Zion and within Jerusalem, and his glory is before his elders." This imagery invokes the scene of Moses and the seventy elders in Exod 24:9-11. In Isa 24:23, however, the elders are no longer with Moses but with Yhwh upon Mount Zion and within Jerusalem. There is no mention of the temple here. One question that can be posed in this context is the following: How were these concepts as found in Isaiah interpreted by the priestly circles who were simultaneously giving the Pentateuch its shape?[29]

At the end of Isa 30, the penultimate chapter of the five woe-oracles (cf. 28:1; 29:1, 15; 30:1; 31:1), Yhwh in his thundering wrath places the nations in a yoke (30:27-28). The addressees (plural "you") are invited to sing songs and to play flutes. With the sound of drums and zithers in the background, God fights "with wave-offering-battles" (Buber: *"Schwungopfer-Kämpfen"*) either against Assyria (בה; *kethib*) or against them (בם; *qere*) (v. 32). The topheth, the burning place, has also long been prepared for the king (30:33). In its literary context, this is a reference to the Assyrian king (v. 31). It is still an open question, however, whether the original reading was *"mōlek"* (Moloch) rather than *"melek"* (king) (cf. 2 Kgs 23:10; Jer 7:31-32; 19:5-6, 11-12).[30]

After the five *hoy*-oracles that structure chapters 28–31, a new section is started with Isa 32. Its opening is programmatic: "Behold, a king will reign in righteousness." The parallel colon, "and princes will rule with justice" (32:1b), suggests that here it is human kingship that is in view, albeit of a very sober kind, without any trace of an idealized order of peace with paradisiacal features

29. The redactional and compositional processes behind the Pentateuch and the prophetic books appear to be far more closely related than has been assumed so far. There is still much more work to be done in this area!

30. Cf. Kaiser, *Jes 13–39*, p. 247. Amongst others, the following author is in favour of the MT: Jan Kreuch, *Unheil und Heil bei Jesaja: Studien zur Entstehung des Assur-Zyklus Jesaja 28–31*, Wissenschaftliche Monographien zum Alten und Neuen Testament 130 (Neukirchen-Vluyn: Neukirchener Verlag, 2011), pp. 368-69.

(cf. Isa 11).[31] This fits well with the theory that Isa 32:1 is making use of an old proverb.[32] However, the hope for the righteous rule of a human king along with his officials that comes to expression in Isa 32:1-5 is immediately supplanted in Isa 33 by the expectation of Yhwh himself as king. Although one may question the identity of the king in v. 17 ("Your eyes will see the king in his beauty; they will see a broad-open land"), in v. 22 the confession of a we-group that Yhwh is king is unambiguous: "For Yhwh is our judge, Yhwh is our lawgiver, Yhwh is our king. He saves us." The indestructibility of Zion that is celebrated in chapter 33 and "historically" documented with the defeat of Sennacherib, the great Assyrian king, in chapters 36–37, is grounded in the kingship of Yhwh. This kingship is proclaimed here for the first time by a group in the form of a collective confession ("our king").[33] Within the context of the development of the book in its final form, this group can only be the core Isaianic community that consists of those disciples whose eyes and ears are no longer blocked (cf. 6:9-10; 29:9-12; 32:3-4; 33:17).[34] The sole kingship of Yhwh does not only overcome Assyria, Babylon, and all other powers, it also overcomes Edom, which is destroyed by the God of Israel before the eyes of all the nations so that no other kingdom may be named there (34:12). Against this background, the battle for Jerusalem in Isa 36–37 is not only a struggle for the city of God, it is also a struggle for Yhwh's claim to exclusive kingship, i.e. his autarchy over Israel and the nations.

Within the dramaturgy of the book of Isaiah, the narratives that have been taken over with small but significant modifications from 2 Kgs 18–20, namely the siege of Jerusalem by Sennacherib, the miraculous deliverance of both the city and the fatally ill Hezekiah, and the visit of the Babylonian legation (Isa 36–39), acquire a special function. Rather than being a mere appendix, as has been claimed, they are the center of this prophetic document's textual world. Yhwh, the universal king, saves his city and those within it who trust in him

31. So Ernst-Joachim Waschke, "Jesaja 33 und seine redaktionelle Funktion im Protojesajabuch," in Markus Witte, ed., *Gott und Mensch im Dialog,* Beihefte zur Zeitschrift für alttestamentliche Wissenschaft 345/I (Berlin: De Gruyter, 2004), pp. 517-32 (here: p. 531) — with justified criticism of the interpretation by Ulrich Berges, *Das Buch Jesaja: Komposition und Endgestalt,* Herders Biblische Studien 16 (Freiburg i.Br.: Herder, 1998), pp 233-34.

32. Williamson, *Variations,* pp. 62-66; similarly: Williamson, "Messianic Texts," pp. 265-66.

33. Willem A. M. Beuken, *Isaiah II,* vol. 2, *Isaiah 28–39,* Historical Commentary on the Old Testament (Leuven: Peeters, 2000), pp. 274-75.

34. Ulrich Berges, "Hören und Sehen: Das anthropologische Rüstzeug für den Gottesknecht im Jesajabuch," in Christian Frevel, ed., *Biblische Anthropologie: Neue Einsichten aus dem Alten Testament,* Quaestiones Disputatae 237 (Freiburg i.Br.: Herder, 2010), pp. 256-78.

against all the arrogant attacks of enemy nations, here exemplified by the failed attempt of Assyria in the year 701. Hezekiah's payment of tribute in 2 Kgs 18:13-16 indicates that the historical reality was in fact quite different, but the book of Isaiah naturally makes no reference to this event, for how can a pious king pay tribute rather than trust in Yhwh's help?

Yet it is not only the king of Assyria and thereby all kingdoms who cannot overcome Zion, the Mountain of God, and Jerusalem, the city of God. The Davidic line itself appears to come to an end when Isaiah announces to King Hezekiah that all the treasure of the king's house will be carried off to Babylon and a number of his sons will serve the king of Babylon as "eunuchs/court officials" (39:6-7; סריסים). This clears the way for the kingship of Yhwh, which he promptly assumes in Isa 40:9 in the form of a shepherd who cares for his herd.

At this juncture, it is necessary to highlight specifically the use of the keyword "kingdom" (ממלכה) as opposed to "king." In the entire book of Isaiah it only has a positive connotation in its first use in 9:6. The rule of the messianic child with its four throne names — yet without a royal title — shall be great and there will be no end to peace upon the throne of David and over *his kingdom.*[35] After this, all further uses of the term are negatively connoted (10:10; 13:4, 19; 14:16; 17:3; 19:2; 23:11, 17; also in 47:5; 60:12). It cannot be a coincidence that the last instance in the oracles against the nations speaks of "*all* kingdoms of the earth" (23:17). This is then taken up in the only two other instances in Proto-Isaiah, namely in the prayer of Hezekiah (37:16, 20).

All in all, the central theological position of Isa 1–39 is clear: Yhwh is *the* king of the world (Isa 6). He reveals himself over and against *all the kingdoms of the earth* as a powerful saviour and the one and only God.[36]

III. King and Kings in Isaiah 40–66

In contrast to Isa 1–39, the title "king" is only used in Isa 40-66 in the singular for Yhwh. Yhwh is the king of Jacob (41:21) and Israel (44:6). He is Israel's creator, "your king" (43:15; מלככם). The messenger of Zion proclaims to Zion that "your God is king" (52:7; מלך אלהיך). "Kings" (מלכים) in the plural only

35. Seebass, *Herrscherverheißungen,* p. 18 and p. 76, draws our attention to the fact that in 11:1-8 there is no trace of vocabulary from the semantic field of "dominion" and "power"!

36. Schultz, *King,* p. 154: "Yahweh the divine king is sovereign over the nations and accomplishes his purpose through and despite human kings."

appears in these chapters in a passive and not (or no longer) in a dominating role. The one whom Yhwh has called out of the East subjugates "kings" (41:2). Before him Yhwh strips kings of their robes and disarms them (45:1). Kings see the servant of the powerful ones (49:7; עבד משלים) and prostrate themselves for the sake of Yhwh. They become Zion's nurses (49:23) and shut their mouths before the suffering servant who has been exalted into the heights (52:15). Just as in Edom there will no longer be a kingdom (34:12), so will Babylon no longer have a throne (47:1); it will no longer be called "mistress of kingdoms" (47:5; גברת ממלכות).

In chapters 60–62, which are closely related to Isa 40–55, kings are portrayed in a very similar manner: They travel to Zion's brilliant light and are ready to minister to it (60:10). Kings are brought to her day and night as either prisoners or as offerers of gifts (60:11); Zion will drink at the breast of kings (60:16). The final instance of "king" in the book of Isaiah brings this image to a climax. All kings see Zion's glory and she will be called by a new name that has been given by the mouth of Yhwh (62:2). Zion is elevated to the royal position of city of God: "And you will be a magnificent crown in the hand of Yhwh and a royal diadem (וצנוף מלוכה בכף אלהיך; *qere*) in the hand of your God" (Isa 62:3). The crown, however, is not placed upon Zion: Yhwh keeps it in his hand.

IV. Yhwh Is King — And Who Is His Royal Servant?

The point of departure for this question is the result of the analysis carried out above. In the book of Isaiah, the only undisputed king and true author of the destinies of Israel and the nations is Yhwh himself. In contrast to what is often claimed in exegesis, Cyrus — unlike Nebuchadnezzar in the book of Jeremiah (Jer 25:9; 27:6) — is not the royal servant of Yhwh. The Persian is only Yhwh's military and political instrument for the implementation of his plan.[37] Within the context of the debate between Yhwh and the imperial gods concerning the identity of the one and only true divinity, Cyrus and the servant play complementary roles. The Persian takes care of the fall of Babylon and the liberation of the people of God; the servant is responsible for correctly interpreting this epochal change by means of his proclamation. Cyrus creates the facts, the

37. Sebastian Grätz sees this differently. Cf. Sebastian Grätz, "Die unglaubliche Botschaft: Erwägungen zum vierten Lied des Gottesknechts in Jes 52,13-53,12," *Scandinavian Journal of the Old Testament* 18 (2004): 184-207.

servant — in his capacity as mediator of the covenant and light of the nations — interprets them in relation to Yhwh. Cyrus follows the plan without knowing Yhwh; the servant, however, has received the spirit of God in order to proclaim what is right, i.e. to witness before Israel and the nations to Yhwh's control of history. The servant renders this witness not with many words but by means of his own destiny.

In accordance with the book of Isaiah's orientation to accentuate the unique kingship of Yhwh, the servant is directed towards Yhwh's sphere of influence and takes on royal characteristics. He is described, for example, as "high and lofty" (52:13; cf. Isa 6:1). It is from the outset unlikely that the servant's royal mien has been taken either exclusively or primarily from ancient Near Eastern royal ideology,[38] for in the book of Isaiah Cyrus is specifically not called a king and the Judean kings are not ideologically glorified. This is also contradicted by the fact that although there are connections between Cyrus and the servant, the differences are greater. Both are grasped by Yhwh (42:6; 45:1), called by him (Cyrus: 45:3-4; 46:11; 48:15; Servant: 42:6; 49:1) and both implement his will (44:28; 48:14; 53:10). Yet, in contrast to the servant, whom Yhwh commissioned while in his mother's womb (49:1), Cyrus does not know the God of Israel (45:4). Whereas the Persian operates using military power (41:2-3; 45:1-3; 46:11; 48:14), the servant is weak and sorely afflicted (42:2-3; 49:7; 50:6-7; 52:13–53:12). Cyrus certainly conquers the nations, but it is only the servant who brings them torah and light (42:4, 6; 49:6; 52:15). The servant's mission only really begins once the Persian's mission has been accomplished, i.e. after the end of Babylon in Isa 46–47.[39] Rainer Kessler expresses the difference between Cyrus and the servant figure in the following manner: "Cyrus always remains distinct from Jacob/Israel. The relationship between Israel and the *eved* is different, for these two entities are closely related to each other. This is not only because Israel is explicitly referred to as the *eved*, it is also due to the *eved*'s special mission to Israel as well as his consistent anonymity. In contrast to Cyrus, this makes the boundary between Israel and *eved* fluid."[40]

38. Thus Antti Laato, *The Servant of YHWH and Cyrus: A Reinterpretation of the Exilic Messianic Programme in Isaiah 40–55*, Coniectanea Biblica. Old Testament Series 35 (Stockholm: Almqvist & Wiksell International, 1992), p. 155, with particular proximity to the Josianic royal ideology; Grätz, "Unglaubliche Botschaft," pp. 187-207, expands Laato's Akkadian evidence for ancient Near Eastern royal ideology to include ancient Persian.

39. Cf. Ulrich Berges, "How Babylon Became Merciless: A Subversive Re-Reading of Isaiah 47.6," in Jill Middlemas et al., eds., *The Centre and the Periphery: A European Tribute to Walter Brueggemann*, Hebrew Bible Monographs 27 (Sheffield: Phoenix Press, 2010), pp. 145-58.

40. Rainer Kessler, "Kyros und der Eved bei Deuterojesaja: Gottes Handeln in Macht und

In contrast to the practice of Duhm and many after him,[41] all exegesis is obliged to respect the intentional interweaving of these two identities that takes place both within and outside of the Servant Songs. Rainer Kessler makes use of the concept of "perspectival identification" in order to understand this interplay between *eved* and Jacob, thereby overcoming the dichotomy between an "individual and collective interpretation" of the servant of God.[42]

In addition to the servant, another figure who similarly enters into Yhwh's sphere of influence is Zion, the rehabilitated royal bride who has been raised out of the dust. Her royal diadem, however, is not to be found upon her head but in the hand of God (Isa 62:3). Just like the servant, her exaltation is entirely dependent upon Yhwh as the only true king. Just like the servant, Zion too is both a literary individual as well as a social collective. The purpose of both of their missions goes well beyond that which an individual is capable of accomplishing, namely the actualization of Yhwh's covenant with his people in such a manner that it may be a light to attract all the nations of the world (42:6; 49:6, 8). Just like all true prophets, the servant is equipped with the word of God as a weapon (49:2). The servant's confession that he has fully exhausted himself in his attempt to bring Jacob/Israel back to Yhwh (vv. 4-5) articulates his disappointment at only having been able to motivate a small portion of the exiles to return home to Zion/Jerusalem. The experience of failure has been an element of the prophetic mission since Moses (cf. Num 11:14-15; Elijah in 1 Kgs 19:4-8; Isa 8:16-18; Jer 15:10-11 and 20:7-10). The servant's reward, however, does not consist in the alleviation of his task but in its expansion. As a light to the nations he must make the salvation of Yhwh visible unto the ends of the earth (v. 6). This can only happen when Zion becomes a light to the nations (cf. Isa 60–62).

The servant consists of all those who live as disciples in a community of learning with Yhwh. As the third Servant Song pregnantly puts it: "Adonai

---

Schwäche," in Marlene Crüsemann and Carsten Jochum-Bortfeld, eds., *Christus und seine Geschwister. Christologie im Umfeld der Bibel in gerechter Sprache* (Gütersloh: Gütersloher Verlagshaus, 2009), pp. 141-58 (here p. 150).

41. Jürgen Werlitz, *Redaktion und Komposition: Zur Rückfrage hinter die Endgestalt von Jesaja 40–55*, Bonner Biblische Beiträge 122 (Berlin: Philo Verlagsgesellschaft, 1999), p. 31, fn. 81, summarizes the following parallels: address as servant (41:8-9; 42:1); election (41:8-9; 42:1); calling (41:9; 48:12; 49:1); formation from the womb (44:2, 24; 49:5); formation into a servant (44:21; 49:5); reception of the spirit (44:3; 42:1); Yhwh holds the servant (41:10; 42:1); the servant is honored by God (43:4; 49:5); the judgement of the servant (40:27; 49:4); Yhwh's glorification in him (44:23; 49:3).

42. Kessler, *Kyros*, pp. 150-51.

Yhwh has given me the tongue of disciples (לשון למודים), so that I know how to sustain the weary. He wakes me, indeed morning for morning he wakens my ear so that I hear like disciples (אזן לשמע כלמודים)." Apart from 50:4, the word "students/disciples" only appears in 8:16 (Isaiah seals the torah in his disciples) and 54:13 (all the children of Zion shall be called students of Yhwh). This particular formulation may also be due to an allusion to the Mosaic concept of a community of learning as found in Deuteronomy. But here, it is not Moses but Yhwh himself who is the teacher of the descendants of the servant and the children of Zion. The prophetic stylization becomes clear in 51:16: "I have placed my word in your mouth and have covered you with the shadow of my hand in order to pitch the heavens [like a tent] and to lay the foundations of the earth and to say to Zion: 'You are my people!' " The prophetic commission to preach the word (cf. Deut 18:18) is thereby transferred to the community in Zion as the true servant Jacob/Israel.[43]

V. The Royal Servant as the True Community of Zion

The suffering and exaltation of the community of Zion is literarily developed in the fourth Servant Song in a prophetic manner. Here the servant is a new entity oriented to the destiny of Zion, rather than an extension or continuation of the Davidic kingdom of Proto-Isaiah.[44] Exegetes must pay more attention than has been the case so far to the positioning of Isa 53 between the "Zion chapters" of 52 and 54, which also speak of the miraculous exaltation of the city of God to royal dignity.[45] In 52:13 the servant is raised to the heights of the divine king. The connections to Isaiah's throne vision in chapter 6 are manifold: In 52:13 the kings of the nations shut their mouths in response to the unexpected exaltation of the servant, in 6:6-8 the lips of Isaiah were opened. The purpose of the hardening of Israel's heart was to prevent it from converting and thereby bring about their healing (6:10). Now, however, a collectivity con-

43. In 59:21 this prophetic ability is perpetuated in the offspring, in all those within Jacob (!) who turn away from sin.

44. The one whose jubilee we are celebrating will forgive me when I do not follow his interpretation of the fourth Servant Song as concerning the fate of an individual (see Blenkinsopp, *Isaiah 40–55*, pp. 344-57).

45. See Ulrich Berges, "Zion and the Kingship of YHWH in Isaiah 40–55," in Archibald L. H. M. van Wieringen and Annemarieke van der Woude, eds., *"Enlarge the Site of Your Tent": The City as Unifying Theme in Isaiah*, Oudtestamentische Studiën 58 (Leiden: Brill, 2011), pp. 95-119.

fesses that "through his wounds we are healed" (53:5). Whoever confesses this has had the hardness of their heart removed and now belongs to the disciples of the prophet and the servant and are simultaneously the children of Zion (53:10; 54:3).[46]

Those of the "many," i.e. Israel as a whole, who manage to reassess the returnees from the Golah and the Diaspora in this manner belong to the "we," i.e. to the offspring of the servant and Lady Zion, the "desolate" one who has never been in labour (54:1; לא חלה). Despite the different word, this is an allusion to the "sickness" (חלי) of the servant (53:3, 4, 10). The exaltation of the servant to the highest heights after being beaten and insulted mirrors what will happen to the royal bride after she suffers the deepest humiliation. When this happens to the servant, i.e. to the faithful community of the servants in Zion,[47] the kings of the nations will shut their mouths and see what has never been told them and apprehend what they have never heard (52:15): "That which has never been recounted or heard in the whole world will become manifest. The servant Zion, who has been disfigured by his blows, will raise himself like a king, high and very lofty."[48]

This correlating and interweaving of Zion and the servant is continued in Isa 54, for behind the precious stones (vv. 11-12) that Yhwh uses to rebuild the miserable, storm-tossed and unconsoled city of Zion (cf. Lam 4:1-2) are her children, who are all "Yhwh's students," as the immediately following verse makes clear (54:13; cf. 8:16; 50:4). They have been promised great peace (54:13), which connects them to "the covenant of my peace" (54:10) that is clearly made for Zion. The destinies of Zion and the servants are inseparably intertwined. The security that God guarantees to Zion (54:16) is proclaimed to be the inheritance of the servants (54:17). Just as the Levites did not receive a portion of the land, living instead entirely from their service to Yhwh (e.g. Num 18:20; Deut 12:12; 14:27), so should the servants — who play a central role in the last two chapters of the book of Isaiah (65:8, 9, 13, 14, 15; 66:14) — depend entirely upon the support of God.

46. See Zoltán Kustár, *"Durch seine Wunden sind wir geheilt": Eine Untersuchung zur Metaphorik von Israels Krankheit und Heilung im Jesajabuch,* Beiträge zur Wissenschaft vom Alten und Neuen Testament 154 (Stuttgart: Kohlhammer, 2002).

47. Gordon P. Hugenberger, "The Servant of the Lord in the 'Servant Songs' of Isaiah: A Second Moses Figure," in Satterthwaite et al., eds., *The Lord's Anointed,* pp. 105-40, rejects the collective interpretation of servant but nevertheless comes to a collective understanding by means of his "Mosaic identity" (especially p. 139).

48. Eckart Otto, *Krieg und Frieden in der Hebräischen Bibel und im Alten Orient: Aspekte für eine Friedensordnung in der Moderne* (Stuttgart: Kohlhammer Verlag, 1999), p. 135.

It is this proximity of the community of the servant to Zion — and not something like a Davidic renaissance — that is responsible for the activation of the Davidic motif in Isaiah 55:1-5. By means of a "הוי-call," which otherwise always introduces a woe oracle (e.g. Isa 5:8, 11, 18, 20; 10:1; 13:1; 45:9-10) but which here is to be understood as an urgent appeal (cf. Zech 2:10-11), the addressees are faced with the alternative of either joining the servants or rejecting them.[49] It is only with the servants that Yhwh establishes an "eternal covenant" according to his steadfast promises of faithfulness to David (55:3).[50] In contrast to Ezek 34:23-24 this promise is not applied to a "David *redivivus*" in the capacity of servant of Yhwh but to the servants as a collectivity. In other words, the David tradition is applied to the servants rather than being developed in terms of a dynasty. They are the bearers of the Davidic promises (cf. Ps 89:38, 50[37, 49]). They are the ones that Yhwh has raised up to be a "witness to the nations," to be a prince and a commander of the peoples (Isa 55:4).[51] These functions no longer refer to the political dominion which Yhwh had temporarily transferred to Cyrus as his anointed one and shepherd (44:28; 45:1); they refer to the role of leading people from the nations to the God who glorifies himself in Zion (55:5).[52] The servant's mission of being a light to the nations (42:6; 49:6) is carried forward in the witness of the servants to the nations. In addition to this, the witnessing function of that part of the Golah that is willing to return home (43:10, 12; 44:8) has been passed on to those who have either joined or will join the community of the servant in Zion.[53]

49. Raymond de Hoop, "The Interpretation of Isaiah 56:1-9: Comfort or Criticism?" *Journal of Biblical Literature* 127 (2008): 671-95, works out a critical note for the almost unchallenged beginning of Trito-Isaiah. In contrast, see Fritz Maas, "Tritojesaja" in Fritz Maas, ed., *Das Ferne und das Nahe Wort,* Beihefte zur Zeitschrift für Alttestamentliche Wissenschaft 105 (Berlin: Töpelmann, 1967), pp. 153-63 (especially 157).

50. Ulrich Berges, *Neuer Anfang und neuer Davidbund in Tritojesaja* (forthcoming).

51. According to Ernst-Joachim Waschke, "Die Königsvorstellung nach den 'letzten Worten Davids' (2 Sam 23,1-7)," in Uwe Becker and Jürgen van Oorschot, eds., *Das Alte Testament — ein Geschichtsbuch?! Geschichtsschreibung oder Geschichtsüberlieferung im antiken Israel,* Arbeiten zur Bibel und ihrer Geschichte 17 (Leipzig: Evangelische Verlagsgesellschaft, 2005), pp. 129-44, this post-exilic text shows that "in addition to the priesthood and the circles of elite laity there [must] have been other groups who had not given up the memory of David as king or the hope for his kingdom" (pp. 141-42).

52. Cf. Williamson, *Variations,* p. 140: "The title 'king' is reserved for God himself, but Israel takes over the status and functions regarding the nations that in pre-exilic times the king had with regard to Israel."

53. For socio-historical classification of these servants, see Werlitz, *Redaktion,* p. 321: "According to the opinion that is developed here, those who were responsible for the composition of Isa. 40–55 were a group of returnees who had a connection with the pre-exilic guild

In addition to prophetic and royal dignity, the servants also ascribe priestly characteristics to themselves. This is also done by means of Zion (Isa 61).[54] The focal point of Isa 60–62 is the divine gift of the spirit to the community of the righteous upon Zion. Just as those exiles who were willing to return home as the servant of Yhwh for the sake of implementing his will were gifted with his spirit (cf. 42:1; 44:3; 48:16), so too do their offspring commit themselves to restoring Jerusalem according to God's will. Yet the previous commitment to liberation from Babylon and the Diaspora (cf. 42:7; 49:9) has now been transformed into a battle for liberation from economic oppression.

Isaiah 61:6 brings Exod 19:6 into play, which talks of the priestly function of the people of God in the midst of the nations. Exodus 19:6 also begins with ואתם ("but you"). In Isa 61:6 it is those who have been gifted with the spirit of God who are told: "But you shall be priests of Yhwh" and "servants of our God" (61:6). Prophetic charisma and priestly dignity are united in the servants, who may have come from circles which, while not being priestly, were connected to the temple.[55] The promise to those who mourn in Zion that their double portion of shame shall be recompensed with a double portion of the land (61:7) also points in this direction. They will not only receive the wealth of the nations, as "priests of Yhwh" they will also receive a second piece of property in their countries.[56] This also reveals a Levitical colouring:[57] The tradents responsible for the final form of the book of Isaiah understand themselves to be "priests of Yhwh" for the nations.[58]

---

of temple singers and who, after their return in the 20's or 30's of the 6th century B.C.E., had apparently reconnected with this group of cultic personnel."

54. G. P. Hugenberger, "Servant of the Lord," also comes to the conclusion that the servant is characterized by royal and priestly traits, albeit by different means (". . . prophetic, royal, and priestly traits in the portrait of the servant") (p. 139).

55. That which is true in general for the scribes of the OT is particularly true for the authors and redactors of the book of Isaiah: "One can only say so much, that it must have been scribal circles who had access to historiographic, legal, wisdom, prophetic, and priestly traditions or who descended from this milieu." See Reinhard G. Kratz, "Zwischen Elephantine und Qumran: Das Alte Testament im Rahmen des Antiken Judentums," in Lemaire, *Congress Volume Ljubljana 2007,* pp. 128-46 (here p. 132).

56. Berges, *Das Buch Jesaja,* p. 451.

57. On the guilds of Levitical singers as the tradents responsible for the final formation of the book of Isaiah, see Berges, *Farewell,* pp. 575-95 (especially pp. 584-88). In relation to the Psalter, see Susan E. Gillingham, "The Levitical Singers and the Editing of the Hebrew Psalter," in Erich Zenger, ed., *The Composition of the Book of Psalms,* Bibliotheca Ephemeridum Theologicarum Lovaniensium 238 (Leuven: Peeters Publishers, 2010), pp. 91-123.

58. Those whom Otto Kaiser considers to be the tradents of Isa 1–12, namely "Levitical

The proximity to the cult is continued in 61:8, where Yhwh says that he loves justice and hates robbery. It was the sons of Eli, the servants of Yhwh (1 Sam 2:11; 3:1; cf. 61:6 [servants of our God]), who did not keep the law of the priests (1 Sam 2:13) and who sinned both against God and those who offered sacrifices. Such an abuse of one's office will not take place on Zion and amongst the community of Zion. The cult will be pleasing to God — in contrast to Isa 1 as well as in Isa 66.

Yhwh establishes his "eternal covenant" (61:8) with the faithful community of Zion, the "oaks of righteousness" (v. 3).[59] Whereas the promises in 55:3 referred to royal-Davidic dignity and those in 59:21 to Mosaic-prophetic dignity, here in 61:8 the reference is to priestly dignity. With this final instance of the term "covenant" in the book of Isaiah, all authority is transferred to the community of the servants in Zion.

Conclusion

The themes of "king/kingship" and "servant/servants" in the book of Isaiah do not stand within a single line of development. As such, one cannot say that in the post-exilic period the royal servant and the servants who follow him simply applied royal honor to themselves. Such a simplification would obscure the fact that in the book of Isaiah king/kinship and earthly dominion are always situated under the primacy of exclusive divine sovereignty. Even the expectation of a Davidic heir to the throne in Isa 7, 9, 11 avoids the title of "*melek*," for Yhwh himself is king (Isa 6 and 33). This is also the credo of Isa 40–55, where it is no longer a matter of political rule but rather the recognition of the one and only God. This is the task of the servant and the servants to Israel and the nations from the very beginning of the second section of the book. The servant and the servants do not acquire their royal mien by adopting elements of ancient Near Eastern royal ideology, but rather

circles," are most certainly responsible for the final section of the book of Isaiah: "In the form of the guilds of singers in the second temple they assumed the heritage of the pre-exilic cult prophets, whom possibly also descended from their ranks." Otto Kaiser, *Das Buch des Propheten Jesaja. Kapitel 1–12*, Das Alte Testament Deutsch 17 (5th ed., Göttingen: Vandenhoeck & Ruprecht, 1981), pp. 24-25.

59. See Ulrich Berges, "Überlegungen zur Bundestheologie in Jes 40–66," in Christoph Dohmen and Christian Frevel, eds., *Für immer verbündet: Studien zur Bundestheologie der Bibel*, Stuttgarter Bibelstudien 211 (Stuttgart: Verlag Katholisches Bibelwerk, 2007), pp. 19-26.

through their perspectival identification with Zion, the bride and mother who was once spurned but has now been rescued by Yhwh, the divine king. The post-exilic hope for a new future heir to the throne from the house of David — as can be found in Jeremiah, Ezekiel, Micah, or Amos — plays no role in the final form of the book of Isaiah. The Davidic-messianic triptych of Isa 7, 9, 11 that came to find such a significant echo within the Christian tradition is thereby overshadowed, even replaced, by the only true and abiding kingship of Yhwh.

Regardless of whether one works synchronically or diachronically, it is impossible to make a connection between the expectation of a king in Proto-Isaiah and the figure of the servant in Deutero-Isaiah without taking into account the servants as the children of the maltreated servant and despised mother Zion. They are the missing link between "king" and "servant" in the book of Isaiah. However, they do not support a post-exilic movement hoping for the renaissance of a "David *redivivus.*" Quite the contrary: They apply the divine expressions of faithfulness to David (55:3) to themselves as the true servant of God. But not only that: They also apply to themselves Mosaic-prophetic and even high-priestly characteristics. The remoteness of this conception from that of a royal-Davidic restoration can also be seen in the selectivity with which Isa 11:6-9 is cited in Isa 65:25. The image of peace amongst the animals serves solely to illustrate the longed-for absence of violence that will characterize the New Jerusalem. They can happily do without the image of the branch from the root of Jesse. As the "servant of rulers" (Isa 49:7), every form of human-earthly dominion is deeply suspect to them.[60] The hope for a future righteous Davidide that is fomented in Isa 7, 9, and 11 does not fall on fertile ground.[61] For them, Yhwh alone belongs upon the throne that surpasses all human categories (Isa 66:1). With this skepticism of power they are anything other than a "royal servant"!

60. Cf. Werner H. Schmidt, "Die Ohnmacht des Messias. Zur Überlieferungsgeschichte der messianischen Weissagungen im Alten Testament," in Struppe, ed., *Messiasbild,* pp. 67-88: "The declaration of belief in the power of God that grew within the Old Testament in tandem with an increasing emphasis upon his transcendence came to be combined with a declaration of belief in the powerlessness of his representative on earth" (p. 87).

61. See also Williamson, *Variations,* p. 120, who is similarly unable to perceive any dependence between Isa 55:3 and the "messianic texts" in Isa 1–39.

Eschatology in the Book of Isaiah

Marvin A. Sweeney

I

The book of Isaiah is the best-known and most widely read prophetic book in both Judaism and Christianity. In both traditions, Isaiah is read as an eschatological text that anticipates fundamental change in the world for Jerusalem, Israel and Judah, the nations, and creation at large. Isaiah is read as a *Haphtarah* text, i.e., a prophetic reading that accompanies the weekly reading of the *Torah* in the Jewish worship service, more frequently than any other book of the Prophets.[1] Readings from Isaiah appear eight times among the ten *haphtarot* texts read during the three weeks of admonition and the seven weeks of consolation prior to Rosh ha-Shanah, the Jewish New Year, which celebrates God's sovereignty and renewal of creation at the beginning of each New Year. Isaiah is cited more frequently than any other book of the Hebrew Bible — with the exception of the book of Psalms — in the Christian New Testament. In Christianity's reading of Isaiah, the book is employed extensively in the gospel traditions to foretell the coming and significance of Jesus Christ as the inauguration of a new age in the history of humankind.[2]

The superscription of Isaiah in Isaiah 1:1 identifies the entire book as "the vision of Isaiah ben Amoz which he saw concerning Jerusalem and Judah in

1. For discussion of the *Haphtarot* in Jewish tradition, see now, Michael Fishbane, *Haftarot* (JPS Bible Commentary; Philadelphia: Jewish Publication Society, 2002).

2. For discussion of the reading of Isaiah in the Gospels and in the New Testament as a whole, see now, Steve Moyise and Maarten J. J. Menken, *Isaiah in the New Testament* (London and New York: T and T Clark, 2005).

the reigns of Uzziah, Jotham, Ahaz, and Hezekiah, kings of Judah." Although the superscription suggests that the entire sixty-six chapters of the book present the vision of the late-eighth-century B.C.E. prophet, interpreters from the Middle Ages on (e.g., Abraham Ibn Ezra, d. 1167 C.E.) have recognized that major portions of the book were written by later, anonymous figures from the exilic period of the sixth century B.C.E. and perhaps also in the early-Persian period during the late-sixth through the fifth centuries when Jews began to return from Babylonian exile to Jerusalem in order to rebuild the Jerusalem Temple and to reestablish Jewish life in the land of Israel.[3] Isaiah 1–39 largely presents the words and activities of Isaiah ben Amoz during the latter half of the eighth century B.C.E., Isa 40–55 presents the words of an anonymous Exilic-period prophet generally known as Deutero- or Second Isaiah, and Isa 56–66 presents the oracles of anonymous early-Persian period prophets known collectively as Trito- or Third Isaiah. In addition, major redactional work appears to have shaped each of the three major portions of the book.

Despite its lengthy and complex compositional history, the book of Isaiah is designed to be read as a single coherent work that presents the vision of Isaiah ben Amoz over some four centuries from the late-eighth through the fifth century and perhaps beyond.[4] Readers tend to emphasize the royal or messianic aspects of the book in assessing its eschatological perspectives.[5] Nevertheless, the book of Isaiah is fundamentally concerned with Zion or the city of Jerusalem, insofar as Jerusalem is the site of YHWH's holy Temple, which in turn symbolizes YHWH's role as the sovereign creator of the entire universe, including Israel, Judah, and the nations at large.[6] Although the de-

3. For discussion of the history of interpretation of Isaiah, see Brevard S. Childs, *Introduction to the Old Testament as Scripture* (Philadelphia: Fortress, 1979), pp. 316-18; Christopher R. Seitz, William R. Millar, Richard J. Clifford, "Isaiah, Book of," *ABD* 3:472-507.

4. For discussion of the formation and literary form of the book of Isaiah as a whole, see my *The Prophetic Literature* (IBT; Nashville: Abingdon, 2005), pp. 45-84; cf. M. Sweeney, *Isaiah 1–39, with an Introduction to Prophetic Literature* (FOTL 16; Grand Rapids: Eerdmans, 1996). For alternative treatments of Isaiah, see Joseph Blenkinsopp, *Isaiah 1–39* (AB 19; New York: Doubleday, 2000); Joseph Blenkinsopp, *Isaiah 40–55* (AB 19A; New York: Doubleday, 2002); Joseph Blenkinsopp, *Isaiah 56–66* (AB 19B; New York: Doubleday, 2003); Brevard S. Childs, *Isaiah: A Commentary* (OTL; Louisville: Westminster John Knox, 2001).

5. See, e.g., Hugo Gressmann, *Der Messias* (FRLANT 43; Göttingen: Vandenhoeck & Ruprecht, 1929); Sigmund Mowinckel, *He That Cometh: The Messiah Concept in the Old Testament and Later Judaism* (trans. G. W. Anderson; Nashville: Abingdon, [1954]); Joseph Klausner, *The Messianic Idea in Israel: From Its Beginning to the Completion of the Mishnah* (trans. William F. Stinespring; New York: Macmillan, 1955), esp. pp. 52-71.

6. Christopher R. Seitz, *Zion's Final Destiny: The Development of the Book of Isaiah: A*

struction of the Jerusalem Temple is never expressly mentioned in the book, the concerns with the impending threat to Jerusalem by the Assyrians, the return to Jerusalem by exiled Jews at the time of the downfall of the Babylonian empire, and the efforts to restore Jerusalem to its role as the seat of YHWH's sovereignty over Israel and Judah, the nations, and all creation define the eschatological perspective of the entire book. Indeed, the two-part literary structure of the book of Isaiah as a whole points to its concern with the eschatological revelation of YHWH's sovereignty at Zion, first from the standpoint of YHWH's plans to reveal divine sovereignty over all creation from Zion in Isa 1–33 and second from the standpoint of the realization of those plans in Isa 34–66:[7]

THE VISION OF ISAIAH BEN AMOZ
PROPHETIC EXHORTATION TO JERUSALEM/JUDAH
TO ADHERE TO YHWH
Isaiah 1-66

I. Concerning YHWH's plans to reveal worldwide sovereignty at Zion	1:1–33:24
A. Prologue to the book of Isaiah: Introductory parenesis concerning YHWH's intentions to purify Jerusalem	1:1-31
B. Prophetic instruction concerning YHWH's projected plans to reveal worldwide sovereignty at Zion: Announcement of the Day of YHWH	2:1–33:24
1. Prophetic announcement concerning the preparation of Zion for its role as the center for YHWH's worldwide sovereignty	2:1–4:6
2. Prophetic instruction concerning the significance of Assyrian judgment against Jacob/Israel: restoration of Davidic rule	5:1–12:6
3. Prophetic announcement concerning the preparation of the nations for YHWH's worldwide sovereignty	13:1–27:13
a. Announcements concerning the nations	13:1–23:18

Reappraisal of Isaiah 36–39 (Minneapolis: Fortress, 1991); Sweeney, *Isaiah 1–39*, pp. 31-62; idem, *The Prophetic Literature*, pp. 45-84.

7. For discussion of the following structure analysis of the book of Isaiah, see my *Isaiah 1–39*, pp. 31-62; Sweeney, *The Prophetic Literature*, pp. 45-84.

b. Restoration for Zion/Israel at the center of the nations	24:1–27:13
4. Prophetic instruction concerning YHWH's plans for Jerusalem: announcement of a royal savior	28:1–33:24
II. Concerning the realization of YHWH's plans for revealing worldwide sovereignty at Zion	34:1–66:24
A. Prophetic instruction concerning the realization of YHWH's sovereignty at Zion	34:1–54:17
1. Prophetic instruction concerning YHWH's power to return redeemed exiles to Zion	34:1–35:10
2. Royal narratives concerning YHWH's deliverance of Jerusalem and Hezekiah	36:1–39:8
3. Prophetic instruction that YHWH is maintaining covenant and restoring Zion	40:1–54:17
a. Renewed prophetic commission to announce YHWH's restoration of Zion	40:1-11
b. Contention: YHWH is master of creation	40:12-31
c. Contention: YHWH is master of human events	41:1–42:13
d. Contention: YHWH is redeemer of Israel	42:14–44:23
e. Contention: YHWH will use Cyrus for the restoration of Zion	44:24–48:22
f. Contention: YHWH is restoring Zion	49:1–54:17
B. Prophetic exhortation to adhere to YHWH's covenant	55:1–66:24
1. Exhortation proper to adhere to YHWH	55:1-13
2. Substantiation: prophetic instruction concerning reconstituted people in Jerusalem	56:1–66:24
a. Prophetic instruction concerning proper observance of YHWH's covenant	56:1–59:21
b. Prophetic announcement of restoration for the people	60:1–62:12
c. Prophetic instruction concerning the process of restoration for the people	63:1–66:24

Altogether, the major sub-units that appear within the larger literary structure of the book of Isaiah are designed to proclaim YHWH's divine sovereignty in relation to the major events that changed Jerusalem and the world from the eighth through the fifth centuries B.C.E. These events include the Assyrian invasions of the late-eighth century B.C.E. that devastated Israel and Judah and left Jerusalem isolated; the Babylonian exile of the sixth-century B.C.E. in which

Jews who survived the Babylonian invasions of Judah and the destruction of Jerusalem and the Temple were forcibly relocated to Babylonia; the rise of the Persian monarch Cyrus to power over Babylonia in the late-sixth century which would enable Jews to return to Jerusalem to rebuild the Temple and the city; and the challenges faced by returning Jews during the fifth century B.C.E. as they carried out the restoration of Jerusalem and the Temple. The book of Isaiah therefore functions as an example of theodicy insofar as it attempts to explain the disasters that overtook Jerusalem and Israel/Judah at large as a deliberate act of YHWH that would demonstrate divine power and righteousness in the world rather than as the result of YHWH's failure to protect Jerusalem and Israel/Judah in accordance with the Zion/Davidic covenant tradition (e.g., Isa 8:23–9:6[9:1-7]; 11:1-16; 55:1-13). Indeed, the book of Isaiah modifies the Zion/Davidic tradition by positing that YHWH brought about the exile of Jerusalem and authorized a foreign monarch, King Cyrus of Persia, to serve as the divinely designated monarch in place of the Davidic kings.

II

Isaiah's eschatological perspective appears throughout the entire book. The eschatological perspective is defined by its concern with YHWH's role as sovereign of creation at large; the role of Zion and the Temple at the center of creation; the status of Israel and Judah as the people bound by covenant with YHWH; the status of the monarchy that serves on behalf of YHWH and the people; the role of the nations within creation; and the status and role of creation itself. Key texts play an important role in defining the eschatological perspectives of the book as a whole and the sub-units that constitute the present form of Isaiah.

The prologue for the book in Isaiah 1 presents an encapsulated overview of the message of the book as a whole.[8] Following the superscription in Isa 1:1, Isa 1:2-31 presents a series of oracles that state the basic concerns of the book with the prophet's announcements of divine judgment against Jerusalem and its anticipated restoration once the punishment is over. The cosmic dimensions of this scenario are signaled in v. 2 in which the prophet calls heaven and earth to hear the accusations of rebellion leveled against the people of Israel, and vv.

8. Georg Fohrer, "Jesaja 1 als Zusammenfassung der Verkündigung Jesajas," *Studien zur alttestamentlichen Prophetie (1949-1965)* (BZAW 99: Berlin: Töpelmann, 1967), pp. 148-66; Sweeney, *Isaiah 1–39*, pp. 63-87.

18-20 present YHWH's offer of reconciliation to those who would repent. Verses 27-28 present the interrelated themes of judgment and restoration by announcing that Zion and those of her people who repent will be delivered during the course of judgment whereas those characterized as rebels and sinners will perish. The image of a wilted tree that burns for lack of water in vv. 29-31 metaphorically portrays the judgment in natural or cosmic terms.[9]

The presentation of the prophet's instruction concerning YHWH's plans to reveal worldwide sovereignty at Zion in Isa 2:1–33:24 focuses especially on the concept of the Day of YHWH. The Day of YHWH is of uncertain origin, although it appears to derive from the holy war traditions of ancient Israel in which YHWH's defeat of enemies that threatened Israel and Judah was celebrated liturgically in the Jerusalem Temple and perhaps in other Israelite sanctuaries as well.[10] Although the tradition focused originally on YHWH's protection of Israel, many of the biblical prophets employed it as a means to announce YHWH's judgment against Israel or Judah as part of a process by which YHWH would purge the people of impurity attributed to the failure to observe YHWH's expectations. Thus the Day of YHWH tradition is widely read by interpreters as an expression of an eschatological scenario in which Israel/Judah and the world at large are transformed, purified, and sanctified by YHWH.[11] The process of transformation appears throughout the major textual sub-units that constitute Isa 2:1–33:24.

Isaiah 2–4 begins the sequence with the prophet's announcement of the preparation of Zion for its role as the site for the manifestation of YHWH's sovereignty in the world.[12] The transformation of Zion and the world of the nations at large is evident in the initial oracle in Isa 2:2-4, which portrays the nations streaming to Zion to receive YHWH's *Torah* or Instruction "in the later days," and to inaugurate an era of peace among the nations in which they would beat their swords into plowshares and their spears into pruning hooks. Many interpreters read the Hebrew phrase, *bĕʾaḥărît hayyāmîm,* "in the later days," as a reference to "the end of days," but this is a mistaken reading influenced by the Greek version of the term, *en tais eschatais ʿēmerais,* "in the final

9. For discussion of tree imagery in the book of Isaiah, see Kirsten Nielsen, *There Is Hope for a Tree: The Tree as Metaphor in Isaiah* (trans. C. and F. Crowley; JSOTSup 65; Sheffield: JSOT Press, 1989).

10. For discussion of the Day of YHWH tradition, see esp. K. J. Cathcart, "Day of YHWH," *ABD* 2:84-85.

11. E.g., Hugo Gressmann, *Der Ursprung der israelitisch-jüdischen Eschatologie* (FRLANT 6; Göttingen: Vandenhoeck & Ruprecht, 1905), pp. 141-58.

12. Sweeney, *Isaiah 1–39,* pp. 87-112.

days." The Hebrew phrase is simply a common reference to a future time.[13] Zion of course designates the site of YHWH's Temple in Jerusalem to which the nations will come to learn and to worship. Although this oracle is frequently identified as an exilic-period composition, it presents a fundamental concern of the book as a whole, viz., the resulting peace that will ensue when Israel and the nations recognize the ideal of YHWH's worldwide sovereignty at Zion.[14] The exhortational or persuasive dimensions of the book emerge in Isa 2:5 in which Jacob or Israel is invited to join the nations streaming to Zion. Such an appeal is directed to the readers of Isaiah who are asked to recognize the impending restoration of Zion as an act of YHWH that was planned from the outset of Jerusalem's and Israel's/Judah's afflictions. A lengthy portrayal of the Day of YHWH then follows in Isa 2:6-22 in which all that is lifted up, self-aggrandized, and arrogant is brought down by YHWH's power on the Day of YHWH. The frequent use of the formula "and it shall come to pass in that day" and its variants in Isaiah is designed to refer the reader back to this initial presentation of the Day of YHWH. Portrayals of judgment against the men and women of Jerusalem in Isa 3:1–4:1 then introduce a portrayal of the future beauty, glory, and splendor of YHWH's holy presence at Zion following the purging of the people. The images of cloud, smoke, and flame over the shrine on Mt. Zion are common symbols of YHWH's presence in the wilderness Tabernacle and the Jerusalem Temple. Altogether, the portrayal of YHWH's purge of Jerusalem and Israel in Isa 2–4 facilitates the recognition of YHWH at Zion by both the so-called remnant of Israel/Judah and the nations. Interpreters in the aftermath of the Shoah or Holocaust have recognized that such a theological schema has tremendous problems insofar as it charges that the victims of violence must have deserved the violence inflicted upon them.[15]

13. For discussion of the phrase, *bĕʾaḥărît hayyāmîm,* see Simon J. De Vries, *From Old Revelation to New: A Tradition-Historical and Redaction-Critical Study of Temporal Transitions in Prophetic Prediction* (Grand Rapids: Eerdmans, 1995), pp. 89-95. See also his discussion of the phrase *bayyôm hahûʾ*, "in that day" (pp. 38-63), which does not refer to the end of time but only to the future; cf. Peter Andreas Munch, *The Expression bajjôm hāhûʾ: Is It an Eschatological Terminus Technicus?* (Oslo: Jacob Dybwad, 1936), who likewise argues that the expression is simply a reference to a future time.

14. Cf. Hans Wildberger, *Isaiah 1–12* (CC; trans. Thomas T. Trapp; Minneapolis: Fortress, 1991), pp. 81-96, who provides an overview of research and ultimately concludes that the oracle was composed by Isaiah.

15. E.g., Richard L. Rubenstein, *After Auschwitz: Radical Theology and Contemporary Judaism* (Indianapolis: Bobbs-Merrill, 1966); cf. Marvin A. Sweeney, *Reading the Hebrew Bible after the Shoah: Engaging Holocaust Theology* (Minneapolis: Fortress, 2008).

Isaiah 5–12 shifts the focus from Jerusalem to Israel and Judah at large in an effort to portray the significance of the Assyrian invasions of the region as an act of YHWH that will lead to the restoration of righteous Davidic rule.[16] Much of the material in this block derives from either Isaiah ben Amoz himself or from a seventh-century redaction of Isaiah that was designed to support King Josiah's program of national restoration and religious reform. The unit begins with a sequence of oracles in Isaiah 5 that warn of YHWH's coming punishment of Israel and Judah by means of the invading Assyrian army. Isaiah's account of his vision of YHWH in the Jerusalem Temple in Isa 6 presents his commissioning as a prophet and once again portrays YHWH's plans to purge the people so that they may be reconstituted like a tree that is cut down and burned so that it might grow once again. The imagery of Isaiah's vision of YHWH is drawn from the Temple itself, viz., YHWH's throne is identified with the Ark of the Covenant housed in the Holy of Holies in the Temple; YHWH's train which fills the Temple is identified with the smoke of the incense altars that fill the Temple with an amorphous and sweet-smelling presence; the Seraphim or fiery attendants of YHWH are identified with the flickering lights of the Temple Menorahs or candelabra whose seven-branched lights are visible within the cloud of incense smoke.[17] Isaiah's vision is particularly problematic insofar as YHWH demands that the prophet render the people blind, deaf, and incapable of understanding so that they will not be able to repent, escape the punishment, and thereby thwart YHWH's plans. The narrative account of the prophet's encounter with King Ahaz in Isa 7:1–9:6 emphasizes Isaiah's view that the people will be reduced to a remnant in order to realize YHWH's plans. When Ahaz refuses to accept Isaiah's assurances that YHWH will deliver Jerusalem despite the loss of so much of the population, the prophet then announces judgment against Ahaz, Jerusalem, and Judah in the form of an Assyrian invasion that inundates the land like a flood. Although Isaiah's oracles to Ahaz emphasize judgment, they also contain elements of subsequent restoration. One such sign of YHWH's intentions to restore Jerusalem following the period of punishment is the announcement in Isa 7:14-16 of the birth of a son named Immanuel to a young woman (see also Isa 8:8). The name Immanuel in Hebrew, *ʿimmānû ʾēl,* means "God is with us." Although this announcement is employed in the NT as an indication of the virgin birth of Jesus, the Hebrew term, *ʿalmâ,* simply means "young woman" rather than

16. Sweeney, *Isaiah 1–39,* pp. 112-211.

17. Sweeney, *The Prophetic Literature* (IBT; Nashville: Abingdon, 2005), p. 59.

"virgin," as suggested by the Greek term, *parthenos*, employed in the LXX version of Isa 7:14 and in Matt 1:23.

Isaiah portrays the emergence of a righteous Davidic king (Isa 8:23–9:6[9:1-7]) following statements concerning his frustrations as he declares his intention to bind up the testimony and Torah among his disciples. The question of YHWH's role in disaster appears once again as Isaiah declares that he will wait for YHWH, who hides the divine face from Jacob (Isa 8:16-17). Although the people will walk in darkness, they will ultimately see a brilliant light that will signal the end of oppression and the reign of a new righteous Davidic monarch. Insofar as the new monarch is described as "a child born to us, a wonderful counselor, and a prince of peace," most interpreters maintain that this passage refers to the birth of King Hezekiah ben Ahaz, the next king of Judah. The passage continues with further condemnation of Israel in Isa 9:7-20, but it shifts to condemnation of the Assyrian king in Isa 10:1-34, who arrogantly threatens Jerusalem and claims that his victories have come by his own efforts rather than those of YHWH. As a result, Isa 10:33-34 employs the natural imagery of a tree once again to portray the Assyrian king metaphorically as an overgrown olive tree that must be beaten with a rod to lop off its branches and harvest its produce. The metaphor continues in Isa 11:1-16 in which the new Davidic king is portrayed as a shoot that grows out of the stump of Jesse and a twig that grows from his stock. The new king is identified as a wise and sweet-smelling figure who inaugurates a new period of righteous Davidic rule in which the lion lies down with the lamb, a signal is displayed to the nations, Ephraim and Judah are reunited to establish their rule over the nations in the region, and the exiles of Israel and Judah are returned to the land from Assyria and Egypt. The return of the exiles is portrayed as the result of YHWH's drying up and striking the Nile and Euphrates Rivers. The use of such natural and Eden-like imagery lends itself to eschatological readings of the book in which Israel's restoration signals a fundamental transformation in the world. The authorship of Isa 11:1-16 is disputed as interpreters assign it to Isaiah ben Amoz, the Josian redaction, or to exilic or post-exilic authors. Nevertheless it reiterates the scenario of restoration in the aftermath of disaster that plays such an important role in defining the theological perspective of Isaiah. The unit closes with a thanksgiving hymn in Isa 12, which both cites language from the Song of the Sea in Exod 15 to celebrate YHWH's deliverance of Israel once again and presupposes the setting of the Jerusalem Temple where such a hymn would be sung.

Isaiah 13–27 shifts the focus of the book from Israel to the nations and YHWH's role in prompting their recognition of divine sovereignty in creation by bringing punishment against them and gathering them at Zion for a banquet that is identified with liturgical worship and sacrificial meal.[18]

The segment of this sub-unit in Isa 13–23 focuses on YHWH's punishment of the nations. Although many interpreters presuppose that all of the nations of the world are included here, it is striking to note that the nations identified in these chapters are those that were conquered by the Persian empire in the late-sixth and early-fifth centuries B.C.E., i.e., Babylon (Isa 13:1–14:23); Assyria (Isa 14:24-27); Philistia (Isa 14:28-32); Moab (Isa 15:1–16:14; Damascus/Aram and Israel (Isa 17:1-14); Ethiopia/Cush (Isa 18:1-7); Egypt (Isa 19:1–20:6); the Desert of the Sea or Babylon (Isa 21:1-10); Dumah or Edom (Isa 21:11-12); the Arabian desert (Isa 21:13-17); the Valley of Vision or Jerusalem (Isa 22:1-25); and Tyre (Isa 23:1-18). Although many of these oracles may be attributed to Isaiah ben Amoz, they have been redacted to identify YHWH's sovereignty over the nations with Persia's conquest of southwest Asia and northeast Africa. YHWH's role in subduing the nations is evident at the outset in the oracle concerning Babylon in Isa 13:1–14:23 in which YHWH's heavenly armies respond to the raised standard to attack Babylon on the Day of YHWH. The depiction of the resulting downfall of Babylon — the preeminent nation of the world, the downfall of its king, and the resulting impact on creation recalls Isa 2:6-22 concerning the Day of YHWH and the downfall of all that is high and lifted up among the nations and in creation. The brief oracle concerning Assyria makes the point that Babylon's fall echoes that of Assyria in Isa 14:24-27 insofar as YHWH had planned long ago to bring down the nations on YHWH's holy mountain Zion. The following oracle concerning Philistia in Isa 14:28-32 becomes a sign that YHWH has established Zion, and the oracle concerning Moab in Isa 15:1–16:14 is identified as a word that YHWH spoke long ago. The oracle concerning Damascus and Israel in Isa 17:1-14 emphasizes that YHWH is their maker, and it concludes with a metaphorical portrayal of YHWH's defeat of the nations as YHWH's subduing of the sea at creation. The oracle concerning Ethiopia in Isa 18:1-7 emphasizes the tribute brought to YHWH at Zion, and the oracle concerning Egypt in Isa 19:1–20:6 emphasizes how the Nile will dry up as Egypt recognizes and submits to YHWH. The oracles concerning the Desert of the Sea, Dumah, and Arabia in Isa 21 point to YHWH's advance by mention of Elam and Media, the allies of Persia, the watchman in Seir who watches for YHWH's advance, and the fall of the desert to YHWH's sovereignty. The oracle concerning the Valley of Vision in Isa 22 identifies Jerusalem's downfall with YHWH's advance and emphasizes once

18. Sweeney, *Isaiah 1–39*, pp. 212-353.

again that it was planned long ago. The oracle concerning Tyre in Isa 23 attributes Phoenicia's demise to YHWH, and anticipates a seventy-year period of restoration (cf. Jer 25; 29).

Interpreters generally consider Isa 24–27 to be an exilic or post-exilic period apocalyptic or proto-apocalyptic text.[19] Although its composition post-dates that of many of the oracles concerning the nations, Isa 24–27 plays an important role in relation to Isa 13–23 by pointing to YHWH's efforts to gather the nations at Zion as the culmination of the oracles concerning the nations. The eschatological perspectives of Isa 24–27 are very clear, viz., these chapters point to the withering of creation as a signal that human beings have violated the divine covenant that maintains the order and stability of creation; the coastlands begin to sing liturgical hymns as even the farthest reaches of the earth recognize YHWH; the world undergoes divine punishment as YHWH's sovereignty is revealed on Mt. Zion; the nations gather on Zion for a banquet that constitutes liturgical recognition of YHWH; liturgical song breaks out in Judah as the righteous city (Jerusalem) is restored and YHWH's righteousness is vindicated; Leviathan, the mythological chaos dragon, is slain in the sea; and YHWH's vineyard (cf. Isa 5:1-7) is restored as the calves graze in Eden-like tranquility and the exiles are restored from Egypt and Assyria. Even death is metaphorically overcome as the rebirth of the new world is likened to a woman giving birth (Isa 26:13-19).

The final sub-unit concerned with YHWH's anticipated sovereignty over the world appears in Isa 28–33, which focuses on Zion or Jerusalem and the emergence of a royal savior.[20] The sequence of oracles, most of which derive from Isaiah, are organized to demonstrate YHWH's actions in relation to Jerusalem to prepare it for its role as the center for YHWH's sovereignty over the world. Isaiah 28 maintains that YHWH is bringing Assyrian invaders to purge the leadership of Israel and Judah. Isaiah 29 emphasizes that the assault against Zion itself is designed to purge Jerusalem and that the blind and the deaf (cf. Isaiah 6) will one day understand the divine purpose. Isaiah 30 takes up the question of YHWH's delay in delivering the people by highlighting YHWH's dissatisfaction with Jerusalem's embassy to Egypt. Isaiah 31 again warns against reliance on Egypt and calls upon the people to return to YHWH. The climax of this sub-unit appears in Isa 32–33, which focus on the downfall of the oppressor and the rise of the royal savior of Israel. As the righteous king

19. See also Donald C. Polaski, *Authorizing an End: The Isaiah Apocalypse and Intertextuality* (BibInt 50; Leiden: Brill, 2001).

20. Sweeney, *Isaiah 1–39*, pp. 353-433.

emerges, justice and peace will prevail throughout the land and the eyes, ears, and minds of the people will be opened to comprehend YHWH's actions. At that point, the oppressor will fall as YHWH is exalted in Zion. The text calls upon its readers to behold the king in his beauty, to gaze upon a secure Zion or Jerusalem, and to recognize YHWH as king.

Whereas Isa 1–33 anticipates the revelation of YHWH's sovereignty in creation, Isa 34–66 announces that the revelation of YHWH's sovereignty is at hand. The eschatological perspectives of the second portion of the book continue those of the first, viz., concern with YHWH's role as sovereign of creation; the role of Zion and the Temple at the center of creation; Israel's covenant relationship with YHWH; the role of the monarchy and Davidic covenant; the role of the nations; and the status and role of creation in YHWH's plans.[21]

Isaiah 34:1–54:17 constitutes the first of two major sub-units of the second part of the book. Although this sub-unit contains material composed during the late-seventh-century reign of Josiah, the exilic period of the sixth century B.C.E., and the early Persian period during the late-sixth and fifth centuries, it is organized to present this material as Isaiah's instruction concerning the realization of YHWH's sovereignty at Zion.

Isaiah 34:1–35:10 introduces this sub-unit with a prophetic instruction concerning YHWH's power to return the redeemed exiles to Zion, which reiterates the theme of the Day of YHWH in its portrayal of divine punishment against the nations and restoration of the exiles to Zion.[22] YHWH's sword strikes Edom in particular as a representative of the nations, and Edom's demise is portrayed as an act of sacrifice. YHWH's actions have an impact on all creation, which responds with withering at the punishment and rejoicing at the restoration of Zion. These chapters call upon the reader to search out these matters in the scroll of YHWH, i.e., the book of Isaiah, and they reiterate the theme of Isaiah's inaugural vision (Isa 6) by announcing the open eyes and ears of the blind and deaf as they witness YHWH's actions.

Isaiah 36:1–39:8 then follows with a presentation of the royal narratives concerning YHWH's deliverance of Jerusalem and Hezekiah at the time of the Assyrian invasion of Judah in 701 B.C.E.[23] Although these narratives depict events from the late eighth century, they appear to have been composed during the seventh-century reign of Josiah to promote adherence to YHWH as part

21. Sweeney, *The Prophetic Literature*, pp. 69-83.

22. Sweeney, *Isaiah 1–39*, pp. 434-54.

23. Sweeney, *Isaiah 1–39*, pp. 454-511; contra Seitz, *Zion's Final Destiny*.

of his program of religious reform and national restoration. Hezekiah's actions at the time of the Assyrian invasion are deliberately contrasted with those of Ahaz in Isa 7:1–9:6. Whereas Ahaz rejects Isaiah's advice to rely on YHWH alone in a time of crisis and sees the subjugation of Jerusalem and Judah, Hezekiah ultimately turns to YHWH and sees the deliverance of Jerusalem, the deaths of one hundred and eighty-five thousand Assyrian troops, and the assassination of Sennacherib by his own sons in the temple of his god. Insofar as these narratives were designed to promote faith in YHWH during a time of crisis, they serve as an appropriate introduction to the works of Second Isaiah, who calls upon the readers of the book to recognize YHWH's sovereignty and actions in the world beginning in Isa 40.

The key sub-unit appears in Isa 40:1–54:17, which presents a series of arguments that YHWH maintains the covenant with Israel and acts to restore Zion. This block constitutes the bulk of the material attributed to the anonymous sixth-century prophet Second Isaiah, although within the context of the book as a whole it is presented as part of the vision of Isaiah ben Amoz.[24] Insofar as Isa 40:12–48:22 focuses on Jacob, the eponymous ancestor of northern Israel, and Isa 49:1–54:17 focuses on Bat Zion, the feminine personification of Jerusalem, this block of material draws out the earlier concerns of the Josian reform to restore the unity of the twelve tribes of Israel around the Jerusalem Temple when the exiled northern kingdom would return "home" to Jerusalem. Of course, such a scenario accounts for the realities of the Babylonian exile. The passage presents a fundamental change in creation as it calls upon its readers to open their eyes, ears, and minds, to search past tradition, and to recognize YHWH's fidelity to the covenant with Israel even as Cyrus emerges as YHWH's divinely designated Messiah and Temple builder to replace the defunct house of David.

The sub-unit begins in Isa 40:1-11 with the prophet's commission to announce YHWH's restoration of Zion. The passage draws upon motifs from the Exodus tradition as it envisions creation acting to clear a road in the wilderness for YHWH's return to Zion. In addition to portraying a new Exodus — this time from Babylon — the passage addresses the question of YHWH's credibility and fidelity by emphasizing that God's word stands forever. Isaiah 40:12-31 then follows with an oracular block that argues that YHWH is the master of creation. By drawing on past tradition to identify YHWH as creator, Isa 40:12-31 builds the case that readers of the book should open their eyes, ears,

24. See also Roy F. Melugin, *The Formation of Isaiah 40–55* (BZAW 141; Berlin: Walter de Gruyter, 1976).

and minds once again to recognize that YHWH will act on behalf of Jacob. Isaiah 41:1–42:13 argues that YHWH is the master of human events, who upholds the divine servant to serve as a light to the nations who will recognize YHWH. Isaiah 42:14–44:23 attempts to answer concerns with YHWH's silence during the period of exile by arguing that YHWH is the redeemer of Israel. Again, all creation is affected as YHWH calls upon deaf and blind to open their ears and eyes to recognize YHWH's actions concerning Israel, the nations, and creation at large. Here, the prophet maintains that whereas YHWH punished Jacob for sins, the time has now come to redeem YHWH's servant Jacob as the people, much like their ancestral namesake who returned from Aram and whose bones were brought back from Egypt, return to the land of Israel from exile in Babylonia. Isaiah 44:24–48:22 then contends that YHWH will designate Cyrus as the divinely-chosen Messiah who will build the Temple and restore Zion. Such a contention is particularly remarkable insofar as Second Isaiah does not envision the restoration of a Davidic king, but looks to a foreign king as YHWH's agent at the time of Babylon's downfall and Israel's/Jacob's return to Jerusalem from Babylonian exile.

The culmination of this block appears in Isa 49:1–54:17 which contends that YHWH is restoring Zion. The passage gives a special emphasis to the ambiguous figure of the servant of YHWH in Isa 49:1-13, here identified as Israel in Isa 49:3 and commissioned to bring Jacob back to YHWH in Isa 49:5, who seems to function both as Israel per se and YHWH's agent who will act to restore Israel.[25] The focus shifts to Zion per se in Isa 49:14–52:12. The passage draws on the classical portrayal of the marriage between YHWH and Zion to personify Zion as YHWH's forsaken bride, but it assures her that YHWH will restore her as bride and signal the nations to return her scattered children to her as well.[26] Although the passage contends that Zion was forsaken or punished for her sins — which thereby defends YHWH against charges of weakness or wrongdoing — it also contends that YHWH's role as creator enables

25. For discussion of the so-called Servant Songs in Isaiah, see now, Bernd Janowski and Peter Stuhlmacher, editors, *The Suffering Servant: Isaiah 53 in Jewish and Christian Sources* (trans. Daniel P. Bailey; Grand Rapids and Cambridge: Eerdmans, 2004); T. N. D. Mettinger, *A Farewell to the Servant Songs: A Critical Examination of an Exegetical Axiom* (Lund: Gleerup, 1983).

26. See Patricia Tull Willey, "The Servant of YHWH and Daughter Zion: Alternating Visions of YHWH's Community," *Society of Biblical Literature 1995 Seminar Papers* (ed. Eugene Lovering; Atlanta: Society of Biblical Literature, 1995), pp. 267-303; Patricia Tull Willey, *Remember the Former Things: The Recollection of Previous Texts in Second Isaiah* (SBLDS 161; Atlanta: Scholars Press, 1997), pp. 229-61.

YHWH to restore the marriage. The image of the servant appears once again in Isa 50:4-9 who is punished but waits for divine deliverance. The full announcement of Zion's salvation then appears in Isa 51:1–52:12 with announcements that YHWH will act, Zion's suffering is over, Zion will be comforted, YHWH will return, and that her people should maintain purity as they depart to follow YHWH once again. The exaltation of the suffering servant follows in Isa 52:13–53:12, and the portrayal of Zion as restored bride and mother concludes the block in Isa 54:1-17 as YHWH declares that divine fidelity and the covenant of peace will never be compromised.

The concluding segment of the book of Isaiah appears in Isa 55:1–66:24 as a prophetic exhortation to adhere to YHWH's covenant as articulated throughout the book. Although Isa 55 is generally recognized as the work of Second Isaiah and Isa 56–66 as the work of Third Isaiah, the block has been edited so that the exhortation in Isa 55 defines the overall concerns and perspectives of the entire block. Indeed, Isa 55 is a key passage in the eschatological perspective of the book of Isaiah insofar as it redefines the Davidic covenant in relation to the earlier contentions in Isa 44:28 and 45:1 that King Cyrus of Persia is YHWH's divinely chosen Messiah and Temple builder. Insofar as no Davidic king will emerge in the concluding portions of the book of Isaiah — or in the Persian period for that matter — Isa 55 applies the Davidic covenant to the entire nation of Israel and maintains that this was YHWH's plan from the beginning (cf. Isa 55:8, 11).[27] This is a remarkable example of theodicy insofar as it defends YHWH against charges that the exile and dissolution of the Davidic monarchy occurred because YHWH lacked the will or power to defend Israel, Jerusalem, or the house of David. From an eschatological perspective, the passage marks a major change in Israel's self-understanding now that a Davidic king will no longer rule the restored nation.

The substantiation necessary to support the exhortation appears in Isa 56–66, which is generally ascribed to Trito-Isaiah, as prophetic instruction concerning the reconstituted people in Jerusalem. The oracles in this block are organized into three major sub-units concerned with various aspects of the restoration of the nation and its covenant with YHWH. The first sub-unit in Isa 56:1–59:21 provides instruction concerning proper observance of the covenant. Many interpreters note that foreigners and eunuchs are now included

27. Marvin A. Sweeney, "The Reconceptualization of the Davidic Covenant in Isaiah," *Studies in the Book of Isaiah* (ed. J. Van Ruiten and M. Vervenne; BETL 132; Leuven: Peeters, 1997), pp. 41-61.

in the covenant, but they are also enjoined to observe YHWH's expectations, particularly the Shabbat and Temple sacrifice or worship, in order to do what is right and just. Such actions entail an early form of conversion to Judaism. Isaiah 60:1–62:12 announce the restoration of the people as YHWH's glory shines, the exiled of Israel are returned to Jerusalem by the nations of the world, and the nations work to rebuild Jerusalem's walls. The segment concludes with YHWH's oath that Zion's deliverer has come and that the people will now be known as "the Holy People," "Sought Out," and "the City Not Forsaken" (Isa 62:12). The final sub-unit in Isa 63:1–66:24 presents prophetic instruction concerning the process of restoration. The portrayal of YHWH's punishment against Edom in Isa 63:1-6 echoes the earlier references to Edom's impending downfall in Isa 34. Although this sub-unit envisions a process of return that is imminent, it is clearly not yet accomplished. It refers to those who are sinful who are still in need of repentance or punishment as it envisions the return of the exiles. A particularly striking aspect of the projected restoration is YHWH's declaration in Isa 66:1 that "heaven is my throne and earth is my footstool," which recounts the role of the Temple and the Holy of Holies in particular as YHWH's throne room on earth. Within the context of the book as a whole, this statement identifies YHWH as the sovereign who will reign in Jerusalem in place of the earlier Davidic monarchs and Cyrus of Persia. Once again, the rebirth of Zion is likened to a woman giving birth to a child. Although many interpreters mistakenly read Isa 66:18-21 as indication that some among the nations will be chosen as Levitical priests, a close reading of the passage indicates that the nations will return the exiles to Zion and that the priests will be chosen from the exiles.[28] In the end, the restoration of Zion entails the creation of a new heaven and earth, i.e., the restoration of Zion fundamentally changes creation as YHWH's sovereignty is recognized. The final reference to the corpses of the wicked underlines the exhortational character of Isa 63–66 — and indeed of the book of Isaiah as a whole — as a call to recognize YHWH's sovereignty and join in YHWH's covenant.

28. Brooks Schramm, *The Opponents of Third Isaiah: Reconstructing the Cultic History of the Restoration* (JSOTSup 193; Sheffield: Sheffield Academic Press, 1995), pp. 171-73; cf. Marvin A. Sweeney, "Prophetic Exegesis in Isaiah 65–66," *Writing and Reading the Scroll of Isaiah: Studies of an Interpretive Tradition* (ed. Craig Evans; VTSup 70/1; Leiden: Brill, 1997), pp. 455-74.

III

Although the book of Isaiah includes materials from at least three different periods of composition, it has been formed into a coherent literary work that articulates a distinctive eschatological perspective concerning the changes that took place in the world of Israel and Judah from the late-eighth through the fifth centuries B.C.E. Whereas Isaiah ben Amoz argued that YHWH would punish Israel and Judah with Assyria in order to purge the nation and to restore righteous Davidic rule, the final form of the book extends that perspective to account for the Babylonian exile and the Persian period restoration. Central to the book's concern is the question of YHWH's relationship with Jerusalem and the world of creation and the nations at large. Whereas Isaiah ben Amoz envisions righteous Davidic rule, the full book of Isaiah acknowledges the dissolution of Davidic kingship and argues instead that YHWH is the true sovereign of Jerusalem, Israel, the nations, and all creation, and that Jerusalem, the site of YHWH's Temple, will emerge as the site for the revelation of YHWH's sovereignty throughout all creation.

Consumerism, Idolatry, and Environmental Limits in Isaiah

Patricia K. Tull

A key trope in Isaiah is "high" and "low" — often representing appropriate or inappropriate postures before God.[1] This trope is used against the imperial tyrant of the day, the arrogant king of Assyria, who like a tree grown too high and mighty will be laid low (Isa 10:33). But he is not alone. Babylon (13:10), Moab (25:11-12), the wealthy of Samaria and Judah (5:14), and humanity in general (5:15), and those living on high (26:5) are viewed as forgetting their place and needing to be brought down to size by the God who alone is high and exalted (6:1).

As John Barton has pointed out, such self-aggrandizement is seen in Isaiah as a habit of thought underlying more specific sins of social, economic, and legal injustice. Barton notes a natural-law theology in Isaiah, where "the universe forms an ordered whole in which each creature should know its place; and God's place, if we may speak so, is to be supreme."[2] Humans who resist this order fail, he says, to accept their rightful place in the world.

As Barton points out, this moral order shows up very close to the book's beginning. Following the prophet's first exhortations to set aside evil and learn to carry out social justice, Isa 1:19-20 lays out two distinct alternatives for worshipers, posed as mirror opposites: (1) Be willing and obedient toward God, and eat the good of the land; or (2) Refuse and rebel, and be eaten by the

1. The discussion in this paper is adapted from chapter 4 of my book *Inhabiting Eden: Christians, the Bible, and the Ecological Crisis* (Louisville: Westminster John Knox, 2013). I am delighted to offer this discussion in tribute to Joseph Blenkinsopp, from whose writings I have learned much about Isaiah, biblical scholarship, and historical imagination.

2. John Barton, "Ethics in Isaiah of Jerusalem," *JTS* (1981): 1-18 (8).

sword. Shortly after this, in Isaiah's second chapter, two different portraits appear, portraits that could hardly be more distinct, mirroring each other through opposition.

We encounter first the well-known description of the world's nations coming to Jerusalem to learn from God (2:1-5). The temple mount is raised up as the highest mountain and, like a river defying gravity, peoples flow upward to it.[3] As they adopt Israel's God as their judge, arbiter, and teacher, they reshape their weapons of destruction into tools for agricultural growth:

> 1The word that Isaiah son of Amoz saw concerning Judah and Jerusalem.[4]
> 2In days to come
> the mountain of the LORD's house
> will be established at the peak of the mountains,
> and will be lifted up above the hills,
> and all the nations will stream to it.
> 3and many peoples will come, and they will say,
> "Come, let us go up to the mountain of the LORD,
> to the house of the God of Jacob,
> that he may teach us his ways,
> so we may walk in his paths."
> From Zion will come teaching,
> and the word of the LORD from Jerusalem.
> 4God will judge between nations,
> and arbitrate for many peoples.
> They will beat their swords into plowshares,
> and their spears into pruning knives.
> Nation will not take up sword against nation,
> and they will no longer train for war.
> 5House of Jacob,
> come, let us walk in the light of the LORD.

If these first few verses of chapter 2 dream of a bright future, the rest of the chapter comes across as a nightmare. There a very different picture emerges: a

3. So notes Jonathan Magonet in "Isaiah's Mountain or the Shape of Things to Come," *Prooftexts* 11 (1991): 173-81.

4. Disagreement continues concerning the origin of this passage, which is found nearly identically, though in a very different setting, in Mic 4. More scholars believe it to have originated with Isaiah than with Micah, since it fits Isaiah's general message and vocabulary more closely. Yet even more believe it to have been a later composition added to both. For present purposes, this otherwise interesting question will be set aside.

complex, chaotic vision of human disregard for God and of God's terrifying show of power. As in Hans Memling's *Last Judgment,* which shows souls ascending to heaven's gates on one side and souls descending to hell's mouth on the other, in these two portraits utopia and dystopia are set side by side. The relationship between these two juxtaposed visions is not spelled out. Perhaps, as in the Memling tryptic, and as many have suggested, they show two alternative futures. Or perhaps, as Joseph Jensen has suggested, the second vision describes the present state of affairs that temporarily, but not finally, blocks realization of the ideal future, "a stage on the way to Yhwh's salvation."[5]

Both of these visions involve the nations coming to Judah, and both involve weapons of war. Both depict humans submitting themselves to a deity. Yet there the similarities break into contrasts.[6] Rather than coming to God's mountain to learn from Israel's God, foreigners are bringing their own commodities and information sources into the land. Rather than walking in their creator's path, they worship their own creations. Rather than streaming upward, they are bowing downward. Rather than destroying weaponry, they proliferate it. Rather than peace and harmony, they find — as the vision continues to unfold — terror and humiliation. Strikingly, if the first vision is easily translated, textually clear, poetically balanced, and spiritually satisfying, the second is none of these. Instead, the drumbeat of recurring jaggedly repetitive refrains puts the problems of disorder on full display.[7]

The passage begins in 2:6-8 by building to introduce the first of three

5. Joseph Jensen, "Weal and Woe in Isaiah: Consistency and Continuity," *CBQ* 43 (1981): 167-187 (186).

6. Jensen, "Weal and Woe," p. 184. Brevard Childs (*Isaiah* [OTL; Louisville: Westminster John Knox, 2001], pp. 32-33) likewise outlines a series of ironic oppositions between these two visions.

7. The redaction history of this passage has inspired much discussion. On the one hand, vv. 12-16 strike most readers as being especially consistent with the prophet's own language. But on the other hand, referring to idols as "the work of their hands, what their own fingers have made" resonates with Deuteronomistic thought, and other disorders such as sudden changes from third person to second person, repeated phrases, and evidently parenthetical thoughts seem to indicate the passage's growth. For thorough discussions see especially Joseph Blenkinsopp, "Fragments of Ancient Exegesis in an Isaian Poem (Isa 2:6-22)," *ZAW* 93 (1981): 51-62; and H. G. M. Williamson, "The Formation of Isaiah 2.6-22," in *Biblical and Near Eastern Essays: Studies in Honour of Kevin J. Cathcart* (ed. Carmel McCarthy and John F. Healey; London: T&T Clark, 2004), pp. 57-67. Blenkinsopp sees as the basic core vv. 6-8 (without the Deuteronomic addition), an indictment, and 12-16, a verdict, linked by v. 10. Williamson mostly agrees, though he sees vv. 10-17+19 as having been assembled in an ABCBA structure, though not necessarily by the first author, and believes vv. 6-8 to have been an originally separate poem. For purposes of this paper, details of the passage's probably complex redactional history are less important than the impact of the resulting whole.

interwoven themes. Translational uncertainties remain, particularly in verse 6, but the general sense is evident:

> 6For you have abandoned your people,
> house of Jacob [*or* the house of Jacob].[8]
> They are full of sorcerers[9] from the east
> and fortune tellers like the Philistines,
> and they clasp hands with foreigners
> [*or* and they are teeming with foreign children].[10]
> 7Their land is filled with silver and gold,
> and there is no end to their treasures.
> Their land is filled with horses,
> and there is no end to their chariots.
> 8Their land is filled with idols . . .[11]

We expect here something like "and there is no end to their gods," or "images," or some other parallel.[12] But instead, drawing attention to itself and renewing interest through variation, the rhythm is broken, and sustained attention is directed toward the final objects with which the land is filled:

> 8Their land is filled with idols;
> they bow down to the work of their hands,
> to what their own fingers have made.

8. Translators and commentators differ over whether "house of Jacob" should be read as an appositive, in which case the addressee is God (as in KJV, RSV, NJB, and NIV), or as vocative, addressing the house of Jacob itself (as in NRSV and Tanakh).

9. Hebrew lacks an object. Many translators supply קסמים "sorcerers," paralleling עננים, possibly lost early in transmission by haplography because of its similarity to מקדם. Other translators supply a similar presumed object.

10. The meaning of this phrase is uncertain partly on account of the unusual verb ישׂפיקו. It can be taken as meaning "to clap" or "clasp" on the basis of Job 27:23 (see also Num 24:10 and Lam 2:15), in which case ילדי is emended to ידי. Otherwise it can be taken as a verb meaning "to be sufficient; abundant" (cf. 1 Kgs 20:10; Job 20:22; 36:18).

11. The word used for "idols" here, אלילים, an evidently derogatory term derived from the adjective אליל, "vain, worthless," is one of more than a dozen scriptural words commonly translated as "idols." It is found more often in First Isaiah than in the rest of Scripture combined, and is by far this section of the book's favored term, found four times in this chapter (vv. 8, 18, and twice in 20), as well as at 10:10, 11; 19:1, 3; and twice at 31:7. By way of contrast, the terms פסל and פסיל are favored in Second Isaiah.

12. In fact, some commentators have suggested that the expected line has dropped out, and two lines substituted in its place; see for instance Joseph Blenkinsopp, *Isaiah 1–39: A New Translation with Introduction and Commentary* (AB 19; New York: Doubleday, 2000), pp. 192-93.

In marked contrast to the prior passage, in which the nations approaching Jerusalem learn the ways of Judah's God and, as a result, reject their war weapons, here the nations bring to Judah their foreign diviners and handmade gods, material wealth, and military technology. All these foreign commodities — wealth, costly war weapons bought with wealth, and human-made idols, may appear to promise freedom from divine authority, but instead, ironically, they are depicted as ushering in slavery, as the people bow down to inert objects. Contrasting markedly with the swords-into-plowshares passage, in which even the nations were coming to Israel's God, here even the Israelites are worshiping foreign deities. Greed, militarism, and idolatrous worship go hand in hand, debasing those who think power and wealth will bring stature, as we will see even more clearly when the idols return in verses 18 and 20.

After these verses introduce idolatry both in the form of literal objects of worship and in the metaphorical sense of desiderata through which humans perennially seek security — information, wealth, and weapons — a second theme, that of human humiliation, becomes explicit:

> 9 And humanity will be brought down;
>   each person laid low — do not lift them up!
> 10 Go into the rock,
>   and hide yourself in the dust
> from the terror of the LORD,
>   and from the splendor of God's majesty!
> 11 People's proud eyes will be brought down,
>   and humanity's haughtiness laid low,
>   and the LORD alone will be exalted on that day.

In the prior poem it was the mountain of the LORD's house that had been raised high (נשׂא), and nations streamed upward toward it, peoples proposing to ascend to it. But not so in this poem. Instead, in a series of refrains in verses 9 and 11, and returning in 17, two parallel nouns, which may be rendered as "people" (אדם) and "everyone," or "humanity" (איש/אנשים), and two verbs, "be humbled" (שׁחח) and "be brought low" (נפל), are wound together in various configurations, followed the last two times by the contrasting line "the LORD alone will be exalted (שׂגב) on that day."[13] People who were aloft not

13. These verses may have accumulated by accretion, as Blenkinsopp suggests, since they do not comprise a refrain as regular as those found in chaps. 5 and 9–10. Nevertheless, as they stand now they create a broken, repetitive, building pattern. Their "editorial debris" (to quote Blenkinsopp, "Fragments," p. 56) dramatizes well the accretion of foreign debris listed in vv.

because they were going up to God but because they were aloof from God will not be lifted up (אל תשׂא להם, v. 9, literally "do not lift them up," often translated "do not forgive them"), but humbled, ironically separated from God, who alone is "high and lifted up" (6:1, רם ונשׂא).

The third theme emerges in the haunting visual image that intertwines with and finally concludes this section. It begins in verse 10, quoted above, and will return twice more, in verses 19 and 21. Instead of ascending to God, here humanity tries in vain to dig beneath rock and dust to escape God. If people abase themselves by worshiping idols in verse 8, they abase themselves even further through futile attempts to crawl into fissures and dusty holes to hide in terror from the one they have betrayed. But hiding will not suffice; as Amos already said, "Though they dig into Sheol, from there my hand will take them" (9:2).

Three themes have now been introduced — idolatry, humbling, and hiding. By the passage's end these will have each appeared three times. Before this, however, once the contrast of high and low has been established, the passage's center emerges in verses 12-16, five consecutive verses built upon close repetition of the preposition על, which covers a range of positions: not only "against," but, more spatially, "upon," "over," and "above." The Geneva Bible captures the syntax most directly, and is echoed in this translation:

> 12 For the day of the LORD of hosts
> is upon all that is proud and haughty,
> upon all that is lofty and high,[14]
> 13 upon all the cedars of Lebanon, high and lofty,
> upon all the oaks of Bashan,
> 14 upon all the high mountains,
> upon all the lofty hills,
> 15 upon every tall tower,
> upon every fortified wall,
> 16 upon all the ships of Tarshish,
> upon all the lovely boats.

Everything in the landscape that can be called tall, including several traditional symbols of might, are listed as objects of this one preposition. In verse 2 the

6-8 as filling the land of Judah, as well as the debris of useless idols tossed to the moles and bats further on in v. 20.

14. The Hebrew here says ושׁפל, "and it will be brought low." Many translations correct; cf. LXX.

mountain of the LORD's house had been lifted up; Isaiah will later see the Lord sitting on a throne in the temple, high and lifted up. But here, nothing can get away with being high. Nothing is immune to the threatening, violent storm, neither trees nor mountains, and certainly not the human-made landscape of towers, walls, and cargo ships. The mixing of both the natural and the manufactured suggests that if even the mighty in creation cannot resist God, then certainly neither can the strongest products of human engineering. This section bears kinship to Ps 29, in which God's voice breaks, even shatters, the cedars of Lebanon (v. 5) and twists the oaks, stripping the forest bare (v. 9).

Tantalizing here is the role the cedars of Lebanon play in the culture surrounding this passage — and possibly the oaks of Bashan as well, which only appear in Scripture alongside Lebanon's cedars (see Ezek 27:6; Zech 11:2). These mighty forests were not simply wonders of nature but, beginning at least with Sumerian civilization, sources of commercial wealth so tempting that over the course of centuries they were clear-cut nearly to extinction. The story of Gilgamesh describes the Sumerian god Enlil as protector of the cedar forests. When Gilgamesh and his lumberjacking companions strip the mountains, leaving bare rock, Enlil "sent down a series of ecological curses on the offenders: 'May the food you eat be eaten by fire; may the water you drink be drunk by fire.'"[15] As both Scripture and ancient Near Eastern royal inscriptions attest, the cedars of Lebanon were prized resources, used not only in building palaces such as Solomon's (1 Kgs 5:5-6), but in the creation of mighty Tyrean ships that made marine trade possible (Ezek 27:5). Assyrian inscriptions and friezes, such as that by Sargon II now housed in the Louvre, depict the felling and transport of lumber from the cedar forests.[16] Isaiah 37:24 criticizes Sennacherib's boasts of felling the remotest of trees, and Isa 14:8 describes the trees themselves rejoicing that royal death has saved them from a Mesopotamian tyrant's axe. Thus the cedars of Lebanon came to signify not only natural strength and beauty, but also imperial commerce, a theme reinforced here by the wooden merchant ships, lovely perhaps on account of the glorious luxuries they carry.

15. Rania Masri, "The Cedars of Lebanon: Significance, Awareness and Management of the *Cedrus Libani* in Lebanon," http://almashriq.hiof.no/lebanon/300/360/363/363.7/transcript.html. See likewise Ched Myers, "'The Cedar Has Fallen!': The Prophetic Word vs. Imperial Clear-Cutting," in *Earth and Word: Classic Sermons on Saving the Planet* (ed. David Rhoads; New York: Continuum, 2007), pp. 211-23.

16. Department of Near Eastern Antiquities, "Frieze of the Transport of Timber," http://www.louvre.fr/en/oeuvre-notices/frieze-transportation-timber. See likewise Assyrian royal references to the procuring of cedar at: http://archaeotype.dalton.org/archaeotype_library/royal.html#15.

The three themes of idolatry, humbling, and hiding return together in the final portion:

> 17 People's pride will be brought down,
>   and human haughtiness laid low.
> The LORD alone will be exalted on that day,
>   18 and the idols will completely pass away.
> 19 And they will go into rocky caves
>   and dusty holes
> before the terror of the LORD
>   and the splendor of God's majesty
>   arising to overawe the earth.
> 20 On that day people will throw away
>   to the moles and to the bats
> their gods of silver and gods of gold
>   which they made for themselves to worship.
> 21 They will hide in clefts of rocks
>   and crevices of cliffs
> before the terror of the LORD
>   and the splendor of God's majesty
>   arising to overawe the earth.
> 22 Turn yourselves away from humans
>   who have mere breath in their nostrils,
>   for of what account are they?

Finally the pictures converge: in an almost cartoonish image, humans fleeing God drop everything and run, discarding their silver and gold idols, which litter the paths of animals who have no use for them. So much for the wealth of the land.

These two pictures stand side by side in Isa 2 — a joyous scene of pilgrimage toward God, ushering in peace and prosperity, and a terrifying scene of judgment against all that would rival God's majesty, ushering in loss and humiliation. In the theocentric world of verses 2-5, the vision of even foreign nations voluntarily approaching and learning goads Judeans to seek their own God. In the splintered world of verses 6-22, the futility of ignoring God's status ends up compelling unwilling, terrified humiliation, as if to say that the divinely created cosmos will return to its own equilibrium whether humanity cooperates or not.

Similar messages prevail throughout Isaiah, which asserts repeatedly that

God has a plan for the future (עצה, Isa 14:24-26; 19:12-17; 23:8-9; 25:1; 28:29), and that human plans will be thwarted (7:5-7; 8:10; 19:2; 29:15; 30:1-3). Attention to God and God's plans leads to human wisdom and environmental stability, but consumption of (and, ultimately, consumption by) lesser ends leads to destruction and waste. The theme is echoed in the woe oracles wrapped around the core of the first twelve chapters, the oracles that begin in chapter 5 by railing against those who add house to house and join field to field (5:8-9), and who taunt God's plans (5:19), and end in chapter 10 with a bitter cry against those who wrongfully turn even the legal process to their profit (10:1-2). It is seen in the visions of Babylon's downfall in chapter 13. And it is seen in the protoapocalyptic vision of chapter 24, in which:

> The earth dries up and wilts . . .
> The earth lies polluted under its inhabitants,
>   for they have transgressed teachings,
> swept aside law, broken the ancient covenant. (vv. 4-5)

Politically, this opposition between seeking and resisting God is played out in the lethal dramas of the late eighth century B.C.E., in which Isaiah commends the decidedly unpopular ethic of trusting God rather than weapons or nations, especially when he opposes Hezekiah's attempts to court favor with Egypt for protection from Assyria (29:15; 30:1-7; 31:1-3). In this thinking there is no room for trusting God in prayer while hedging one's bets with action, no room for the pragmatic philosophy of *True Grit*'s old-school Presbyterian, the young protagonist Mattie Ross ("The author of all things watches over me, and I have a fine horse").

Connections between pride and downfall are rendered self-evident in Scripture not only by their sheer prevalence, but also by their spatial metaphors of high and low. But what can we make of the connection between pride and idolatry? On the surface, these seem to be two opposite moves — one a standing tall and the other a groveling down. Yet this poem places the two together. This is a very important question that I want to pursue in relation to not only Isaiah but also later thinking.

But first I would like to cast a glance at where this trope, "idols of silver and gold," found in verse 20, takes us. It's a widespread description in Scripture, shared with the Pentateuch (Exod 20:23; Deut 7:25; 29:17), several other prophets (Isa 40:19; 46:6; Jer 10:3-9; Hos 8:4; Hab 2:18-19) and the Psalms (115:4; 135:15). The description with which this passage begins of a land filled with endless silver, gold, weapons, and idols suggests parallels among these objects, but does not spell out an explicit correspondence between idolatry and material greed. At most it suggests a common impulse to stockpile the kinds of objects in which one might place trust, representing wealth, power, and supernatural favor.

Yet these two topics, greed and idolatry, are both widespread within Isaiah. Later on, in the writings of Philo and in the New Testament, the love of money is explicitly viewed as idolatry. Philo writes that the first commandment "condemns strongly the money-lovers who procure gold and silver coins from every side and treasure their hoard like a divine image in a sanctuary, believing it to be a source of blessing and happiness of every kind."[17] Greed and idolatry are equated in Eph 5:5 and Col 3:5 as sins precluding participation in God's realm. Jesus similarly positions wealth as a rival god: "No one can serve two masters. . . . You cannot serve God and wealth" (Matt 6:24; Luke 16:13). The theme is also echoed in the early church. John Chrysostom, for instance, in his commentary on this Isaiah passage, criticizes the sin of hoarding:

> The prophet was not criticizing the use of these possessions [silver and horses], but the misuse of them. When he said, "Woe to the mighty," he was not condemning them for having possessions but for hoarding so much more than they needed.[18]

Contemporary people resist imagery like that found in verses 9-22. Following so many tragic attempts to engineer divine judgment, from the Crusades and Spanish Inquisition to televangelistic explanations of Hurricane Katrina, the metaphor of divine wrath no longer conveys what it may have once been intended to convey. There is nevertheless an important warning here. The sad picture in Isaiah of a land littered with objects of consumption, with silver, gold, chariots, and discarded idols, seems strangely reminiscent of our contemporary landscape where, if anything, the scatter of debris has been magnified to degrees the prophets could hardly have imagined. The objects filling the land to no end today, offloaded in cargo crates from farther east than those that filled Judah, now inspire bumper stickers unrecognizable to a traditional religious consciousness, sayings such as "I'm spending my grandchildren's inheritance," and "the one who dies with most toys wins." There is a

17. Philo, *On the Special Laws* 1:21-22; see Brian S. Rosner, "The Concept of Idolatry," *Themelios* 24.3 (May 1999): 21-30 (27).

18. John Chrysostom, *Commentary on Isaiah 2:7*, as quoted in Steven A. McKinion, *Isaiah 1–39* (Ancient Christian Commentary on Scripture: Old Testament 10; Downers Grove, Ill.: InterVarsity Press, 2004), p. 29.

recognizable malaise in this restless cycle of buying and discarding. Nearly everyone living in middle-class Western society today has spent a lifetime surrounded by a consumer culture so pervasive that it is difficult to imagine its absence.

A friend of mine tells of her daughter, a high school student, who after growing up in privilege spent a summer in Kenya among the poor. She returned with a radically changed understanding of the materialism she had taken for granted before, and proceeded to give away most of her possessions. She realized at an early age what the prophet said long ago: that what we own owns us, and this realization became a turning point for her life and vocation. If in our travels or our imaginations we have glimpsed other possibilities, we may find ourselves questioning the seeming inevitability of our role as consumers of disposable items.

In a disturbing yet wonderfully entertaining article published in *The Atlantic* in 1999 entitled "The Market as God," theologian Harvey Cox narrates the gospel of Wall Street, voicing its quasi-theological myths. He describes the economic market as an omniscient, omnipotent, omnivorous deity, demanding to be kept happy under all circumstances. Foreshadowing more recent developments, Cox says, "At times [the market's] appetite may seem excessive — a $35 billion bailout here, a $50 billion one there — but the alternative to assuaging its hunger is too terrible to contemplate."[19] He described a phenomenon heard regularly on market news: "The market's fickle will is clarified by daily reports from Wall Street and other sensory organs of finance [which tell us] on a day-to-day basis that The Market is 'apprehensive,' 'relieved,' 'nervous,' or even at times 'jubilant.'"[20] In short, he points out, while we may think we own the stocks, they may in fact own us — own not only those whose portfolios they inhabit, but everyone affected by their rising and falling fortunes.

Like Wall Street, the American public is also regularly psychoanalyzed by economic measures. The "consumer confidence index" is a monthly gauge of the optimism about employment and income expressed by potential shoppers, an index used to help manufacturers and retailers predict the future of sales. It is based on the perception that Americans who expect to make more money will spend this money. It evidently does measure spending patterns with some

19. Harvey Cox, "The Market as God: Living in the New Dispensation," http://www.theatlantic.com/magazine/archive/1999/03/the-market-as-god/6397/1/.

20. Cox, "Market as God." The Marketplace report is even accompanied by the appropriate mood music — "We're in the Money" when the Dow Jones Industrial Average climbs and "Stormy Weather" when it slumps. Never, "I've Got Plenty of Nothing, and Nothing's Plenty for Me."

accuracy. But labeling this behavior as confidence seems perverse. If shopping is linked with confidence and failure to shop with its lack, one wonders what becomes of our self-image as humans, and as citizens. Does authentic confidence lead to shopping, or more naturally to singing, or tackling a difficult problem, or writing a check to help vaccinate poor children?

According to this index's underlying assumptions, Americans have become so well trained for spending that we are no longer regulated by what is needed to feed, clothe, and shelter our families, but by how much money we have (or worse, expect to have). Yet there are reasons behind this compulsion. No generation before ours has been so intensely beset by the instruction to buy. It is almost as difficult to imagine a world free of billboards, internet ads, flyers, jingles, and corporate sponsorships of programs, arenas, and even school buses, as it is to imagine nations turning swords into plowshares. Perhaps it is even more difficult: while the ravages of war are clear, many people are not as aware of the damage done by servitude to material desire — damage to human wellbeing, and damage to the natural world.

Realities the prophets foresaw from a distance — perhaps, as some suggest, because they themselves witnessed such environmental devastations as the denuding of Lebanon's hills for commercial gain — have become increasingly tragic today. Dr. Kristen Shrader-Frechette teaches environmental biology and ethics at the University of Notre Dame. She has served on the EPA's science advisory board, and has advised the Centers for Disease Control, NASA, and the Department of Energy, as well as several foreign governments and the U.N. She directs the Center for Environmental Justice and Children's Health, which works *pro bono* with community groups around the world to assess ecological health dangers and to inform residents of their rights and risks. In her 2007 book entitled *Taking Action, Saving Lives,* Shrader-Frechette points out the serious health risks of industrial pollutants, especially to children's vulnerable and fast-growing bodies.[21] She argues that because U.S. citizens enjoy the benefits of products and services that generate air and water pollutants, "ordinary citizens have ethical responsibilities to use traditional democratic tools to help prevent threats to life and health."[22]

Shrader-Frechette points out that estimates from the U.S. National Cancer Institute show industrial pollution contributing to 60,000 premature American cancer deaths annually — three times larger than the annual number of

21. Kristin Shrader-Frechette, *Taking Action, Saving Lives: Our Duties to Protect Environmental and Public Health* (Oxford: Oxford University Press, 2007).

22. Shrader-Frechette, *Taking Action,* p. 6.

murders.[23] She carefully documents the damage done among the poor by factories positioned in their neighborhoods creating the luxury goods. It is not only factories and their polluting emissions that end up next to the poor, but also landfills that receive these possessions when they are no longer wanted.

What the debris of consumerism does to the natural world is another part of the story. Writer Annie Leonard began studying the cycles of consumerism when she noticed the piles of trash awaiting pick-up on the streets of New York City. She followed the trash to Fresh Kills Landfill on Staten Island, whose peaks were eighty feet taller than the Statue of Liberty.[24] This enormity inspired her to research the life cycle of complex products, what happens as they are mined, manufactured, transported, consumed, and discarded. At every step in the process, from the extraction of raw resources to the production of goods, from their distribution to their consumption and final disposal, the ecological waste is far greater than we may think. Yet most people have learned to take such waste for granted, presuming that the ecosystem contains infinitely available resources and capacity to heal itself from all that we may toss at it.

The damage done to the natural world and to poorer people by an economic system based on growth and spending is recognizable to some. What is harder to recognize, because we are so embedded within it, is the damage done to consumers themselves, the very people whose purchasing power fuels the engine of waste. This, I believe, is where Isa 2 can help us out. To understand it more deeply, we will first take a turn through a more recent history.

At the turn of the twentieth century economist Thorstein Veblen examined critically, and often wryly, the stratum of society given to what he called "conspicuous consumption," that is, the open use of what money could buy to assert one's importance and position. As far as he could tell, the perceived purpose of money among the wealthy was not to meet needs, but to buy status:

23. Shrader-Frechette, *Taking Action,* p. 17, citing U.S. Department of Health and Human Services and National Cancer Institute (NCI), "Health Status Objectives," *Cancer* 16:1 (1991): 416-40. This figure was confirmed in a 2005 study by the U.S. National Academy of Science: J. Michael McGinnis, "Attributable Risk in Practice," in Institute of Medicine, *Estimating the Contributions of Lifestyle-Related Factors to Preventable Death* (Washington, D.C.: National Academy Press, 2005), pp. 17-19.

24. Annie Leonard, *The Story of Stuff: How Our Obsession with Stuff Is Trashing the Planet, Our Communities, and Our Health — and a Vision for Change* (New York: Free Press, 2010), p. ix.

> In any community where goods are held in severalty it is necessary . . . that an individual should possess as large a portion of goods as others with whom he is accustomed to class himself; and it is extremely gratifying to possess something more than others. But as fast as a person makes new acquisitions, and becomes accustomed to the resulting new standard of wealth, the new standard forthwith ceases to afford appreciably greater satisfaction than the earlier standard did. The tendency in any case is constantly to make the present pecuniary standard the point of departure for a fresh increase of wealth; and this in turn gives rise to a new standard of sufficiency and a new pecuniary classification of one's self as compared with one's neighbours.[25]

In other words, when luxuries create self-image, the answer to the question, "How much is enough?" is inevitably "just a little more." There is indeed no end to such treasures.

Veblen's conspicuously wealthy were engaged in a race against neighbors, a race of affluence, or more precisely, of perceived affluence in the form of conspicuous consumption. But in contrast with these few, most of the American public at the time valued thrift. By the late 1920s it was becoming clear to manufacturers that the increasing productivity of their factories was outstripping a frugal public's inclination to buy. In order for the leisure class's wealth to increase, ordinary citizens had to be taught to want more goods.[26] Workers and unions favored rebalancing overproduction by reducing the work week. But many business owners, perceiving that shorter work weeks would erode profits, called thrift a "buyer's strike." They rolled out guilt-seeking slogans such as "Your Purchases Keep America Employed."[27] In 1927 industrial relations counselor E. S. Cowdrick called for "the new economic gospel of consumption," not because the American public was demanding it, but because it was not. In 1929, President Herbert Hoover's Committee on Recent Economic Changes reported that because "wants are almost insatiable" and "one

25. Thorstein Veblen, *The Theory of the Leisure Class: An Economic Study of Institutions* (Norwood, Mass.: Norwood Press, 1899), p. 31.

26. This history is detailed by Jeffrey Kaplan in "The Gospel of Consumption," *Orion Magazine*, May-June 2008 (http://www.orionmagazine.org/index.php/articles/article/2962/).

27. Benjamin Kline Hunnicutt, *Work without End: Abandoning Shorter Hours for the Right to Work* (Philadelphia: Temple University Press, 1988), p. 38. Such slogans sound strangely familiar today, when consumer spending is closely linked to the monthly jobs report, as if the only employment possible were the making of commodities for individual consumption, and not education, the arts, or infrastructure.

want satisfied makes room for another," therefore, "economically we have a boundless field before us," to be exploited by what the committee called "carefully predeveloped consumption."[28] With those ends in mind, the modern advertising industry was born.

Yet like a sugar high, the desires created by advertising leave buyers empty. The key to understanding this is in the otherwise puzzling link Isaiah draws between pride and idolatry. Here the prophet put an ancient finger on a characteristic of the human condition that has come to fruition in our generation. Barton draws a link between pride and idolatry in this passage by viewing them as "two examples of the effect of failing to observe order in the world,"[29] a folly that can lead to one of two possible consequences:

> On the one hand, they come to overestimate their own importance . . . and this pride leads to a delight in prestige and the accumulation of riches and status symbols. On the other hand, they fail to see where their trust and confidence should properly be placed, and rely on sources of strength other than God.[30]

Yet the relationship can be even more tightly drawn. The Catholic theologian Russell Reno makes use of St. Augustine's discussion of self-love to trace out the connection in ways quire reminiscent of Isaiah, though without referring to either the prophet or this passage. In Augustine's thinking, he says, to turn one's back on God is to attempt to make the self one's central concern. To do so is a mistake, for according to Augustine, as Reno puts it:

> No false love can be successful, because it has no place, no truth, in which to come to rest. . . . We can try to make ourselves happy with wealth, but neither the luster of coins nor their ability to bring us all the merchant's cargo is powerful enough to bring us peace. . . . All the more so with pride: it can evacuate the soul of love of God, but it cannot fill us with self-love, for the self has nothing to offer itself other than the capacity to glorify God.[31]

Both pride and idolatry arise from the same mistaken denial of what we were made to be. They lead to the same sad conclusion, the inability to find satisfaction:

28. Hunnicutt, *Work without End,* p. 44.
29. Barton, "Ethics in Isaiah," p. 9.
30. Barton, "Ethics in Isaiah," p. 9.
31. R. R. Reno, "Pride and Idolatry," *Interpretation* 167 (April 2006): 166-78 (172-73).

> While we may attempt, in pride, to make ourselves our own ground and the source of our own happiness, we cannot succeed, for we have nothing to give ourselves other than our reality as creatures whose true happiness is in God alone. . . . We should expect, then, that pride will fail, and in failing, it becomes not its opposite, which is humility, but instead the perversion of a perversion, the redoubled futility of slavery to idols of our own fabrication.[32]

In other words, just as misuse of the created world for purposes for which it was not intended yields ecological crisis, so, according to Augustine as read by Reno, misuse of ourselves for purposes for which we were not made leaves a personal and social vacuum that is succinctly expressed in Augustine's well-known prayer, "You have made us for yourself, O Lord, and our heart is restless until it rests in you." "The inevitable slide from pride to idolatry should not surprise us," Reno comments. "We are made for love, and our desire is to give ourselves away, not to draw in upon ourselves as the source and ground of our happiness. . . . Pride's project of finding rest in the self will always find concrete expression as the worship of idols."[33]

Neuroscientist Patrick McNamara, examining the role of religion around the world in the development of human conscious agency, similarly noted that the self is not a thing but a process, fragile, transient, always in flux. "When it attaches itself to unworthy objects," he said, "slavery is the result. When, however, it lets go of these attachments and instead yokes itself up with 'God' [however, in one's culture, God is understood], illumination and freedom are the result."[34] Likewise David Bryant, citing Wolfhart Pannenberg's concept of human "exocentrism," says, "We are fundamentally centered on what is outside of us rather than on ourselves."[35] He continues:

> Human fulfillment comes through an other-directedness that takes us beyond all individual beings to the ultimate horizon within which we know and have to do with all particular beings, to God. As the horizon of beings, the divine life includes all creation, so that we cannot serve God without having regard for creation.[36]

32. Reno, "Pride and Idolatry," p. 173.

33. Reno, "Pride and Idolatry," p. 180.

34. Patrick McNamara, *Neuroscience of Religious Experience* (Cambridge: Cambridge University Press, 2009), p. 147.

35. David J. Bryant, "Imago Dei, Imagination, and Ecological Responsibility," *Theology Today* 57.1 (2000): 35-50 (43), citing Wolfhart Pannenberg, *Anthropology in Theological Perspective* (Philadelphia: Westminster, 1985), pp. 63-74.

36. Bryant, "Imago Dei," p. 43.

Cultural observers indeed note the consumer overload, the "affluenza" afflicting many, appearing as stress-related symptoms such as headaches, hyperacidity, heart palpitations, depression, anxiety, sleeplessness, irritability, all harking back to a lack of "margins" in the American lifestyle. Psychologist Richard Ryan echoes Augustine when he notes that as consumers "we keep looking outside ourselves for satisfactions that can only come from within."[37]

Western society needs desperately to regain understanding of where satisfaction lies for humans, and what a life well lived actually is. Reno saw this as a fully theological conundrum, but perhaps his vision can be balanced by that of biologist E. O. Wilson. An atheist himself, Wilson appeals to religious leaders, saying that science and religion, as two of society's most powerful forces, could be making common cause in defense of an ecosystem both science and religion value.[38] Wilson points out what he calls human "biophilia," love for the biosphere, which enlarges and satisfies. This larger world is not something separate from human culture. Rather, it is the world inside of which human culture is only nested. Even such complex structures as the human economic system live inside this ecosphere, and can act as destructive or cooperative forces within it.

In Isaiah's symbolic world, a shift from consumerism to biophilia might be viewed as dethroning human powers to give place to God and God's creation. In the end, though, it is humans ourselves whose souls are enlarged by making sure that the human-made objects in our lives — whether these are swords, spears, treasures, iPhones, economic indicators, or multinational corporations — regain their place as tools to further wellbeing, and cease to retain the power to assert themselves as gods that we must serve.

When Jesus said "you cannot serve God and wealth," he was speaking to a culture that knew too well the ubiquity of masters on all levels from the household to the empire. He appears to have had no need to say, "And don't even think you can avoid serving any masters at all!" In Matt 6:25-34, immediately after this saying, Jesus offers sound advice against many anxieties, including the anxiety of consumerism: "Look at the birds" whom God feeds, and "consider the lilies of the field" whom God clothes in bright array. Most religious traditions offer similar paths toward the wisdom of serving not manufactured objects but the world we did not make at all, the world of which we ourselves are a part.

37. John De Graaf, David Wann, and Thomas H. Naylor, *Affluenza: The All-Consuming Epidemic,* 2nd ed. (San Francisco: Berrett-Koehler Publishers, 2005), p. 115.

38. E. O. Wilson, *The Creation: An Appeal to Save Life on Earth* (New York: W. W. Norton & Co., 2006), p. 5.

Isaiah 2:2-5 envisions the nations streaming to God for teaching that helps them turn to more fruitful employment than war-mongering, that helps them transform their technology from weapons to the agricultural tools needed for carrying out the vocation given humans in the creation story, the vocation to till and keep the earth (Gen 2:15), or as more recent translations suggest, to "serve (עבד) and preserve (שמר)" it.[39] The scenario reverses the story of Eden, depicting the nations eventually returning to this original vocation. As Brigitte Kahl has pointed out, God's words to the first man, "until you return to the ground," hold a double meaning:

> The "back to the earth" of Gen 3:19 has been almost exclusively remembered at the tombs of the dead. Its challenge to Christian life practices was seldom heard. But the text very explicitly talks about a change of direction, for the Hebrew word for *return* implies also the theological dimension of repentance, turning back to God.[40]

Blenkinsopp has shown that "back to nature" themes appear frequently in Isaiah, opposing the commercial excesses enjoyed by the royal cities Samaria and Jerusalem. Several passages depict inhabitants being slaughtered or deported, and their cities returning to pastoral land inhabited not by humans but by wild animals.[41] Other passages, however, such as Isa 2:2-5, reflect a hope of returning to a lost Eden.[42] Long before the current generation of ecological prophets arose, Isaiah envisioned that the earth will return to its own equilibrium whether humans cooperate or not, whether, that is, our "return to the ground" takes the form of extinction or of cultural transformation.

39. See for instance Ellen Davis, *Scripture, Culture, and Agriculture: An Agrarian Reading of the Bible* (Cambridge: Cambridge University Press, 2009), pp. 29-30.

40. Brigitte Kahl, "Fratricide and Ecocide: Rereading Genesis 2–4," in *Earth Habitat: Eco-Injustice and the Church's Response* (ed. Dieter Hessel and Larry Rasmussen; Minneapolis: Fortress, 2001), p. 57.

41. Joseph Blenkinsopp, "Cityscape to Landscape: The 'Back to Nature' Theme in Isaiah 1–35," in *"Every City Shall Be Forsaken": Urbanism and Prophecy in Ancient Israel and the Near East* (ed. Lester Grabbe and Robert Haak; JSOTSup 330; Sheffield: Sheffield Academic Press, 2001), pp. 35-44 (39).

42. Blenkinsopp, "Cityscape to Landscape," p. 43.

Isaiah's Interpretive Revolution: How Isaiah's Formation Influenced Early Jewish and Christian Interpretation

Jacob Stromberg

"The history of the interpretation of Isaiah begins in the book itself."[1]

The origins of Ancient Judaism intertwine with the beginnings of scriptural exegesis. As Michael Fishbane puts it: "Classical and traditional Jewish culture is fundamentally a text culture — formed, informed, and reformed by Scripture . . . and its interpretation."[2] Scriptural interpretation, as a mode of religious imagination, comes into full view in the Late Second Temple period. By most accounts, its cultivation in this period promises to be one of the keys that will help unlock our understanding of much that followed. Seen this way, Second Temple interpretation becomes crucial to understanding the development of Jewish culture: to describe exegesis in this period is to describe a central dynamic in the development of Judaism.

How, then, should one characterize Second Temple interpretation? This, of course, is a matter of some debate. A central issue in this discussion (and the topic of this article) is how best to construe the relationship between the text and its interpretation in this period. More specifically, how should we describe the relationship between what the Bible meant as a product of ancient Israel and what it was later taken to mean in Second Temple Judaism? How

1. Joseph Blenkinsopp, *Opening the Sealed Book: Interpretations of the Book of Isaiah in Late Antiquity* (Grand Rapids, MI: Eerdmans, 2006), p. 7.

2. Michael Fishbane, "Bible Interpretation," in *The Oxford Handbook of Jewish Studies*, ed. M. Goodman et al. (New York: Oxford University Press, 2002), p. 680.

much of this later interpretation was innovation, and how much of it was inheritance? Did the perspectives of these later readers have native roots[3] in what came before? Or were they wholly the product of their own day?

This question receives a bold answer in John Barton's highly influential treatment of the subject. He argues, "The theology and thought-forms of Second Temple Judaism are not just slightly different from the theology and thought-forms of the Old Testament, they represent a radically different system articulated on quite fresh lines."[4] As the subtitle of Barton's book indicates, his study examines "Perceptions of Ancient Prophecy in Israel after the Exile." He treats these perceptions largely under the rubric of "modes of reading." Thus, his statement captures what he sees as the basic *interpretive* dynamic at play in Second Temple Judaism. It was a full-scale rereading of the Hebrew Bible, an interpretive *tour de force.* Only to a very "small extent" did the Bible itself contribute to these later perceptions.[5] Put this way, there emerges a radical discontinuity between what the Bible originally meant and what it was later taken to mean.

Barton is hardly alone in his assessment. James Kugel has characterized biblical interpretation at the turn of the common era as "a massive rewriting."[6] It was an interpretive revolution that produced a fundamentally changed document — not because the words themselves had changed, but because their meaning had. On this showing, Second Temple interpretation (and with it the communities defined by this) appears to be largely an innovation with very few semantic antecedents in its textual past.

That interpretation took place on an impressive scale in this period and that it was highly innovative cannot be gainsaid; and yet such a construal hardly represents the whole picture. To begin with, as Barton clearly shows, the Hebrew Bible cannot be separated neatly from Second Temple Judaism.[7] Though the origins of the Hebrew Bible can be traced back hundreds of years before this period, the Hebrew Bible is nevertheless in many ways a product of it. Much work has shown that the textual form of individual books and the shape of the emerging scriptural collection itself were still in flux during this period. Indeed, some biblical books are wholly the product of it.

3. Cf. Fishbane, "Bible Interpretation," p. 681.

4. John Barton, *Oracles of God: Perceptions of Ancient Prophecy in Israel after the Exile* (New York: Oxford University Press, 1988), p. 151.

5. Cf. Barton, *Oracles,* p. 150.

6. James L. Kugel, *How to Read the Bible: A Guide to Scripture Then and Now* (New York: Free Press, 2007), p. 672.

7. Barton, *Oracles;* cf. Kugel, *How,* pp. 568, 681-84.

For many scholars, this period witnessed the last stages of the Bible's formation intersecting with the beginnings of its early interpretation.[8] There existed a confluence of composition and interpretation that has been preserved in the textual record. This truth has been demonstrated and elaborated in manifold ways since the discovery of the Dead Sea Scrolls, though the insight itself goes back much further than that. It simply will not do, then, to put the Bible of ancient Israel on one side of the equation and its interpretation in Second Temple Judaism on the other. The evidence itself belies a clean break.

Indeed, a closer look at Barton's work reveals that the real contrast he perceives is not actually between Second Temple Judaism and the Hebrew Bible as such. Rather, the contrast he finds again and again is really between "classical" prophecy in Israel (represented by the pre-exilic figures Amos, Hosea, Isaiah, etc.) and perceptions of such ancient prophecy in Second Temple Judaism. This is a very different contrast. Thus, rather than a radical rereading of, say, the prophetic book Isaiah, Barton discerns a reconfiguration of the prophet himself. Throughout Barton's book it is evident that the real contrast is between these historical figures (as modern scholarship has reconstructed them) and their interpretation in the late Second Temple period.

But one need not read between the lines of Barton's work to see that this is a contrast he is consciously emphasizing. He is quite explicit about this from the start. The pre-exilic classical prophets are to be compared with material from roughly 250 BCE to 250 C.E. with a special "bias to the earlier part of that period and a considerable interest in later Old Testament books which somewhat antedate its upper limit," in other words, the late Second Temple period. He is also quite explicit in placing far less emphasis on writings from the sixth or fifth centuries BCE, and in allowing very little weight at all to fall on redactional additions to the prophetic books.[9] Thus, knowing full well that the prophetic books are the product of extensive redaction (no small amount of which took place in the sixth and fifth centuries), Barton is deliberately identifying a certain gap in the data upon which his argument builds.

It is precisely to this gap that Barton draws attention at the end of his book,

8. See, e.g., Reinhard G. Kratz, *Prophetenstudien: Kleine Schriften II* (FAT 74; Tübingen: Mohr Siebeck, 2011), pp. 32-48; Joseph Blenkinsopp, *Isaiah 56–66* (AB 19B; New York: Doubleday, 2003); Odil H. Steck, *Studien zu Tritojesaja* (BZAW 203; Berlin: Walter de Gruyter, 1991). Of course, the now classic treatment of this phenomenon as it occurred in a variety of periods is Michael Fishbane, *Biblical Interpretation in Ancient Israel* (Oxford: Clarendon Press, 1985).

9. Barton, *Oracles*, pp. 5-7.

as an area needing further study, should one want to understand more fully the role of the prophetic books in the development he seeks to uncover — the decisive break between what pre-exilic classical prophecy actually was and what it was later perceived to be by those readers in the late Second Temple Period. This break, Barton argues, was "a segment of the time-line of history, not a Euclidean point on it," that is, the break took place over a period of time, the beginning of which saw the cessation of the activity of the classical prophets, and the ending of which was marked "by the coming into existence of a fixed corpus of prophetic scriptures." Between these two points were the collection and editing of the prophetic books, about which he concludes, "we may say that there is a 'tunnel' period between the activity of named prophets and the emergence of finished books bearing their names, and that it is during that period that the shift in perception described in the present study must have begun to take place."[10]

In other words, the formation of prophetic literature and this shift in perspective were not only coextensive for a time; but it was precisely when the prophets were being edited that the whole process began, making the redaction of these books paramount (even if frustratingly difficult to access) evidence for the origins of this whole development.[11] While Barton gives some attention to the collecting and editing of the prophets, he largely brackets this out and regards it as an area for future research, a reasonable decision given the vast breadth of material covered in his book. In one sense, then, missing from the argument are the books themselves — that is, the books in their redacted forms, the forms emerging from the tunnel which saw the beginning of a shift in perspective later proving decisive for early readers.

Thus, to seek to fill this gap in the development traced by Barton is to address a basic question: What role did these books play in this process? How did they reconfigure the classical prophets? What portraits did they paint? And how did these portraits mediate the prophetic message to later readers? After all, late Second Temple interpreters knew nothing of a critically reconstructed Amos or Isaiah; instead, they had the books bearing their names, the portraits of the prophets. This point is especially crucial in dealing with a book like Isaiah, because, though it preserves the words of the eighth-century

10. Barton, *Oracles*, p. 271.

11. Some of the tradents of this literature may have been conscious of a shift in what is called prophecy, seeking to register this awareness in their work. Cf. Christopher Seitz, "The Divine Council: Temporal Transition and New Prophecy in the Book of Isaiah," *JBL* 109 (1990): 229-247.

prophet, the book itself is ultimately the product of early Second Temple times — placing us squarely within the very period under consideration.

All this to say, any characterization of biblical interpretation in the Second Temple period must reckon with two points: (1) the liminal position held by many biblical books at the point of their final composition, preserving sources reaching back into ancient Israel, but being redacted into their final form in this late period; and (2) the role the books themselves played (in their final redacted form) in mediating the messages of these ancient figures to later readers. (Accepting the common charge that redaction criticism often yields uncertain results, I cannot see how this line of inquiry can be gotten around, once one has set the goal as historical understanding. Reconstructing the historical figures of the prophets requires redaction critical work no less than does understanding the final form of the prophetic literature, for both begin with the text we have — a redacted text — and move from there along the same path, albeit in opposite directions.[12])

I would argue that, despite Barton's suggestion that this is an area worthy of future research, this crucial stage in the process of interpretation has yet to be fully appreciated, and that consideration of this stage results in a much subtler and more complex understanding of the Bible and its later readers than is often on offer to students of reception history. Scholars interested in early exegesis need to give careful consideration to that stage of interpretation embedded in the composition and editing of the Bible itself, particularly as this was undertaken in the early Second Temple period, just after the exile.

With this in mind and returning to the subtitle of Barton's work, I would like to revisit "Perceptions of Ancient Prophecy in Israel after the Exile." To do so, I focus on the book of Isaiah, a book whose composition presents an important moment in the history Barton and Kugel seek to trace. Where Kugel sees a *metaphorical* rewriting of the Hebrew Bible by late Second Temple interpreters, I will argue that Isaiah was *literally* rewritten by early Second Temple readers, scribes active just after the exile. The result, I would maintain, is fraught with interpretive decision. The post-exilic shaping of Isaiah itself represents an interpretive revolution. And this was of the greatest hermeneutical consequence for how the book would be read later in the period concerned.

12. Reconstructing the original prophets and their messages requires redaction criticism in reverse.

The Role of Interpretation in the Composition of Isaiah

In the book of Isaiah we have a consummate example of the way composition intersects with interpretation in this period. Its composition history begins in the period of the classical prophets (with the eighth-century Judean prophet Isaiah) and extends into the early Second Temple period, after the exile when the book was given its final form.[13] Its composition history, therefore, spans the period Barton describes, and so potentially offers in itself a rather tidy exemplar of the process he outlines, a reconfiguration of the classical prophets in the Second Temple Period. In other words, Isaiah presents us with the words of a classical prophet framed by an editor of the early Second Temple period.

13. Isaiah 24–27 may date to a later time. Cf. J. Hibbard, *Intertextuality in Isaiah 24–27: The Reuse and Evocation of Earlier Texts and Traditions* (FAT/II 16; Tübingen: Mohr Siebeck, 2006), pp. 32-36. Also a few scholars would date 56-66 to the Hellenistic period. Both passages would still be earlier than the texts discussed here (found in 1QS 8 and the Gospels), so that the debate is largely immaterial to the present argument. Nevertheless, I do not regard a Hellenistic dating of 56-66 to be very probable. So far as I am aware, the best evidence for a Hellenistic dating of the final form of TI comes in 66:22-24, which outlines the conditions that were to obtain in the "new heavens and earth." The righteous seed will endure; all flesh will worship; but the bodies of those who rebel will be an "abomination" (דראון), a word whose occurrence in a similar scenario at the end of Daniel has suggested to many some form of literary influence: "many will awake from sleep in the dusty earth, some to everlasting life and others to reproach and everlasting abomination (דראון)" (Dan 12:2). This word occurs nowhere else in the entire Hebrew Bible. There are, however, significant differences between the outlook of Isa 66:24 and Dan 12:2 (e.g. "corpses" in Isaiah, but resurrected bodies in Daniel) that suggest this is not simply a case of the Isaiah text having been added so late that it reflects the later perspective of Daniel; *pace* Claus Westermann, *Das Buch Jesaia, 40–66* (ATD 19; Göttingen: Vandenhoeck & Ruprecht, 1966), p. 340; Karl Marti, *Das Buch Jesaja* (KHAT; Tübingen: Mohr Siebeck, 1900), p. 414. It seems much more probable that Daniel is alluding back to Isaiah; so, e.g., James A. Montgomery, *A Critical and Exegetical Commentary on the Book of Daniel* (ICC; Edinburgh: T & T Clark, 1927), p. 472; Fishbane, *Biblical Interpretation in Ancient Israel*, p. 493. This would explain the difference between the two passages, and is supported by the probable influence of Isa 53 on Dan 12:3 (the verse immediately following 12:2), as well as strong evidence suggesting Isaiah exerted a great deal of influence in the preceding chapter. On Daniel 11 in this respect, see Andrew Teeter, "Isaiah and the King of As/syria in Daniel's Final Vision: On the Rhetoric of Inner-Scriptural Allusion and the Hermeneutics of 'Mantological Exegesis,'" in *A Teacher for All Generations: Essays in Honor of James C. VanderKam*, ed. Eric F. Mason et al. (JSJSup 153/1; Leiden: Brill, 2012), pp. 169-199. On the reference to Isa 53, see Blenkinsopp, *Opening*, p. 22; John J. Collins, *Daniel* (Minneapolis: Fortress Press, 1993), p. 393; Fishbane, *Biblical Interpretation in Ancient Israel*, p. 493; Harold L. Ginsberg, "The Oldest Interpretation of the Suffering Servant," *VT* 3 (1953): 400-404.

From beginning to end Isaiah's composition lasted at least two hundred years, during which time massive change (social, political, theological, linguistic, etc.) will have put sufficient distance between the prophet's original oracles and their later readers such that there arose the need for someone to interpret their sense.[14] This role was of necessity adopted by the redactors of the book, who were charged with the task of making sense of the ancient oracles for others, but who first had to make sense of these texts for themselves — the one no doubt feeding back into the other. And so this history of composition was fraught with exegesis (conscious and unconscious — but always necessary), fragments of which can now be read off Isaiah's textured surface.

This textured surface stems from two related textual processes at play in the book's formation: (1) earlier texts were redacted in the light of later ones; and (2) later texts allude to and interpret earlier ones. So, for example, many scholars argue that the post-exilic TI alludes to earlier exilic and pre-exilic texts from chs. 1–55. At the same time, many also suspect that this earlier material has at points been edited in the light of TI. Thus, the interplay of texts can be traced in both directions. Significantly, both processes are hermeneutical, in that they reflect the interpretive decisions of later editors and are intended to influence later readers.[15]

With that in mind, I now turn to the book of Isaiah and to two representative examples within it illustrating the confluence of composition and interpretation so crucial to understanding the reconfiguration of the prophet. In each example we will see the textual remains of an interpretive revolution that took place in the post-exilic rewriting of Isaiah. For each, we will also see that

14. Cf. James L. Kugel, *Traditions of the Bible: A Guide to the Bible As It Was at the Start of the Common Era* (Cambridge, Mass.: Harvard University Press, 1998), pp. 3-4.

15. Too much has been written on this to properly document it here. I simply list a few works in relation to the post-exilic stratum of the book. See Joseph Blenkinsopp, *Isaiah 1–39* (AB 19; New York: Doubleday, 2000); Joseph Blenkinsopp, *Isaiah 40–55* (AB 19A; New York: Doubleday, 2002); Blenkinsopp, *Isaiah 56–66;* Steck, *Studien,* p. 203; Wim A. M. Beuken, "Isaiah Chapters lxv–lxvi: Trito-Isaiah and the Closure of the Book of Isaiah," in *Congress Volume Leuven 1989,* ed. J. A. Emerton, VTSup (Leiden: Brill, 1991), pp. 204-21; Marvin A. Sweeney, "Prophetic Exegesis in Isaiah 65–66," in *Writing and Reading the Scroll of Isaiah: Studies of an Interpretive Tradition,* ed. C. Broyles and C. Evans (VTSup 70/1; Leiden: Brill, 1997), pp. 455-74; Hugh G. M. Williamson, *A Critical and Exegetical Commentary on Isaiah 1–27, 1: Isaiah 1–5* (ICC; London: T. & T. Clark International, 2006), pp. 7-11, 126-62. I have sought to give my own account of this problem in Jacob Stromberg, *Isaiah After Exile: The Author of Third Isaiah as Reader and Redactor of the Book* (Oxford: Oxford University Press, 2011). Further literature discussing these phenomena in all stages of the book's history can be found in Jacob Stromberg, *An Introduction to the Study of Isaiah* (London: T & T Clark, 2011).

this interpretive revolution was of the greatest hermeneutical consequence for the readers of the late Second Temple Period.

Isaiah: A Spokesman to His Contemporaries, or a Prophet for the Future?

The first redactional text I would like to consider relates to a mode of reading that Barton regards as distinctive of the late Second Temple Period. In this mode of reading, later interpreters understood prophecy to be "the utterance or writing of oracles whose fulfillment lies in *the far distant future*."[16] This perception of the scope of ancient prophecy dominated its interpretation in this later period. The prophets of old had foreseen days long after their own.

As Barton notes, this view stands in sharp contrast to modern critical reconstructions of the classical prophets. In these reconstructions, the ancient prophets — whose message was characterized by "challenge, protest, and moral seriousness"[17] — "had been charged with a message of *immediate* concern to their own contemporaries."[18] Contrary to the perceptions of late Second Temple readers, then, the concerns of the real ancient prophets lay in their own day.

Barton's characterization of the classical pre-exilic prophets seems to me to be entirely plausible, so long as it remains at the level of historical description.[19] Much in the first thirty-nine chapters of Isaiah would seem to support

16. Barton, *Oracles,* p. 197. The italics are mine.

17. Barton, *Oracles,* p. 267.

18. Barton, *Oracles,* p. 180. The italics are mine.

19. A challenge to the view that the message of the classical prophets was largely negative has been issued by some recent work comparing Isaiah with Assyrian prophecies. See, e.g., Matthijs J. de Jong, "Biblical Prophecy — A Scribal Enterprise: The Old Testament Prophecy of Unconditional Judgement Considered as a Literary Phenomenon," *VT* 61 (2011): 39-70; Uwe Becker, *Jesaja — Von der Botschaft zum Buch* (FRLANT 178; Göttingen: Vandenhoeck & Ruprecht, 1997); Matthijs J. de Jong, *Isaiah among the Ancient Near Eastern Prophets: A Comparative Study of the Earliest Stages of the Isaiah Tradition and the Neo-Assyrian Prophecies* (VTSup 117; Leiden: Brill, 2007). See also the interaction between Becker and Barthel in Matthias Köckert, Uwe Becker, and Jörg Barthel, "Das Problem des historischen Jesaja," in *Prophetie in Israel,* ed. I. Fischer, K. Schmid, and H. G. M. Williamson, *Altes Testament und Moderne* (Münster: LIT Verlag, 2003), pp. 105-36. In this whole debate, there is a danger of assuming that the prophets' thought operated in totally static terms; some of these figures, Isaiah for instance, may have developed expectations that reached beyond their own day, on which, see, e.g., Hugh G. M. Williamson, "Hope under Judgement: The Prophets of the Eighth Century BCE," *EQ* 72 (2000): 291-306.

this view. Many of the oracles considered genuine in this part of the book do not seem to look into the future beyond Israel's entanglement with the Assyrian empire, the ruling power in the prophet's day.

If this is an accurate characterization of Isaiah as he actually was and of what he actually said, then why did late Second Temple readers construe him so differently, understanding his message not as a word addressed to those in the eighth century but as one that looked far into the distant future? The answer, I would suggest, is that they read a prophetic book that portrayed the prophet, not as he has been critically reconstructed by modern scholarship, but as he had been construed by the book's post-exilic shape, which they inherited. The book of Isaiah received its final shape in the early part of the Second Temple period, precisely when such perceptions were taking hold according to Barton. It is this shaping that appears in several patently editorial texts in the book. Each of these post-exilic texts reflects the shift in perspective described by Barton. The prophet's words referred not to his own day, but to another — which brings us to our first example.

One of the best-known instances of post-exilic editing in the book of Isaiah comes in ch. 6, the account of the prophet's commission. Although most would still regard at least part of this chapter as a genuine first-person account by the prophet himself,[20] they also find evidence that it has been edited from this very late perspective. Because this chapter portrays the call of the prophet and outlines the divine plan for his ministry, it probably appeared programmatic to later readers, including Isaiah's later editors. This would be the simplest explanation for why this chapter seems to be alluded to in almost every subsequent level of the book's composition.[21] It stands to reason that any editing of this chapter from the post-exilic period will have had a direct impact on how the prophet and his work were perceived and construed at that time. It will have been this reconfiguration *now textualized* that made its way to late Second Temple readers.

20. E.g. Jörg Barthel, *Prophetenwort und Geschichte: Die Jesajaüberlieferung in Jes 6–8 und 28–31* (FAT 19; Tübingen: Mohr Siebeck, 1997), pp. 79-82; Ronald E. Clements, *Jerusalem and the Nations: Studies in the Book of Isaiah* (Sheffield: Sheffield Phoenix Press, 2011), pp. 53-65.

21. Many of these allusions are helpfully gathered together in Ronald E. Clements, "Beyond Tradition History: Deutero-Isaianic Development of First Isaiah's Themes," *JSOT* 31 (1985): 95-113; Hugh G. M. Williamson, *The Book Called Isaiah: Deutero-Isaiah's Role in Composition and Redaction* (Oxford: Clarendon, 1994), pp. 46-51. Further literature on this may be found in Torsten Uhlig, *The Theme of Hardening in the Book of Isaiah* (FAT/II 39; Tübingen: Mohr Siebeck, 2009).

Proposals for the formation of Isaiah 6 differ, but they invariably agree on the last line of the last verse (זרע קדש מצבתה). This line is seen as the product of a later editor who wanted to identify the "stump" (מצבת) of v. 13 as a purified remnant surviving divine judgment on the people. Verse 13 reads:

> Even if a tenth part remain in it,
>   it will be burned again,
> like a terebinth or an oak
>   whose stump (מצבת) remains standing
>   when it is felled.
> The holy seed is its stump (זרע קדש מצבתה).

Many difficulties surround the translation of this verse.[22] However, by almost any account, the comment "the holy seed is its stump" is secondary to it. This comment is clearly a gloss seeking to clarify the מצבת in the earlier composition, a word whose meaning has proven obscure to modern lexicographers. Besides possessing the classic traits of a gloss,[23] the comment looks secondary to its context for quite a different reason.

This is presented most clearly by John Emerton whom we can only summarize here.[24] In brief, he isolates two crucial points: first, the infinitive לבער is best understood in the light of its use elsewhere as signaling the *destruction* of the tenth ("it will be burned again");[25] and, second, this destruction is carried through the next line, the comparison with the trees, because nothing there signals a contrast. As a consequence of these two points, Isa 6:13, minus the last three words, sets out an oracle of unrelenting doom. In this light, the comment "the holy seed is its stump" is obviously secondary, confirming its

22. See especially the treatment in John A. Emerton, "The Translation and Interpretation of Isaiah vi. 13," in *Interpreting the Hebrew Bible: Essays in Honour of E. I. J. Rosenthal,* ed. J. A. Emerton and S. C. Reif (Cambridge: Cambridge University Press, 1982), pp. 85-118. As Emerton shows (p. 89), the LXX reflects an omission, αὐτῆς at the end of the line likely translating the feminine pronoun on מצבתה.

23. The addition captures features characteristic of a gloss (a comment interpreting a difficult word) as well as an interpolation (an addition intended as part of the running text). See Emanuel Tov, "Glosses, Interpolations, and Other Types of Scribal Additions in the Text of the Hebrew Bible," in *Language, Theology, and the Bible: Essays in Honour of James Barr,* ed. S. E. Balentine and J. Barton (Oxford: Clarendon Press, 1994), pp. 41, 47.

24. Emerton, "Isaiah vi. 13," pp. 85-118.

25. As Emerton notes, the meaning of לבער could be translated "to graze," though even then the meaning likely focuses on destruction, so that the point here would not be affected. Cf. Williamson, *Isaiah 1–5,* p. 266.

status as a gloss. Using the residual "stump" someone introduced hope into an otherwise hopeless passage.[26]

If זרע קדש מצבתה is secondary to the original composition, then *when* was it added? In answering this, the first thing to note is that, according to the logic of God's answer to Isaiah in vv. 11-13, the "holy seed" was to survive the exile, which is clearly spoken of in v. 12 ("and the Lord will send [ורחק] people far away, and the forsakenness in the midst of the land will be great"). Hence, the passage itself suggests the remnant "seed" refers to a community alive during, or after, the exile.

It is therefore noteworthy that the only other occurrence of the expression "holy seed" (זרע קדש) in the Hebrew Bible occurs in Ezra 9:2. Because Ezra 9 stems from the post-exilic period, we might expect the same for the addition at the end of Isa 6:13.[27] This suggestion is supported by Ezra 9, which indicates that the phrase "holy seed" finds its origin in that late period. As Fishbane has shown, Ezra 9 combines laws from Deut 7:1-6 and 23:4-9(3-8) to justify the decree that the returnees of Ezra's day should divorce their foreign wives.[28] Deuteronomy's presence in the process described by Fishbane strongly suggests that the expression "the holy seed" in Ezra 9:2 derives from the phrase "holy nation" in Deut 7:2-6. That is, exegetical innovation transformed Deuteronomy's עם קדוש into Ezra's זרע הקדש. In the light of Deuteronomy's role in Ezra 9, this line of influence seems most probable. Thus, Ezra 9 places the origin of the expression "the holy seed" in the post-exilic period, with the exegesis of Deuteronomy.

If this phrase originated in the post-exilic period, then its use in the gloss on Isa 6:13 must stem from that time or later, which would also suggest an explanation for its close parallel to 65:9 where we again read of a righteous remnant called a "seed."[29] To regard the gloss in 6:13 as post-exilic fits nicely with the secondary nature of the line, a position which was established on entirely different grounds above. If so, then it seems we have found our first clue to help unlock that post-exilic perception of the prophet and his message now interwoven throughout the book.

How does this gloss interpret and thereby reconfigure the prophet's message?[30] Beyond the obvious fact that it identifies the stump with a holy rem-

26. See the formulation of Emerton, "Isaiah vi. 13," p. 110.

27. So Blenkinsopp, *Isaiah 1–39*, p. 226.

28. Fishbane, *Biblical Interpretation in Ancient Israel*, p. 117.

29. This point is developed further in Stromberg, *Isaiah After Exile*, pp. 160-74.

30. This question is predicated on the assumption that the reader is supposed to think that what was told the prophet in 6:11-13 would have borne some relation to what he preached,

nant, this post-exilic addition has a larger effect on the scope of the prophet's commission. In Isa 6:8 God calls out, "Whom will I send and who will go for us?" and Isaiah answers, "Here am I, send me." What God says next has no doubt puzzled readers ever since: "Go, say to this people, 'hear but do not understand, see but do not perceive.'" Isaiah was to "make fat" the heart of the people so that they would not hear with their ears or understand with their heart and so turn and be healed (v. 10). Distressed, he asked "עד מתי (how long)" this state of stupor would last (v. 11). God answered, "עד אשר (until) cities are destroyed to the point of being without inhabitant" and people are moved away "and there is a great forsakenness in the land," and until even those who remain in it are destroyed (vv. 11-13). This state of spiritual stupor — effecting a complete devastation of the land — would last until all that remained was a "holy seed." And then, it is implied, it would end. Without the addition of the last three words, the answer given Isaiah would be wholly negative. The addition therefore puts a positive spin on the passage, a glimmer of light at the end of a dark tunnel. A community, righteous in character, would survive to inherit the land.

Since we saw above that the gloss was of post-exilic origin, this interpretive addition effectively extends the scope of the message Isaiah was to bear. Seen through the lens of this late redaction, Isaiah's message looked forward to the post-exilic period or perhaps beyond that to a still further distant future, such as that found in chs. 65–66. Either way, whoever inserted the gloss did not see the temporal scope of Isaiah's commission as limited to the eighth century, but assumed that it looked far beyond the prophet's own day into a future removed from it by at least two hundred years. Embedded in this interpretive gloss is a perspective on the ancient prophet that maps precisely onto the shift in perspective Barton sees in late Second Temple readers. According to the interpretation of this post-exilic editor, Isaiah looked to the remote future from the start.

If the commission of the prophet came to be rendered this way, we can expect to find editorial texts reflecting a similar perspective in other parts of the book now bearing his name. Indeed, I seek to argue precisely this in a recent monograph on Isaiah's post-exilic composition.[31] There, I find evidence that the gloss in 6:13 is part of a larger redactional rewriting of Isaiah in this period. If that is correct, then the perspective in this small addition is indica-

---

an assumption that seems justified in the light of v. 9 and the fact that ch. 6 purports to be a first person account by the prophet himself.

31. Stromberg, *Isaiah After Exile.*

tive of a perspective now woven throughout the whole book from the first chapter to the last.

As with the gloss in 6:13, this pervasive post-exilic redaction illuminates a mode of reading embedded in the book, a conceptual reconfiguration preserved in textual form: the message of the eighth-century Judean prophet was not limited to his contemporaries in the Assyrian period, but spoke of a distant future. An interpretive revolution fueled a massive rewriting of Isaiah after the exile, producing the prophetic book that late Second Temple interpreters would know. Thus, the change in perspective Barton traces (which is so characteristic of these later readers) was already well under way before their time. And so, it was probably the book itself (along with the line of interpretive tradition captured in it) that shaped these later readers.

Reconfiguring the "Way of the Lord"

Because the rewriting of Isaiah is permeated with a mode of reading that later dominated the interpretation of the prophets, we can reasonably infer (as I have done) that the later readers were influenced by the earlier revolution. But do we have any direct evidence that this was so? To demonstrate that this rewriting had such an effect on later readers (and to avoid a wholly circumstantial case that this was so), I would like to discuss the second example of redaction, along with its interpretive influence in the late Second Temple Period. The example I have in mind centers on the interpretation of the exilic Isa 40 in the post-exilic Isa 57. Significantly, both of these passages are thought to draw on Isa 6 through allusion,[32] so that what follows here will have been regarded as ultimately stemming from, as well as construing, the message of the eighth-century prophet. At the same time, because the gloss in 6:13 was seen to derive from the post-exilic period, precisely when ch. 57 was written, the possibility suggests itself that both passages are related to the same compositional strategy. At any rate, the passage from TI reflects an exegetical trans-

32. On allusions in Isa 40:1-8 back to ch. 6, see, e.g., Williamson, *Book,* p. 38; Seitz, "Divine," pp. 229-247. On allusions in Isa 57:14-21 back to ch. 6, see Williamson, *Book,* p. 39; Wolfgang Lau, *Schriftgelehrte Prophetie in Jes 56–66* (BZAW 225; Berlin: Walter de Gruyter, 1994), pp. 120-21; Risto Nurmela, *The Mouth of the Lord Has Spoken: Inner-Biblical Allusions in Second and Third Isaiah* (Lanham, Md.: University Press of America, 2006), pp. 93-94; Benjamin Sommer, *A Prophet Reads Scripture: Allusion in Isaiah 40–66* (Stanford: Stanford University Press, 1998), pp. 91-92, 250-51 n. 53; Blenkinsopp, *Isaiah 56–66,* p. 168. I seek to draw together these elements of 57:14-21 in Stromberg, *Isaiah After Exile,* pp. 165-66.

formation of the earlier text from DI, and elements of this transformation can be shown to have made their way into the interpretation of Isa 40 in the Dead Sea Scrolls and in the New Testament.

The text in question is Isa 57:14-21, which represents a stunning exegetical reconfiguration of DI's prologue, chapter 40. Of the borrowings present in the later post-exilic passage, the clearest instance comes in 57:14.[33]

> Cast up, Cast up (סלו סלו);[34] Clear the way (פנו דרך); Lift up the stumbling block from the way of my people (דרך עמי).

Most would agree that this represents an interpretive transformation of the older imperative in Isa 40:3.[35]

> In the desert, prepare the way of the Lord (פנו דרך יהוה); In the wilderness, make straight a highway (מסלה) for our God.

In the passage, the imperative in 40:3 anticipates the theophany in v. 5. According to the divine voice in Isa 40, the time had come to offer words of reassurance to a beleaguered people: "Speak tenderly to Jerusalem . . . for she has received double from the hand of the Lord for all her sins." "Her service" was complete. It is almost certain that the "service" in view here was the period of Babylonian captivity viewed as a penal sentence levied against the people for their wrongdoing — an idea pervading the exilic DI. The end of this sentence signaled the beginning of a brighter day, and it was to be initiated by a theophany whose language evokes that of return and restoration elsewhere in DI.[36] This is what the imperative anticipates in Isa 40.

33. The unidentified voice in 57:14 (ואמר) clearly draws on those voices from 40:3, 6 (ואמר) which appear equally anonymous. Beyond these points of contact, the borrowing of ch. 40 likely continued on into 58:1-2, the passage immediately following 57:21. Isaiah 58:1-2 looks as if it could be taking up 40:6-9. In both, the commands issue forth to "call out" (קרא, 40:6; 58:1) and to "lift up your voice" (הרם/הרימי קולך, 40:9; 58:1), though the content to be proclaimed differs considerably in each passage, suggesting again that the later text has developed the earlier. Indeed, the development parallels that between 57:14 and 40:3, by introducing a call to moral preparation (cf. the rest of ch. 58 to which v. 1 is the introduction).

34. 1QIsa[a] adds המסלה as an object (cf. 62:10). In support of the MT, compare the LXX where ὁδοὺς probably translates דרך.

35. So, e.g., Lau, *Prophetie,* pp. 118-20; Walther Zimmerli, "Zur Sprache Tritojesajas," in *Gottes Offenbarung. Gesammelte Aufsätze* (Munich: Kaiser Verlag, 1969), pp. 223-24; Blenkinsopp, *Isaiah 56–66,* pp. 168-70.

36. Thus, the passage leading up to the theophany employs language used elsewhere in DI to describe Jerusalem's restoration and the return of the exiles. Elsewhere in DI, מדבר parallels

In citing this imperative, Isa 57 renews it, again anticipating restoration, one modeled on the exilic vision just described. So, where Isa 40:1 proclaims, "Comfort, comfort my people (נחמו נחמו עמי)," Isa 57:18 promises "comforts" (נחמים) to those addressed. The old promise of restoration is transformed by the new context in ch. 57. Instead of offering comfort to the whole people as does ch. 40, Isa 57 offers comfort only to the humble and crushed of spirit (v. 15). It cautions that "there is no peace for the wicked" (v. 21). This suggests restoration would now be enjoyed only by the righteous, the wicked having no share in it. Such a division in Israel is completely absent in the source text, Isa 40.

This conceptual transformation required specific textual reformulations in the citation itself. In Isa 40:3 it is the "way of the Lord" needing to be cleared, whereas in 57:14 — the citation — it is "the way of my people" needing this. Moreover, the citation adds that it is a "stumbling block" (מכשול) needing to be cleared from the way of the people, a word absent from its source. Thus, while the post-exilic citation renews the "comfort" first offered in Isa 40, it perceives an obstacle blocking the people's enjoyment of it. A "stumbling block" now stands in the way of divine blessing.

What was that obstacle? If context is any guide, the author saw that obstacle as some form of iniquity. The word "iniquity" itself occurs in v. 17 where God announces his anger against the people. Identifying the "stumbling block" with sin also explains why the imperative in v. 14 is followed by the statement in vv. 15-16. One was to "clear the way" because (כי) God dwells with the humble and is willing to relent from his anger. Moreover, failure to heed the imperative to clear the way carried consequences. A stern warning concludes the passage in vv. 19-21, stating that, while divine שלום would become available, "there is no שלום for the wicked, says my God." Such consequences also suggest the obstacle in view was a moral one. Iniquity stood in the way of divine blessing. That was the stumbling block.[37] Accordingly, to remove the stumbling block was to remove iniquity. In its new post-exilic configuration, then, the imperative to "prepare the way" has become moral preparation,[38] an interpretation supported by everything in the context of the citation.[39]

ערבה only at 41:19 (the transformation of the wilderness) and at 51:3 (God comforts Zion making her wilderness like Eden). Elsewhere in DI, דרך parallels מסלה only at 49:11 (the mountains will be made into a way and the highways raised up so that the exiles may return).

37. Compare מכשל עון in Ezek 7:19 and the comments of Moshe Greenberg, *Ezekiel 1–20* (AB 22; Garden City: Doubleday, 1983), p. 153.

38. Cf. Lau, *Prophetie,* pp. 119-220; Zimmerli, "Sprache," pp. 224-25; Blenkinsopp, *Isaiah 56–66,* p. 169.

39. Everything in the chapter leading up to 57:14-21 prepares for this understanding;

We can see just how far this new formulation goes in transforming the original imperative of 40:3, when we compare the different motives generating the source and the citation. In Isa 40, the imperative goes forth because the people had paid for their transgressions so that restoration was coming to all. In Isa 57, the imperative goes forth for precisely the opposite reason: iniquity remained, needing removal before restoration could be enjoyed. The interpretive reconfiguration is striking.[40] Isaiah 57 reaffirms the older promise of salvation, but restricts it to those whose way has been prepared — a hermeneutic evident everywhere in TI.

The new imperative enjoins the addressees to moral preparation and it assumes a division among the people. Neither aspect is present in the source, Isa 40. Both are introduced by the exegetical citation as part of the book's post-exilic composition. For those acquainted with the interpretation of Isa 40 in the late Second Temple Period, this reformulation will sound utterly

---

hence, v. 14 is preceded by a contrast between those who misplace their trust and those who trust in the Lord. Everything that follows the passage urges moral preparation (chs. 58–59), material which also appears to cite ch. 40 (see note 33 above) and which continues with other citations of DI in the same vein (compare, e.g., 58:8b with 52:12b as well as 59:1a with 50:2).

40. I do not regard this as an instance of revision. What distinguishes revision from interpretation is that the former seeks to replace while the latter aims to explicate. Cf. Sommer, *Prophet*, pp. 25-28. In form, commentary may not differ all that much from revision, but in intent they are worlds apart. On this understanding, TI was clearly not written as revision. It was written onto, rather than instead of, the earlier material in chs. 1–55. Indeed, it is highly probable that the preservation of the earlier oracles owed itself to the author(s) of this later post-exilic section of the book: see Stromberg, *Isaiah After Exile*, pp. 143-46. Nevertheless, it may reasonably be asked just how 57:14 reflects interpretation when it represents such a radical reconfiguration of 40:3. Apart from saying that 57 was written as an interpretive lens through which the reader of the book was to approach 40 (so that it is interpretive in this sense), I think it probable that the reformulation of 40:3 stemmed from the fact that this passage was not read in isolation from, but in connection with, other earlier oracles in the book — oracles which will have been regarded as of a piece with 40:3 in the light of their common divine origin. Of paramount significance in this respect is the reference to the "high and lofty one" whose "name is holy" in 57:15 where many detect an allusion to the "holy" one of ch. 6 whose throne is "high and lofty" (see note 32 above). In this light, the exegetical procedure seems to have been to read the offer made in ch. 40 through the textual lens of the holiness and exaltedness of God spoken of in ch. 6, divine traits, both of which will have suggested the element of moral imperative in the light of the author's own negative assessment of the people (e.g. 57:17, 20-21). This procedure produced a new theological synthesis which was grounded in the sense of both passages, and sponsored by the parallels already present between 40:1-8 and ch. 6 (see note 32 above). Such an exegetical blend of earlier Isaianic texts can be discerned at several points in TI, such as in 56:1; 60; and 65 to name just a few. On these see Stromberg, *Isaiah After Exile*, pp. 5 n. 22, 13 n. 7, 74-77, 91-97, 101-09.

familiar. Both moves are found in the exegesis of Isa 40:3 at Qumran and in the NT.

The *Rule of the Community* (1QS) preserves an interpretation of Isa 40:3 that, according to many scholars, reaches back to the very beginnings of the Qumran sect. This interpretation, preserved in column eight of the scroll,[41] appears to recount the exegetical justification for the sect's self-segregation in the Judean wilderness.[42] This passage tells the covenanters of the imperative to separate from evil "by going into the wilderness to prepare there the way of the Lord." This injunction anticipates "the supportive citation from Isa 40:3":[43] "As it is written, "In the wilderness, prepare the way of ****; make straight a highway in the desert for our God." This citation provided straightforward scriptural warrant (even if after the fact) for their formation of a community in the wilderness. To separate from evil required going to the wilderness.

What one was required to do once there — to prepare the way of the Lord — is explicated in the rest of the passage: "This is the study of the Torah which he commanded through the hand of Moses, that they may do according to all that has been revealed." Read this way, preparing the way involved studied obedience to the Torah of Moses as well as separation from "the wicked." Both aspects of the exegesis indicate that Isa 40:3 was taken as an injunction to moral preparation.[44] In the light of the sect's orientation with regard to the future, this preparation probably anticipated a future divine act.[45] And so, the *Rule's* exegesis of Isa 40:3 assumes both aspects of that post-exilic reconfiguration noted above — a division between the righteous and the wicked, and in the light of this, the need for moral preparation. Neither is present in Isa 40 itself; but both appear in the exegetical transformation of this passage in Isa 57.

41. 1QS 8:13-15. Cf. 1QS 9:19-20.

42. The editorial history of the *Rule of the Community* is disputed. The citation of Isa 40:3 here is absent in 4QS^{d} 6, so the interpretation of the citation may be due to an editor. See further George J. Brooke, "Isaiah 40:3 and the Wilderness Community," in *New Qumran Texts and Studies: Proceedings of the First Meeting of the International Organization for Qumran Studies, Paris 1992*, ed. George J. Brooke (STDJ 15; Leiden: Brill, 1994), pp. 117-132; Alison Schofield, *From Qumran to the Yahad: A New Paradigm of Textual Development for the Community Rule* (STDJ 77; Leiden: Brill, 2009), pp. 159-62.

43. Michael Fishbane, "Use, Authority and Interpretation of Mikra at Qumran," in *Mikra: Text, Translation, Reading & Interpretation of the Hebrew Bible in Ancient Judaism & Early Christianity*, ed. Martin Jan Mulder and Harry Sysling (Philadelphia: Fortress Press, 1988), p. 349.

44. Cf. 1QS 9:19-21.

45. Cf. 1QS 9.

Both interpretive moves are also embedded in the Gospel accounts of John the Baptist's desert ministry.[46] These accounts creatively parse the parallelism in Isa 40:3 to portray John as the "voice crying out in the wilderness (φωνὴ βοῶντος ἐν τῇ ἐρήμῳ)." Accordingly, John's message is equated with the Isaianic imperative, "prepare the way of the Lord." Since John's message is portrayed as "the baptism of repentance for the forgiveness of sins"[47] (and because people are said to have gone into the wilderness to meet him for precisely this purpose), the Isaianic imperative — which his ministry was seen to fulfill — was understood in terms of moral preparation. Moreover, because this moral preparation anticipated a great divine act of judgment on the people, the exegesis assumes a division between the righteous and the wicked.

While the exegesis implied in the Gospel accounts differs sharply from aspects of that reading found in the *Rule of the Community*, this only tends to cast their interpretive agreement into sharper relief. Both communities read Isa 40:3 ("prepare the way of the Lord") as a call for moral preparation, seeing the old imperative through the lens of a division among the people. Neither aspect is actually found in Isa 40 itself. But both appear in the post-exilic reconfiguration of this passage in Isa 57.

While neither the *Rule of the Community* nor the Baptist narrative actually cites Isa 57, the interpretive antecedent found in this post-exilic rewriting is too blatant to ignore. The interpretive antecedent in Isa 57 strongly suggests that this passage has generated, or captured a moment in, the history of Isa 40's exegesis that surfaces at Qumran and in the NT.[48] As these texts testify, Isaiah's interpretive revolution after the exile had a direct hermeneutical impact on late Second Temple exegesis.[49] In a very real sense, then, this interpretive revolution prepared the way for Isaiah's later readers.

46. Matt 3:1-6; Mark 1:1-8; Luke 3:4-20; John 1:19-34.

47. E.g. Mark 1:4.

48. Cf. Christian Metzenthin, *Jesaja-Auslegung in Qumran* (ATANT 98; Zürich: Theologischer Verlag Zürich, 2010), p. 185

49. This interpretation of Isa 40:3 has often been seen as significant for the origins of the Qumran community and the early Jesus movement. See, e.g., Blenkinsopp, *Opening*, p. 245; James H. Charlesworth, "Intertextuality: Isaiah 40:3 and the Serek Ha-Yahad," in *The Quest for Context and Meaning: Studies in Biblical Intertextuality in Honor of James A. Sanders*, ed. Craig A. Evans and Shemaryahu Talmon (Leiden: Brill, 1997), p. 223. For a different view see Metzenthin, *Jesaja-Auslegung*, p. 188.

Conclusion

Now, to conclude. Barton likens the activity of Second Temple readers to that of looking into a well. When later "Judaism in its many varieties (including the Christian one) peered into the well of Israel's past and thought that it was looking at [the great figures of the prophets] . . . , it was seeing only its own reflection at the bottom."[50] If my argument has any validity, the interpretive reality of the time was far more complex than this image suggests. It would be closer to the mark to say that late Second Temple readers saw the eighth-century prophet *clothed* in early Second Temple dress: they saw Isaiah after exile. This much seems to be anticipated in Barton's brief discussion of the redaction of the prophets mentioned earlier. At least in the case of Isaiah, the interpretive revolution had preceded late Second Temple Judaism by perhaps as many as three hundred years, and this revolution fueled a massive rewriting of the book. This rewritten Isaiah in turn mediated the prophet to these later readers. Far from merely seeing its own reflection at the bottom of the well, then, later Judaism was heir to a much older exegesis.

50. Barton, *Oracles*, p. 273.

Contributors

Rainer Albertz is Professor of Old Testament at the University of Münster. He is the author of numerous works on ancient Israel, including *Family and Household Religion in Ancient Israel and the Levant* (with R. Schmitt).

Klaus Baltzer is Emeritus Professor of Old Testament in the Protestant Faculty at the University of Munich and author of, among other works on Isaiah, *Deutero-Isaiah: A Commentary* in the Hermeneia series.

Hans M. Barstad is Emeritus Professor of Hebrew and Old Testament Studies at the University of Edinburgh and recent author of *A Brief Guide to the Hebrew Bible.*

Ulrich Berges is Professor of Old Testament at the University of Bonn and author of numerous studies on Isaiah, including *Jesaja 40–48* in the Herders Theologischer Kommentar zum Alten Testament series.

Willem A. M. Beuken is Emeritus Professor of Old Testament at the University of Leuven. He is the author of several studies of Isaiah, including the three-volume commentary on Isaiah 1–39 in the Herders Theologischer Kommentar zum Alten Testament series.

Philip Davies is Emeritus Professor of Biblical Studies at the University of Sheffield and the author of, among other works, *The Origins of Biblical Israel.*

Hyun Chul Paul Kim is Professor of Hebrew Bible and Williams Chair of Biblical Studies at Methodist Theological School in Ohio and author of *You Are My People: An Introduction to the Prophetic Literature* (with L. Stulman).

Peter Marinkovic serves as campus minister at Ludwigs-Maximillians-University of Munich and as adjunct professor in the Department für Kulturwissenschaften.

Andreas Schuele is Professor and Head of the Institute of Old Testament Studies at the University of Leipzig and author of *An Introduction to Biblical Aramaic.*

Jacob Stromberg is Visiting Lecturer in Hebrew Bible/Old Testament at Duke University, the Divinity School. He is the author of *Isaiah after the Exile: The Author of Third Isaiah as Reader and Redactor of the Book.*

Marvin A. Sweeney is Professor of Hebrew Bible at Claremont Lincoln University and Claremont School of Theology. Prof. Sweeney is the author of several books, including *Isaiah 1–39, with an Introduction to Prophetic Literature* in the Forms of Old Testament Literature series.

Lena-Sofia Tiemeyer is Senior Lecturer in Hebrew Bible at the University of Aberdeen and recent author of *For the Comfort of Zion: The Geographical and Theological Location of Isaiah 40–55.*

Patricia K. Tull is A. B. Rhodes Professor Emerita of Old Testament at Louisville Presbyterian Theological Seminary and the author, most recently, of *Inhabiting Eden: Christians, the Bible, and the Ecological Crisis.*

H. G. M. Williamson is Regius Professor of Hebrew at Oxford University. Prof. Williamson is the author of numerous studies on Isaiah, including the three-volume commentary on Isaiah 1–27 in the International Critical Commentary series.